Issues and Crises of Public Administration

Issues and Crises of Public Administration

By

Ranjan Kumar Ramani

2008

CYBER TECH PUBLICATIONS
4264/3, Ansari Road, Daryaganj, New Delhi-110002 (India)
Ph.: 011-23244078. Fax: 011-23280028
E-Mail: cybertechpublicationsdelhi@yahoo.com

ISSUES AND CRISES OF PUBLIC ADMINISTRATION

RANJAN KUMAR RAMANI

First Edition 2008

Published by :

G.S. Rawat for **Cyber Tech Publications**
4264/3, Ansari Road, Daryaganj, New Delhi-110002 (India)
Ph.: 011-23244078. Fax: 011-23280028
E-Mail: cybertechpublicationsdelhi@yahoo.com

Printed at : **Amit Enterprises**, Maujpur, Delhi, (9810878184)

PREFACE

As human society developed and begin to live in communities it gradually made governments, panchayats, etc. which could provide them basic amenities of life and others facilities. After a while government felt need of a machinery which could handle all the important works of it and so Public Administration came to the arena. Public Administration is a government machinery which works in the framework of government to facilitate people justice and peace. Public Administration as a discipline is no new thing to Indian Government, but this so called machinery is not as simple to function, there are a lot of complexities in its functioning.

Everyday as the society is advancing the work of Public Administration is increasing and growing complex.

However there are plethora of books on this topic but this book has its own features. In this book I have endeavoured to bring all those issues and crisis of Public Administration which it is confronting in todays world.

We hope that this book will be of immense help to scholars, general readers and to those who are eager to know more about the functioning of Public Administration.

Your valuable suggestion to improve this book are always welcome.

—*Author*

Contents

1

Public Administration: An Introduction

Public administration can be broadly described as the study and implementation of policy. As a moral endeavour, public administration is linked to pursuing the public good through the creation of civil society and social justice. The adjective 'public' often denotes 'government', though it increasingly encompasses Non-governmental organizations such as those of civil society or any entity and its management not specifically acting in self-interest. The term public administration sometimes is taken to refer to bureaucracy (as in Federal Administration). Although used negatively, bureaucracy is needed to perform day-to-day functions of government. In truth, public administration and bureaucracy are in a sense, the same thing.

HISTORICAL BRIEF

In the development of the science of four generations can be distinguished: one pre-generation and.

The Pre-generation: The pre-generation includes thinkers such as Plato, Aristotle and Machiavelli.

Until the birth of the national state, the emphasis lay principally on the problems of moral and political nature, and on the organization of the public administration. The operation of this administration was a less urgent problem. Machiavelli wrote the book *The Prince*, which offered a guideline for European rulers. The operation of the administration, and not only the organization, also profited from the attention it received in this book. From the 16th century, the national state was the reigning model of the administrative organization in Western Europe. These states needed an organization for the implementation of law and order and for setting up a defensive structure. The need for expert civil servants, with knowledge about taxes, statistics, administration and the military organization grew.

In the 18th century the need for administrative expertise grew even further. Therefore king Frederick William I of Prussia established professorates in Cameralism, an economic and social school of thought within 18th century Prussia to reform society, at the universities of Frankfurt an der Order and Halle. The most well know professor of Cameralism was Johann Heinrich Gottlob Justi (1717-1771), who linked Cameralism and the idea of natural law with each other, but the leading Public Administration scholar at that time was Christian Wolff, who was not a Cameralist. Cameralism is a predecessor of the modern science of public administration.

The First Generation

Lorenz von Stein, since 1855 professor in Vienna, is considered the founder of the science of public administration. In the time of Von Stein the science of public administration was considered to be a form of administrative law, but Von Stein thought that opinion was too restrictive. His opinions were innovative in several respects:

- He considered the science of public administration a melting pot of several disciplines, like sociology, political sciences, administrative law and public finance. In the opinion of Von Stein the science of public administration was an integrating science.
- According to Von Stein the science of public administration was an interaction between theory and practice. He considered the public administration as leading practically, but the theory had to form the base.
- Von Stein thought that the science of public administration should strive to adopt a scientific method.

In the United States Woodrow Wilson was the first to consider the science of public administration important. Wilson was more influential to the science of public administration than Von Stein, primarily due to an article Wilson wrote in 1887 in which he argued in favour of four concepts:

- Separation between politics and the public administration.
- Consideration of the government from a commercial perspective.
- Comparative analysis between political and private organizations and political schemes.
- Reaching effective management by training civil servants and assess their quality.

The separation between politics and the public administration, which Wilson argued, has been the subject of fierce debates for a long time, and the different points of view on this subject differentiate periods in the science of public administration.

The Second Generation

The discussion about the separation between politics and the public administration as argued by Wilson continued to play an important role up to 1945. Luther Gulick and Lyndall Urwick were the founders of the Science of Administration. They integrated the ideas of earlier theorists like Henri Fayol into a comprehensive theory of administration. Gulick and Urwick believed that the thoughts of Fayol offered a systematic treatment of management, which was unique at that time. They believed that this could be applied as well for the management of companies as for administrative sciences. They did not want to separate the two disciplines, but believed a single Science of Administration, which exceeds the borders between the private and the public sector, could exist. Later on the Science of Administration would focus primarily on governmental organizations. The reasoning of the Science of Administration was largely borrowed from the fourteen principles of organization of Fayol.

The Third Generation

After 1945 the third generation arose which questioned the ideas of Wilson and the second generation.

Initially the distinction between politics and the public administration was strongly relativized by the third generation, but the discussion would continue. Because of the unsuccessful American intervention in Vietnam and the Watergate scandal politics got discredited and in the eighties there was again a plea in favour of bureaucracy, especially in the United States. The public administration had to detach itself from politics.

After Louis Brownlow from the University of Chicago chaired the Hoover Commission on the Reorganization of Government, he founded Public Administration Service on the University of Chicago campus (at 1313 E. 60th Street). From 193 until the late 1970s PAS provided consulting services to governments at all levels: cities counties, states, the federal government and many foreign countries.

PUBLIC ADMINISTRATION AS AN ACADEMIC DISCIPLINE

A Public Administrator can fill many voids. The academic field evolved in the United States from both academic political science and law as a separate study in the 1910s. In Europe, notably England and Germany (Max Weber), it started as a separate scholarly field in the 1890s, but it was first taught in Continental universities in the 1720s. The Federalist Papers several times referred to the importance of good administration, and scholars such as John A. Rohr see a long history behind the constitutional legitimacy of government bureaucracy.

A few public administration theorists advocate a bright line differentiation of the professional field from related academic disciplines like political science and sociology. But, in general, the interdisciplinary nature of PA is acknowledged and it is viewed as a field of study rather than a discipline.

As a field, public administration can be compared to business administration, and the MPA viewed as similar to an MBA for those wishing to pursue governmental or non-profit careers. An MPA often entails substantial ethical and sociological aspects not usually found in business schools. There are derivative and related degrees that address public affairs, public policy, and the like. Differences often connote program emphases on policy analysis techniques or other topical focuses such as the study of international affairs as opposed to focuses on constitutional issues such as separation of powers, administrative law, problems of governance and power, and participatory democracy.

Public administration theory is the domain where discussions of the meaning and purpose of government, bureaucracy, budgets, governance, and public affairs take place in the field. In recent years, public administration theory has occasionally connoted a heavy orientation toward critical theory and postmodern philosophical notions of government, governance, and power, but many public administration scholars support a classic definition of the term which gives weight to constitutionality, service, bureaucratic forms of organization, and hierarchical government.

There is minor tradition that holds that the more specific term public management refers to ordinary, routine or typical management concerns, but in the context of achieving public good. Others see public management as a new, economically driven perspective on the operation of government. This latter view is often termed "new public management" by its advocates and can be seen as a reform attempt aimed at re-emphasizing the professional nature of the field versus its academic, moral or disciplinary characteristics.

Bureaucracy

Bureaucracy is a concept in sociology and political science referring to the way that the administrative execution and enforcement of legal rules are socially organized. This office organization is characterized by standardized procedure (rule-following), formal division of responsibility, hierarchy, and impersonal relationships.

Examples of everyday bureaucracies include governments, armed forces, corporations, hospitals, courts, ministries and schools. A few specific examples of bureaucracies are the Department of Motor Vehicles and the College Board.

Origin of the Concept

Bureaucracy is derived from the word bureau, used from the early 18th century in Western Europe not just to refer to a writing desk, but to an office, i.e. a workplace, where officials worked. The original French meaning of the word *bureau* was the baize used to cover desks. The term bureaucracy came into use shortly before the French Revolution of 1789, and from there rapidly spread to other countries. The Greek suffix-*kratia* or *kratos*-means "power" or "rule". Bureaucracy thus basically means office power or office rule, the rule of the officialdom.

In a letter of July 1, 1764, the French Baron de Grimm declared: "We are obsessed by the idea of regulation, and our Masters of Requests refuse to understand that there is an infinity of things in a great state with which a government should not concern itself."

Jean Claude Marie Vincent de Gournay sometimes used to say, "We have an illness in France which bids fair to play havoc with us; this illness is called *bureaumania*." Sometimes he used to invent a fourth or fifth form of government under the heading of "bureaucracy". In another letter of July 15, 1765 Baron Grimm wrote also, "The real spirit of the laws in France is that bureaucracy of which the late Monsieur de Gournay used to complain so greatly; here the offices, clerks, secretaries, inspectors and *intendants* are not appointed to benefit the public interest, indeed the public interest appears to have been established so that offices might exist."

This quote refers to a traditional controversy about bureaucracy, namely the perversion of means and ends so that means become ends in themselves, and the greater good is lost sight of; as a corollary, the substitution of *sectional* interests for the *general* interest. The suggestion here is that, left uncontrolled, the bureaucracy will become increasingly self-serving and corrupt, rather than serving society.

However, bureaucracy existed long before words and theories were devised to describe it in detail. The Chinese Song dynasty (960 AD) for example constructed a centralized bureaucracy staffed with civilian scholar-officials.

This system of rule led to a much greater concentration of power in the hands of the emperor and his palace bureaucracy than was achieved in previous dynasties. The first occurrence of this was in Ancient China, during the Wang dynasty in 380 BC.

Karl Marx and Bureaucracy

In Karl Marx's theory of historical materialism, the historical origin of bureaucracy is to be found in *four* sources: religion, the formation of the state, commerce and technology.

Thus, the earliest bureaucracies consisted of castes of *religious* clergy, officials and scribes operating various rituals, and armed functionaries specifically delegated to keep order. In the historical transition from primitive egalitarian communities to a civil society divided into social classes and estates, occurring from about 10,000 years ago, authority is increasingly centralized in, and enforced by a state apparatus existing separately from society. This state formulates, imposes and enforces laws, and levies taxes, giving rise to an officialdom enacting these functions. Thus, the state mediates in conflicts among the people and keeps those conflicts within acceptable bounds; it also organises the defence of territory. Most importantly, the right of ordinary people to carry and use weapons of force becomes increasingly restricted; forcing other people to do things becomes increasingly the legal right of the state authorities only.

But the growth of trade and commerce adds a new, distinctive dimension to bureaucracy, insofar as it requires the keeping of accounts and the processing/recording of transactions, as well as the enforcement of legal rules governing trade. If resources are increasingly distributed by prices in markets, this requires extensive and complex systems of record-keeping, management and calculation, conforming to legal standards. Eventually, this means that the total amount of work involved in commercial administration outgrows the total amount of work involved in government administration. In modern capitalist society, private sector bureaucracy is *larger* than government bureaucracy, if measured by the number of administrative workers in the division of labour as a whole. Some corporations nowadays have a turnover larger than the national income of whole countries, with large administrations supervising operations.

A fourth source of bureaucracy Marxists have commented on inheres in the technologies of mass production, which require many standardised routines and procedures to be performed.

Even if mechanisation replaces people with machinery, people are still necessary to design, control, supervise and operate the machinery. The technologies chosen may not be the ones that are best for everybody, but which create *incomes* for a particular class of people or maintain their power. This type of bureaucracy is nowadays often called a technocracy, which owes its power to control over specialised technical knowledge or control over critical information.

In Marx's theory, bureaucracy rarely creates new wealth by itself, but rather controls, coordinates and governs the production, distribution and consumption of wealth. The bureaucracy as a social stratum derives its income from the appropriation of part of the social surplus product of human labour. Wealth is appropriated by the bureaucracy by law through fees, taxes, levies, tributes, licensing etc.

Bureaucracy is therefore always a *cost* to society, but this cost may be accepted insofar as it makes social order possible, and maintains it by enforcing the rule of law. Nevertheless there are constant conflicts about this cost, because it has the big effect on the distribution of incomes; all producers will try to get the maximum return from what they produce, and minimise administrative costs. Typically, in epochs of strong economic growth, bureaucracies proliferate; when economic growth declines, a fight breaks out to cut back bureaucratic costs.

Whether or not a bureaucracy as a social stratum can become a genuine ruling class depends greatly on the prevailing property relations and the mode of production of wealth. In capitalist society, the state typically lacks an independent economic base, finances many activities on credit, and is heavily dependent on levying taxes as a source of income. Therefore, its power is limited by the costs which private owners of the productive assets will tolerate. If, however, the state owns the means of production itself, defended by military power, the state bureaucracy can become much more powerful, and act as a ruling class or power elite. Because in that case, it directly controls the sources of new wealth, and manages or distributes the social product. This is the subject of Marxist theories of bureaucratic collectivism.

Marx himself however never theorised this possibility in detail, and it has been the subject of much controversy among Marxists. The core organisational issue in these disputes concerns the degree to which the *administrative* allocation of resources by government authorities and the *market* allocation of resources can achieve the social goal of creating a more free, just and prosperous society. Which decisions should be made by whom, at what level, so that an optimal allocation of resources results? This is just as much a moral-political issue as an economic issue.

Central to the Marxian concept of socialism is the idea of workers' self-management, which assumes the internalisation of a morality and self-discipline among people that would make bureaucratic supervision and control redundant, together with a drastic reorganisation of the division of labour in society. Bureaucracies emerge to mediate conflicts of interest on the basis of laws, but if those conflicts of interest disappear (because resources are allocated directly in a fair way), bureaucracies would also be redundant.

Marx's critics are however skeptical of the feasibility of this kind of socialism, given the continuing need for administration and the rule of law, as well as the propensity of people to put their own self-interest before the communal interest. That is, the argument is that self-interest and the communal interest might *never* coincide, or, at any rate, can always diverge significantly.

Max Weber on Bureaucracy

Max Weber has probably been one of the most influential users of the word in its social science sense. He is well-known for his study of bureaucratization of society; many aspects of modern public administration go back to him; a classic, hierarchically organized civil service of the continental type is — if basically mistakenly — called *"Weberian civil service"*.

However, contrary to popular belief, "bureaucracy" was an English word before Weber; the Oxford English Dictionary cites usage in several different years between 1818 and 1860, prior to Weber's birth in 1864.

Weber described the ideal type bureaucracy in positive terms, considering it to be a more rational and efficient form of organization than the alternatives that preceded it, which he characterized as *charismatic domination* and *traditional domination*. According to his terminology, bureaucracy is part of legal domination. However, he also emphasized that bureaucracy becomes inefficient when a decision must be adopted to an individual case. According to Weber, the attributes of modern bureaucracy include its impersonality, concentration of the means of administration, a levelling effect on social and economic differences and implementation of a system of authority that is practically indestructible.

Weber's analysis of bureaucracy concerns:

- the historical and administrative reasons for the process of bureaucratization (especially in the Western civilisation)
- the impact of the rule of law upon the functioning of bureaucratic organisations
- the typical personal orientation and occupational position of a bureaucratic officials as a status group
- the most important attributes and consequences of bureaucracy in the modern world

A bureaucratic organization is governed by the following seven principles:

1. official business is conducted on a continuous basis
2. official business is conducted with strict accordance to the following rules:
    1. the duty of each official to do certain types of work is delimited in terms of impersonal criteria
    2. the official is given the authority necessary to carry out his assigned functions
    3. the means of coercion at his disposal are strictly limited and conditions of their use strictly defined
3. every official's responsibilities and authority are part of a vertical hierarchy of authority, with respective rights of supervision and appeal

4. officials do not own the resources necessary for the performance of their assigned functions but are accountable for their use of these resources
5. official and private business and income are strictly separated
6. offices cannot be appropriated by their incumbents (inherited, sold, etc.)
7. official business is conducted on the basis of written documents

A bureaucratic official:

- is personally free and appointed to his position on the basis of conduct
- exercises the authority delegated to him in accordance with impersonal rules, and his loyalty is enlisted on behalf of the faithful execution of his official duties
- appointment and job placement are dependent upon his technical qualifications
- administrative work is a full-time occupation
- work is rewarded by a regular salary and prospects of advancement in a lifetime career

An official must exercise his judgment and his skills, but his duty is to place these at the service of a higher authority; ultimately he is responsible only for the impartial execution of assigned tasks and must sacrifice his personal judgment if it runs counter to his official duties. Weber's work has been continued by many, like Robert Michels with his Iron Law of Oligarchy.

Street-level Bureaucracy

Street-level bureaucracy is a term used to refer to a public agency employee who actually performs the actions that implement laws.

Examples of Street-level Bureaucrats: Street-level bureaucrats include police officers, firefighters, and others who "walk the streets" with regular citizens, and provide services to protect, as well as uphold the laws.

System Administrator

A system administrator, or sysadmin, is a person employed to maintain, and operate a computer system or network for a company or other organization. System administrators are often members of an information technology department.

The duties of a system administrator are wide-ranging, and vary widely from one organization to another. Sysadmins are usually charged with installing, supporting, and maintaining servers or other computer systems, and planning for and responding to service outages and other problems. Other duties may include scripting or light programming, project management for systems-related projects, supervising or training computer operators, and being the equivalent of a handyman for computer problems beyond the knowledge of technical support staff.

Skills: The *subject matter* of systems administration includes computer systems and the ways people use them in an organization. This entails a knowledge of operating systems and applications, as well as hardware and software troubleshooting, but also knowledge of the purposes for which people in the organization use the computers.

However, perhaps the most important *skill* to a system administrator is problem solving—frequently under various sorts of constraints and stress. The sysadmin is on call when a computer system goes down or malfunctions, and must be able to quickly and correctly diagnose what is wrong and how best to fix it. System administrators are not software engineers or developers. It is not usually within their duties to design or write new applications software. However, sysadmins must understand the behaviour of software in order to deploy it and to troubleshoot problems, and generally know several programming languages used for scripting or automation of routine tasks.

Particularly when dealing with Internet-facing or business-critical systems, a sysadmin must have a strong grasp of computer security. This includes not merely deploying software patches, but also preventing break-ins and other security problems with preventative measures. In some organizations, computer security administration is a separate role responsible for overall security and the upkeep of firewalls and intrusion detection systems, but all sysadmins are generally responsible for the security of the systems in their keep.

Related Fields: Many organizations staff other jobs related to systems administration. In a larger company, these may all be separate positions within a computer support or Information Services (IS) department. In a smaller group they may be shared by a few sysadmins, or even a single person.

- A database administrator (DBA) maintains a database system, and is responsible for the integrity of the data and the efficiency and performance of the system.
- A network administrator maintains network infrastructure such as switches and routers, and diagnoses problems with these or with the behaviour of network-attached computers.
- A security administrator is a specialist in computer and network security, including the administration of security devices such as firewalls, as well as consulting on general security measures.
- Technical support staff respond to individual users' difficulties with computer systems, provide instructions and sometimes training, and diagnose and solve common problems.
- A computer operator performs routine maintenance and upkeep, such as changing backup tapes or replacing failed drives in a RAID array. Such tasks usually require physical presence in the room with the computer; and while less skilled than sysadmin tasks require a similar level of trust, since the operator has access to possibly sensitive data.

In some organizations, a person may begin as a member of technical support staff or a computer operator, then gain experience on the job to be promoted to a sysadmin position and afterwards an IT Manager.

Training: Unlike many other professions, there is no single path to becoming a system administrator. Few colleges or universities have specific programs for system administration, so many system administrators have a degree in generic fields: computer science, computer engineering, information system management, or even a trade school program. As of 2006, only four U.S. universities, Rochester Institute of Technology, Tufts, Florida State University, Miller-Motte Technical College in AAS in Microcomputer Applications Systems Network Engineer and Michigan Tech have postgraduate programs in system administration. In Europe, Norway, there is a special English-taught MSc programme organized by Oslo University College in cooperation with Oslo University, named "Masters programme in Network and System Administration". The founder of the programme is the creator of ofengine, Mark Burgess.

In addition, because of the practical nature of systems administration and the easy availability of open-source server software, many systems administrators enter the field self-taught. Generally, a prospective administrator will be required to have some experience with the computer system he or she is expected to manage. In some cases, candidates are expected to possess industry certifications such as the Microsoft MCSA or Red Hat RHCE. At the same time, some employers consider reliance on such certifications to be a sign of a poor candidate, or 'paper cert'-someone who has trade-school "book learning" rather than formal theoretical knowledge or hard practical experience.

Sometimes, almost exclusively in smaller sites, the role of system administrator may be given to a skilled user in addition to or in replacement of his or her duties.

Duties of a System Administrator: A system administrator's responsibilities typically include:

- Morning checks of systems/software.
- Performing backups of data.
- Applying operating system updates, and configuration changes.
- Installing and configuring new hardware/software.
- Adding/deleting/creating/modifying user account information, resetting passwords, etc.

- Answering technical queries.
- Responsibility for security.
- Responsibility for documenting the configuration of the system.
- Troubleshooting any reported problems.
- System performance tuning.
- Keeping the network up and running.

In larger organizations, some tasks listed above may be divided among different system administrators or members of different organizational groups. For example, a dedicated individual may apply all system upgrades, a Quality Assurance (QA) team may perform testing and validation, and one or more technical writers may be responsible for all technical documentation written for a company.

In smaller organizations, the system administrator can also perform any number of duties elsewhere associated with other fields:

- Technical support
- Database administrator (DBA)
- Network administrator/analyst/specialist
- Application analyst
- Security administrator
- Programmer

System administrators, in larger organizations, also tend not to be system architects, system engineers, or system designers, however, like many roles in this field, demarcations between systems administration and these other roles are often not well defined in smaller organizations. However, even in larger organizations, senior systems administrators often have skills in these other areas as a result of their working experience.

In smaller organizations, IT/computing specialties are less often discerned in detail, and the term "system administrator" is used in a rather generic way — they are the people who know how the computer systems work and can respond when something fails.

Public Policy

Public policy is a course of action or inaction chosen by public authorities to address a problem. Public policy is expressed in the body of laws, regulations, decisions and actions of government. Policy analysis may be used to formulate public policy and to evaluate its effectiveness. Many public policy analysts earn Ph.D., Master of Public Policy and Master of Public Administration degrees in public policy schools, while others earn specialized degrees, such as an M.Ed for specializing in educational policy or an MSW for specializing in social welfare policy.

Various Definitions: According to William Jenkins in *Policy Analysis: A Political and Organizational Perspective* (1978), a Public Policy is 'a set of interrelated decisions taken by a political actor or group of actors concerning the selection of goals and the means of achieving them within a specified situation where those decisions should, in principle, be within the power of those actors to achieve'. Thus, Jenkins understands Public Policy making to be a process, and not simply a choice.

According to Thomas A. Birkland in *An Introduction to the Policy Process* (2001), there is a lack of a consensus on the definition of public policy. Birkland outlines a few definitions of public policy:

- Clarke E. Cochran, et al.: "The term public policy always refers to the actions of government and the intentions that determine those actions".
- Clarke E. Cochran, et al.: "Public policy is the outcome of the struggle in government over who gets what".
- Thomas Dye: Public policy is "Whatever governments choose to do or not do".
- Charles L. Cochran and Eloise F. Malone: "Public policy consists of political decisions for implementing programs to achieve societal goals".
- B. Guy Peters: "Stated most simply, public policy is the sum of government activities, whether acting directly or through agents, as it has an influence on the life of citizens".

Birkland indicates that the elements common to all definitions of public policy are as follows (p. 20):

- The policy is made in the name of the "public".
- Policy is generally made or initiated by government.
- Policy is interpreted and implemented by public and private actors.
- Policy is what the government intends to do.
- Policy is what the government chooses not to do.

History of Public Policy

According to Birkland: While the study of politics has a long history, the systematic study of public policy, on the other hand, can be said to be a twentieth century creation. It dates, according to Daniel McCool, to 1922, when political scientist Charles Merriam sought to connect the theory and practices of politics to understanding the actual activities of government, that is public policy." (p.4)

Types of Public Policy

Domestic Policy: In government, domestic policy is the counterpart of foreign policy; it consists of all government policy decisions, programs, and actions that primarily deal with internal matters, as opposed to relations with other nation-states. Major areas of domestic policy include tax policy, social security and welfare programs, environmental laws, and regulations on businesses and their practices.

Education Policy: Education policy refers to the collection of laws or rules that govern the operation of education systems. It seeks to answer questions about the purpose of education, the objectives (societal and personal) that it is designed to attain, the methods for attaining them and the tools for measuring their success or failure.

Education being an activity that impacts upon people of all ages, Education policy may be broken down into policy as regards preschool provision, schooling, adult education and training, university education, and so on. Examples of areas subject to debate in education policy, specifically from the field of schools, include school size, class size, school choice, school privatization, tracking, teacher education and certification, teacher pay, teaching methods, curricular content, graduation requirements, school infrastructure investment, and the values that schools are expected to uphold and model.

Education policy analysis is the scholarly study of education policy. Research intended to inform education policy is carried out in a wide variety of institutions and in many academic disciplines. Important researchers are affiliated with departments of psychology, economics, sociology, and human development, in addition to schools and departments of education or public policy. Examples of education policy analysis may be found in such academic journals as *Education Policy Analysis Archives*.

Energy Policy: Energy policy is the manner a given entity (often governmental) has decided to address issues of energy production, distribution and consumption. The attributes of energy policy may include legislation, international treaties, incentives to investment, guidelines for energy conservation, taxation and other public policy techniques.

National Energy Policy

Measures used to Produce an Energy Policy: A national energy policy is comprised by set of measures involving that country's laws, treaties and agency directives. The energy policy of a sovereign nation may include one or more of the following measures:

- statement of national policy regarding energy generation, transmission and usage
- legislation on commercial energy activities (trading, transport, storage, etc.)
- legislation affecting energy use, such as efficiency standards, emission standards
- instructions for state owned energy sector assets and organizations
- active participation in, coordination of and incentives for mineral fuels exploration and other energy-related research and development

- fiscal policies related to energy products and services (taxes, exemptions, subsidies...
- international policy measures such as:
  - o international energy sector treaties and alliances,
  - o general international trade agreements,
  - o special relations with energy-rich countries, including military presence and/or domination.

Frequently the dominant issue of energy policy is the risk of supply-demand mismatch. Current energy policies also address environmental issues. Some governments state explicit energy policy, but, declared or not, each government practices some type of energy policy.

Factors within an Energy Policy: There are a number of elements that are naturally contained in a national energy policy, regardless of which of the above measures was used to arrive at the resultant policy. The chief elements intrinsic to an energy policy are:

- What is the extent of energy self-sufficiency for this nation
- Where future energy sources will derive
- How future energy will be consumed (e.g. among sectors)
- What fraction of the population will be acceptable to endure energy poverty
- What are the goals for future energy intensity, ratio of energy consumed to GDP
- What is the reliability standard for distribution reliability
- What environmental externalities are acceptable and are forecast
- What form of "portable energy" is forecast (e.g. sources of fuel for motor vehicles)
- How will energy efficient hardware (e.g. hybrid vehicles, household appliances) be encouraged
- How can the national policy drive province, state and municipal functions

- What specific mechanisms (e.g. taxes, incentives, manufacturing standards) are in place to implement the total policy

State, Province or Municipal Energy Policy

Even within a state it is proper to talk about energy policies in plural. Influential entities, such as municipal or regional governments and energy industries, will each exercise policy. Policy measures available to these entities are lesser in sovereignty, but may be equally important to national measures. In fact, there are certain activities vital to energy policy which realistically cannot be administered at the national level, such as monitoring energy conservation practices in the process of building construction, which is normally controlled by state-regional and municipal building codes (although can appear basic federal legislation).

Environmental Policy

Environmental policy may refer to either the private sector or the public sector. In the public sector it generally refers to a government's use and creation of the laws, regulations, and other policy mechanisms concerning environmental issues and sustainability. In the private sector it usually refers to the compliance with those tools, or the independent development of self-regulation and rule-making that may go beyond what is required by governments.

The environmental issues generally addressed include air and water pollution, solid waste management, ecosystem management, maintenance of biodiversity, the protection of natural resources, wildlife and endangered species. Policies concerning energy or regulation of toxic substances like pesticides and many types of industrial waste are included in the topic of environmental policy.

Environmental Preservation: Environmental preservation is the act of maintaining the natural state of a particular habitat. In terms of policy making this often means setting aside areas as nature reserves (otherwise known as wildlife reserves). These areas usually restrict or prohibit activities that may cause damage to habitat or wildlife. Such activities may include: logging, hunting, fishing, mining and so on. A government's environmental policy will determine which areas are protected and how.

Foreign Policy

A country's foreign policy is a set of political goals that seeks to outline how that particular country will interact with other countries of the world and, to a lesser extent, non-state actors. Foreign policies generally are designed to help protect a country's national interests, national security, ideological goals, and economic prosperity. This can occur as a result of peaceful cooperation with other nations, or through aggression, war, and exploitation. It may be assumed that foreign policy is as ancient as the human society itself. The twentieth century saw a rapid rise in the importance of foreign policy, with virtually every nation in the world now being able to interact with one another in some diplomatic form.

Nominally, creating foreign policy is usually the job of the head of government and the foreign minister (or equivalent). In some countries the legislature also has considerable oversight. As an exception, in France and in Finland it is the head of state who is responsible for foreign policy, while the head of government mainly deals with internal policy.

In fact, foreign policy is a product of pressure from various groups and classes, political as well as economic. In many countries, foreign policy ranks high on the list of factors that influence public opinion.

International Relations Theory

International relations have been studied and analyzed for centuries, and can partially explain the foreign policy of particular states. However note that International Relations Theory tries to explain the *interaction* in the international system between *all* states (and possibly non-state actors) and does not take into account the specific characteristics of particular states.

The sub-discipline that specialises in the study of foreign policy is known as foreign policy analysis (FPA).

The Politics Series

International relations (IR), a branch of political science, is the study of foreign affairs of and relations among states within the international system, including the roles of states, inter-governmental organizations (IGOs), non-governmental organizations (NGOs), and multinational corporations (MNCs). It is both an academic and public policy field, and can be either positive or normative as it both seeks to analyze as well as formulate foreign policy.

Apart from political science, IR draws upon such diverse fields as economics, history, law, philosophy, geography, sociology, anthropology, psychology, and cultural studies. It involves a diverse range of issues, from globalization and its impacts on societies and state sovereignty to ecological sustainability, nuclear proliferation, nationalism, economic development, terrorism, organized crime, human security, and human rights.

History

The International System: The history of international relations is often traced back to the Peace of Westphalia of 1648, where the modern state system was developed. Prior to this, the European medieval organization of political authority was based on a vaguely hierarchical religious order. Westphalia instituted the notion of sovereignty, which essentially meant that rulers, or sovereigns, would recognize no internal equals within a defined territory, and no external superiors. Classical Greek and Roman authority at times resembled the Westphalian system, but both lacked the notion of sovereignty. Westphalia encouraged the rise of the nation-state and the institutionalization of diplomacy and armies. This particular European system was exported to the Americas, Africa, and Asia via colonialism and the "standards of civilization". The contemporary international system was finally established through decolonization during the Cold War. However, this is somewhat over-simplified. While the nation-state system is considered "modern", many states have not incorporated the system and are termed "pre-modern". Further, a handful of states have moved beyond the nation-state system and can be considered "post-modern". The ability of contemporary IR discourse to explain the relations of these different types of states is disputed.

International Relations Theory: What is explicitly recognized as international relations theory was not developed until after World War I, and is dealt with in more detail below. IR theory, however, has a long tradition of drawing on the work of other social sciences. The use of capitalizations of the 'I' and 'R' in International Relations aims to distinguish the academic discipline of International Relations from the phenomena of international relations. Many cite Thucydides' *History of the Peloponnesian War* as the inspiration for realist theory, with Hobbes' *Leviathan* and Machiavelli's *The Prince* providing further elaboration. Similarly, liberalism draws upon the work of Kant and Rousseau, with the work of the former often being cited as the first elaboration of Democratic Peace Theory. Though contemporary human rights is considerably different than the type of rights envisioned under natural law, Francisco de Vitoria, Hugo Grotius and John Locke offered the first accounts of universal entitlement to certain rights on the basis of common humanity. In the twentieth century, in addition to contemporary theories of liberal internationalism, Marxism has been a durable foundation of international relations.

The Study of IR: Initially, international relations as a distinct field of study was almost entirely British-centred. In 1919, the first Chair in International Politics established at the University of Wales, Aberystwyth, from an endowment given by David Davies, became the first academic position dedicated to IR. In the early 1920s, the London School of Economics' department of International Relations was founded at the behest of Nobel Peace Prize winner Phillip Noel-Baker. While schools dedicated to the study of IR have been founded in Asia and South America, IR as a discipline remains to be studied chiefly in Europe and North America.

Theory

Epistemology and IR Theory: IR theories can be roughly divided into one of two epistemological camps: "positivist" and "post-positivist". Positivist theories aim to replicate the methods of the natural sciences by analysing the impact of material forces. They typically focus on features of international relations such as state interactions, size of military forces, balance of powers etc. Post-positivist epistemology rejects the idea that the social world can be studied in an objective and value-free way. It rejects the central ideas of neo-realism/liberalism, such as rational choice theory, on the grounds that the scientific method cannot be applied to the social world and that a 'science' of IR is impossible.

A key difference between the two positions is that while positivist theories, such as neo-realism, offer causal explanations (such as why and how power is exercised) post-positivist theories focus instead on constitutive questions, for instance what is meant by 'power'; what makes it up, how it is experienced and how it is reproduced. Often, post-positivist theories explicitly promote a normative approach to IR, by considering ethics. This is something which has often been ignored under 'traditional' IR as positivist theories make a distinction between 'facts' and normative judgments, or 'values'.

During the late 1980s/1990 debate between positivists and post-positivists became the dominant debate and has been described as constituting the Third "Great Debate" (Lapid 1989).

Positivist Theories

Liberalism/Idealism/Liberal Internationalism: Liberalism arose after World War I in response to the inability of states to control and limit war in their international relations. Early adherents include Woodrow Wilson and Norman Angell, who argued variously that states mutually gained from cooperation and that war was so destructive to be essentially futile. Liberalism was not recognized as a coherent theory as such until it was collectively and derisively termed idealism by E. H. Carr.

Realism: Realism was a response to liberalism that chiefly denies that states seek to cooperate. Early realists such as E.H. Carr and Hans Morgenthau argued that states are self-interested, power-seeking rational actors. Any cooperation between states is explained as purely incidental. Realists saw World War II as the vindication of their theory. It should be noted that classical writers such as Thucydides, Machiavelli, and Hobbes are often cited as the "founding fathers" of realism by contemporary self-described realists. However, while their work may support realist doctrine, it is not likely that they would have classified themselves as realists (in this sense of the term).

Neorealism: Neorealism is largely the work of Kenneth Waltz (who actually called his theory "structural realism"). While retaining the empirical observations of realism, that international relations are characterized by antagonistic interstate relations, neorealists point to the anarchic structure of the international system as the cause. They reject explanations that take account of states' domestic characteristics. States are compelled by relative gains and balance against concentration of power. Unlike realism, neo-realism seeks to be scientific and more positivist.

Neoliberalism: Neoliberalism seeks to update liberalism by accepting the neorealist presumption that states are the key actors in international relations, but still maintains that non-state actors (NSAs) and intergovernmental organizations (IGOs) matter. Proponents such as Joseph Nye argue that states will cooperate irrespective of relative gains, and are thus concerned with absolute gains. The growing interdependence throughout the Cold War through international institutions means that neo-liberalism is also called liberal institutionalism. This also means that nations are, in essence, free to make their own choices as to how they will go about conducting policy without any international organizations blocking a nation's right to sovereignty. Neoliberalism also contains an economic theory that is based the use of open and free markets with little, if any, government intervention to prevent monopolies and other conglomerates from forming.

Post-positivist/Reflectivist Theories

International Society Theory (the English School): International society theory, also called the English School, focuses on the shared norms and values of states and how they regulate international relations. Examples of such norms include diplomacy, order, and international law. Unlike neo-realism, it is not necessarily positivist. Theorists have focused particularly on humanitarian intervention, and are subdivided between solidarists, who tend to advocate it more, and pluralists, who place greater value in order and sovereignty. Nicholas Wheeler is a prominent solidarist, while Hedley Bull is perhaps the best known pluralist.

Social Constructivism: Social Constructivism encompasses a broad range of theories that aim to address questions of ontology, such as the Structure and agency debate, as well as questions of epistemology, such as the "material/ ideational" debate that concerns the relative role of material forces versus ideas. Constructivism is not a theory of IR, for example in the manner of neo-realism, but instead is a social theory.

Constructivism in IR can be divided into what Hopf (1998) calls 'conventional' and 'critical' constructivism. Common to all varieties of constructivism is an interest in the role that ideational forces play. The most famous constructivist scholar, Alexander Wendt noted in a 1992 article in International Organization (later followed up by a book, *Social Theory of International Politics* (1999)), that "anarchy is what states make of it". By this he means that the anarchical structure that neo-realists claim governs state interaction is in fact a phenomenon that is socially constructed and reproduced by states. For example, if the system is dominated by states that see anarchy as a life or death situation (what Wendt terms a "Hobbesian" anarchy) then the system will be characterised by warfare. If on the other hand anarchy is seen as restricted (a "Lockean" anarchy) then a more peaceful system will exist. Anarchy in this view is constituted by state interaction, rather than accepted as a natural and immutable feature of international life as viewed by neo-realist IR scholars.

Critics, however, abound from both sides of the epistemological divide: Post-positivists say the focus on the state at the expense of ethnicity/race/class/gender makes social constructivism yet another positivist theory. The use of implicit rational choice theory by Wendt has also raised criticisms from scholars such as Steven Smith. Positivist scholars of (neo-) liberalism/realism hold that the theory forgoes too many positivist assumptions for it to be considered positivist.

Critical Theory: Critical international relations theory is the application of 'critical theory' to international relations. Proponents such as Andrew Linklater and Robert Cox focus on the need for human emancipation from States. Hence, it is "critical" of mainstream IR theories that tend to be state-centric.

Marxism: Marxist and Neo-Marxist theories of IR reject the realist/liberal view of state conflict or cooperation; instead focusing on the economic and material aspects. It makes the assumption that the economy trumps other concerns; allowing for the elevation of class as the focus of study. Marxists view the international system as an integrated capitalist system in pursuit of capital accumulation. Thus, the period of colonialism brought in sources for raw materials and captive markets for exports, while decolonialization brought new opportunities in the form of dependence.

Linked in with Marxist theories is dependency theory which argues that developed countries, in their pursuit of power, penetrate developing states through political advisors, missionaries, experts and MNCs to integrate them into the integrated capitalist system in order to appropriate natural resources and foster dependence by developing countries on developed countries.

Marxist theories receive scant attention in the United States where no significant socialist party ever existed. It is more common in parts of Europe and is one of the most important theoretic contributions of Latin American academia, for example through Liberation theology.

Poststructuralist Theories: Poststructuralist theories of IR developed in the 1980s from postmodernist studies in political science. Post-structuralism explores the deconstruction of concepts traditionally not problematic in IR, such as 'power' and 'agency' and examines how the construction of these concepts shapes international relations. The examination of 'narratives' plays an important part in poststructuralist analysis, for example feminist poststructuralist work has examined the role that 'women' play in global society and how they are constructed in war as 'innocent' and 'civilians'.

Examples of post-positivist research include:

- Feminisms ("gendering" war)
- Postcolonialism (challenges the euro-centrism of IR)

INDIAN CIVIL SERVICES

The Indian Civil Service, popularly known by its acronym ICS, originated as the elite civil service of the Indian Government under British colonial rule in India, and continues in the contemporary Civil Services of India, though these are now organised differently.

Colonial Civil Service: There were two exclusive groups of civil servants during the formative stage of British rule in India. The higher employees who entered into "covenants" with the East India Company came to be known as "covenanted" servants, whereas those not signing such agreements came to be known as "uncovenanted". The latter group generally filled the lower positions. This distinction between the covenanted and the uncovenanted virtually came to an end with the constitution of the Imperial Civil Service of India based on the recommendations of the Public Service Commission, 1886-1887, though the phrase "covenanted" continued to be used of anyone in a salaried position with a long term contract-including boxwallahs.

The name *Imperial Civil Service* was changed to Civil Service of India. However, the term *Indian Civil Service* (ICS) persisted. The acronym 'ICS' continued to be used to denote the covenanted civil servants. The Provincial Civil Service was also constituted on the basis of the recommendations of the Aitchison Commission, and this Provincial Service consisted of two cadres, Provincial Civil Service and Subordinate Civil Service.

Further developments took place as a result of the application of the scheme of cadre organization to the administrative departments. Thus, for example, the departments of Forest and Public Works had both the 'imperial, and 'provincial' branches. The basic pattern of the cadre system in the civil service was thus established following the recommendations of the Aitchison Commission.

By 1934, the system of administration in India came gradually to consist of seven All India Services and five Central Departments, all under the control of the secretary of state, and three Central Departments under joint Provincial and Imperial control. The ICS and the Indian Police (Service) were in the 'transferred field', that is, the authority for the control of these services and for making appointments were transferred from the Secretary of State to the provincial governments. It seems relevant to mention that the All India and class I central services were designated as Central Superior Services as early as 1924 in the Lee Commission's report.

After the partition of India, the parts of the service was renamed Central Superior Services (CSP) in Pakistan while the Indian section retained the name *Indian Civil Service.*

Contemporary Indian Civil Service: In spite of relatively contemporary careers like management and IT holding sway over the coúntry's youth, the Civil Services have still not lost the vast popularity enjoyed by them through the years, from the time of the British Raj.

The IAS or Indian Administrative Service replaced the ICS and the pre-independence structure of all-India services, provincial or state services and central or Union government services was retained.

The Constitution provides for more Civil Services branches to be set up by giving the power to the Rajya Sabha to resolve by a two-thirds majority to establish new all-India services or central services. The Indian Forest Service and the Indian Foreign Service are the two services set up under this constitutional provision.

Running the administration of a vast and diverse country like India requires efficient management of its natural, economic and human resources. That, precisely, is the responsibility of the civil services. The country is managed through a number of Central Government agencies in accordance with the policy directions given by the ministries.

The construction of the Civil Services follows a certain pattern. The All India Services, Central Services and State Services constitute the Civil Services.

The Indian Administrative Service (IAS), Indian Police Service (IPS) and Indian Forest Service (IFS) are the three All India Services.

The Indian Foreign Service and Indian Revenue Service are examples of Central Services. There are forty-five other services belonging to Central Services.

The *State Administrative/Civil Service, State Police Service* and *State Forest Service* are among many State services, whose examinations are conducted by individual States of India.

Indian Administrative Service

The Indian Administrative Service (IAS) is one of the three All India Services of the Government of India; other important services being the Indian Police Service (IPS) and the Indian Forest Service (IFS). It is also called the 'Steel frame' of India and of the Government in implementing its policies and decisions effectively.

The precursor of Indian Administrative Service was the Indian Civil Service of the British Raj. ICS officers were generally held in high esteem; known as the 'Collector'. ICS officers were believed to be mostly incorruptible, true managers and good administrators.

Upon independence, the new Republic of India accepted the then serving Indian Civil Service officers who chose to stay on rather than leave for the United Kingdom and renamed the service the Indian Administrative Service.

Selection: The officials of the IAS are involved in civil administration and policy making. They are selected by the Union Public Service Commission through a three-stage combined selection process called the Civil Services Examination, known for being extremely challenging, that recruits officers for 20 other Group A services and five Group B services. Every candidate is asked to choose their preference of services among these. Almost all of them choose IAS as their first choice. The entire selection process lasts fifteen to twenty months. Repeated attempts are allowed (maximum of 4 times). The candidates can choose to be examined in about forty fields, from Civil Engineering and Medicine to Chinese Literature and Accountancy. About 50-70 are selected each year out of the nearly 300,000 appearing. IAS officers are highly regarded in Indian society.

Independence: The Constituent Assembly of India intended that the bureaucracy should be able to speak out freely, without fear of persecution or financial insecurity as an essential element in unifying the nation. The IAS officers are recruited by the Union government on the recommendation of the Union Public Service Commission (UPSC) and posted under various State governments. While the respective State Governments have control over them they can not censure or take disciplinary action against IAS and other All India Services officers without consulting the Union Government and the UPSC.

Designations: The officers of the IAS normally start as Assistant Divisional Magistrates / Sub-Collectors and look after an area that is typically 1,000-5,000 km² in extent and may have a population of 200,000 to 1,000,000. After four years of service, they are promoted to the rank of Under-Secretary to Government of India (equivalent to a Deputy Secretary to a State Government). At sometime in their careers, normally within the first ten years, they are posted as the Collectors/ Deputy Commissioners/ District Magistrates of a district. They will be subsequently promoted as Deputy, Joint, Additional and Principal Secretaries to the Government of India, or to equivalent positions in the Central Government. The head of a State's civil service is called the Chief Secretary and the head of the country's civil service is called the Cabinet Secretary. These positions require at least thirty to thirty five years of service as IAS officers. In addition, the IAS officers are sent to work in all the Attached and Subordinate Offices of the Government of India.

Indian Police Service

The Indian Police Service (IPS) is one of the three All India Services of the Government of India; other important services being the Indian Administrative Service (IAS) and the Indian Forest Service (IFS). The members of the IPS are primarily responsible for managing the policing functions of the states and the central government. These officers deal with all matters pertaining to the Internal Security of India. IPS specialises in all security related issues. Its members, who are all at least university graduates, are the senior officers of the police, with DSPs, Inspectors and Constables belonging to individual state forces.

In its previous incarnation this service was called the Imperial Police. As the name suggests it indeed was an imperial force dedicated to futhering the British Colonial rule in the country. The police and statute governing policing was brought about immediately after the East India Company's rule came to an end in face of the First Indian War of Independence in 1857. A worried British Government brought the country under their direct rule and wanted to create a force which would prevent and quell any rebellion in future. The Indian Police Act 1861 was passed and a force created to protect and perpetuate colonial rule in the country. Thus the nature of the Police Service and the force was hardly in consonance with democratic principles. In 1948, a year after India gained independence, the Imperial Police was replaced by the IPS. Sardar Patel, the first Home Minister of India had a glorious vision for the IPS. He saw it as a service which would work to uphold the rule of law and preserve the unity and intregrity of the newly independent nation.

Indian Forest Service

The Indian Forest Service (IFS) is one of the three All India Services of the Government of India; other important services being the Indian Administrative Service (IAS) and the Indian Police Service (IPS).

History: The Indian Forest Service was created in 1966 for protection, conservation and regeneration of forest resources. The recruitment to this Service is made through the Union Public Service Commission on the basis of annual Competitive Examination. While the service is an All India Service, it is not to be confused with Indian Foreign Service, which is commonly thought to be in the same league as Indian Administrative Service, Indian Police Service and Indian Forest Service. A separate examination, which is slightly different from the Civil

Services Examination as having Science background compulsory for candidates, is held for the Indian Forest Service.

India is one of the first countries in the world to have introduced scientific management of its forests. In 1864 the then British India Government started the Imperial Forest Department and in 1866 appointed Dr. Dietrich Brandis, a German Forest officer, Inspector General of Forests. Having recognized the need to have a premier forest service to manage the varied natural resources of the vast country and to organize the affairs of the Imperial Forest Department, Imperial Forest Service was constituted in 1867.

Having realized the importance of a multi-tier forest administration in the federal and provincial Governments for effective management of forest resources, the British India Government also constituted Provincial Forest Service and Executive & Subordinate Services, which were quite similar to the present day forest administrative hierarchy.

The officers appointed to the Imperial Forest Service from 1867 to 1885 were trained in Germany and France. Thereafter, until 1905 they were trained at Cooper's Hill, London, which had been one of the prestigious professional colleges of Forestry at that time. From 1905 to 1926 the Universities of Oxford, Cambridge and Edinburgh had undertaken the task of training the officers of the Imperial Forest Service. The Imperial Forest Research Institute, Dehra Dun, popularly known all over the world today as FRI, was established at Dehra Dun in the year 1906. The baton to train the IFS officers was passed on to Forest Research Institute, which it did successfully from 1927 to 1932. Subsequently the Indian Forest College (IFC) was established in the year 1938 at Dehra Dun and the officers recruited to the Superior Forest Service by the provinces/states were trained there.

The subject of "Forestry" which was managed by the Federal Government until then, was transferred to the 'Provincial List" by the Government of India Act, 1935 and subsequently recruitment to the Imperial Forest Service was discontinued.

The Indian Forest Service, one of the three All India Services, was constituted in the year 1966 under the All India Services

Act, 1951 by the Government of India. In the Government of India, at the Centre, the Director General of Forests is the highest post. The Director General of Forests is selected from amongst the seniormost PCCFs of all the states.

The main mandate of the service is the implementation of the National Forest Policy which envisages scientific management of forests and to exploit them on a sustained basis for primary timber products, among other things. Since 1935 the management of the forests remained in the hands of the Provincial Governments and even today the Forest Departments are managing the forests of the country under the respective State governments.

Forest Policy: India has an area of 633400 square kilometres notified as forests, representing some 19.27% of geographic area. India is one of the few countries which have a forest policy since 1894, revised in 1952 and again in 1988. The main plank of the current policy is protection, preservation and development of forests.

Creation of Indian Forest Service: The Indian Forest Service (IFS) was created to cater to the need for inter-state coordination and uniformity of approach in dealing with the scientific management of forests and the environment. Mr. Hari Singh was the Inspector General of Forests in 1966 and was instrumental in the creation of the IFS. Being an All India Service, the members are recruited by the Centre but their services are put under the various State cadres, with the privilege of serving both under the State and under the Centre.

Eligibility and Selection: Entry into the Indian Forest Service is open to candidates between the ages of 21 and 30 years, as on 1st July of the year of the examination, with a Bachelor's degree in Science with at least one of the following Subjects: Mathematics, Physics, Chemistry, Botany, Zoology, Geology, Statistics, Veterinary Science and Animal Husbandry; or Bachelor's degree in Engineering (any stream) / Forestry/ Agriculture/ equivalent; or M.B.B.S.

Notification of the Indian Forest Service Examination is generally expected in February. The written examination is conducted in July. The written examination is of the conventional (essay) type. Each paper is of three hours' duration. Applicants appear for tests on: Two compulsory subjects (300 marks each) (i) General English and (ii) General Knowledge. Two optional subjects from a list of 14 subjects including four branches of engineering – Mechanical, Chemical, Civil and Agricultural. Each optional subject has two papers, each paper worth 200 marks. The following combinations of optional subjects are NOT allowed: Chemical Engineering and Chemistry, Mathematics and Statistics, Agricultural Engineering and Agriculture, and Veterinary Science and Animal Husbandry. Candidates who qualify the written examination appear for an Interview of 300 marks. All papers are set only in English and they must be answered in English.

Standards and Syllabus: General English consists of essay writing, precise/summary writing and questions to assess your comprehension and verbal ability in English. General Knowledge paper covers questions relating to the Indian political system, the Constitution of India, history of India, geography (India and world), general science and current events (national and international). Higher secondary level of knowledge is a good base. As for the optional subjects, the level of testing is at least of the Honours degree level. A good bibliography for the subjects provides the base material for study.

Examination: The Indian Forest Service Examination is conducted by the Union Public Service Commission (UPSC). It provides the opportunity for direct entry into employment. The candidates are trained by the government to play a vibrant role at the grassroots level as also in policy formulation. Within the specified age slot (upper age limits are relaxed for SC/ST/ OBC and other categories), a general candidate may get up to four attempts. An OBC candidate is allowed a maximum of seven attempts and there are no limitations on number of attempts for SC/ST candidates.

Interview: As with all conversation rather than a stress exercise. Expected questions could revolve around subjects of academics; current affairs; basic knowledge of forest-related issues / policies and status of their implementation; knowledge of one's state of domicile with respect to geographical features, forest cover, wildlife, economic status, cultural outlook. The interview board wishes to see evidence of leadership qualities, tact, diplomacy, initiative, alertness, observation, mental and physical energy and enthusiasm, love for the outdoors, a sense of adventure, curiosity in surroundings and balance of judgement.

After Selection: Selected candidates are sent for foundation training at the Lal Bahadur Shastri National Academy of Administration, Massourie which is followed by specialised orientation for the Forest Service at the Indira Gandhi National Forest Academy, Dehra Dun with inputs on forests management, wildlife management, soil conservation, engineering survey, tribal welfare and weapon handling. After this comes one year "on the job" field training in the particular state to which the candidate is allotted and on successful completion of probation period on completion of four years of service with reference to the Year of Allotment, the officers are appointed to the Senior Time Scale. On getting the Senior Time Scale the officers are entitled to be posted as the Deputy Conservators of Forests or Divisional Forest Officers in charge of Districts/Forest Divisions.

Indian Foreign Service

The Indian Foreign Service (IFS) is one of the Services of the Government of India; other important services being the Indian Administrative Service (IAS), Indian Police Service (IPS), Indian Forest Service (IFS) and Indian Revenue Service (IRS).

In September 1946, on the eve of India's independence, the Government of India decided to create a service called the Indian Foreign Service for India's diplomatic, consular and commercial representation overseas.

The precursor to Indian Foreign Service can be traced back to September 1783 when Foreign Department was established by the British Raj to conduct business with foreign European powers. In 1947, there was a near seamless transformation of the Foreign department of the British India government into what then became the new Ministry of External Affairs and in 1948 the first batch recruited under the combined Civil service examination system of the Union Public Service Commission joined the service. This system of entry has remained the staple mode of intake into the IFS to this day.

The Indian Foreign Service is not one of the All India Services but still enjoys an equivalent prestige. The three types of civil services in India are the *All India Services, Central Services* and *State Services*. It belongs to the Central Services.

Training: On selection to the Indian Foreign Service through the combined Civil Services examination, the new entrants undergo a multifaceted and comprehensive training programme intended to give them a thorough grounding in diplomatic knowledge, diplomatic qualities and diplomatic skills. First, the probationers will undergo orientation training at the Lal Bahadur Shastri National Academy of Administration, Massourie and then focused training at the Foreign Service Institute in New Delhi. The course involves lectures, attachments with various wings of the Government as well as familiarisation tours both within the country and abroad. The training programme will be for 36 months as a whole.

INDIAN REVENUE SERVICE

The Indian Revenue Service (IRS) is one of the Premier Civil Services (Class-I) of India. IRS comprises of IRS (C&CE)& IRS (IT). IRS officers are concerned with the collection, administration and policy formation of direct (viz. Income, Corporate, Wealth, FBT etc.) & indirect (viz. Central Excise, Service Tax and even Customs Duty) taxes. These officers are the tax administrators of the union of India. They are either under the CBDT (Central board of direct taxes) or CBEC (Central board of Excise & Customs) in the Department of Revenue under the Ministry of Finance.

Selection: Selection is through the *combined civil services examination* conducted by Union Public Service Commission (UPSC) every year. About 400,000 candidates apply, and after a three stage selection process only 400 are selected. Thus only 0.1% pass through, making it one of the most competitive and prestigious examinations of the country. Amongst these 400, the top 200 ranks get the option of choosing between the top 4 Civil Services viz. IAS, IPS, IFS and IRS(IT)/IRS(C&CE).

Training: IRS Officer Trainees (*OTs*, as they are fondly referred to) undergo a 3 month foundational training with their fellow officers from All India Services and other Central Services

(Group A) at Mussorrie (Uttaranchal) followed by a 15 month rigorous professional training in NACEN Faridabad or NADT Nagpur, where they are intensively trained in principles, concepts and advances in Management, Taxation. Public Policy and Law.

Postings: Starting with the prestigious post of Assistant Commissioner, IRS officers rise up to Chief Commissioner level with some fortunate ones reaching the post of Member/ Chairperson-CBDT / CBEC. The Revenue Secretary who heads the Department of Revenue in the Ministry of Finance is usually an IAS officer. They are also deputed to the Vigilance Department, Enforcement Directorate, SEBI, Directorate of Revenue Intelligence, Narcotics Control Bureau, etc. apart from heading various cells in the Ministry of Finance. However the administrative acumen of the service has now started getting recognition of late. One of the previous Chief Election Commissioner was an IRS officer. One of the present member of Union Public Service Commission (UPSC) is also a member of IRS.

Career Prospects: Though the pay is much lower than in private sector, given the high talent and intelligence of the recruits, the unparalleled power, perks, and prestige make up for it. Officers also feel an added sense of satisfaction that comes from directly contributing to the development of the country, revenue being the source of all developmental works of a government. Their contribution can be judged from the fact that with a total strength of around 5000 officers (in direct taxes) and an added 2500 (in indirect taxes), the IRS are responsible for collection of direct/indirect taxes worth tens of thousands of crores of rupees(1 crore = 10 million). Presently only 3% of Indian population comes in the direct tax bracket. Similarly the Service Tax has only started picking up of late due to very few services in the tax net. With the economy booming, the IRS is bound to play an increasingly important role in the affairs of the state. As the country liberalises further, the economic power will shift into private hands with the public-private participation being the keyword. Hence the IRS officers will be at the interaction point between the private industry and the government. This is being recognised in one of the reports of The *Economic Times* which foresees a high demand for IRS officers in the private sector considering their wide range of experience in manning various fiscal and monetary policy centres as well as field formations.

Candidates prefer the IRS above other premier services due to relatively low political interference, greater leisure time, stable tenures, and postings to big cities.

Challenges: As with other government service there are many allegations of corruption. However, even Kautilya/ Chanakya, the Author of Arthauastra mentions that just as it is difficult to prevent a honeybee from tasting honey while collecting it, it is difficult for a revenue collector to remain away from money while collecting it. That apart, however, most of these allegations do not have merit. And even in case of those that have, the system is not beyond repair. The introduction of automated interfaces using electronic technologies have the potential of reducing such shortcomings in the system.

The IRS needs bright, young, honest, and dedicated people with a high sense of morality, integrity and love for the country. The nature of job brings out the jewel in him. An IRS officer on posting is entrusted with the task of completing the Assessment of the tax returns (as in Income Tax, Central Excise and Service Tax) or inter-border physical movements (as in Customs). It requires prolonged verifications and inquiries. An IRS officer gets limited staff to assist him. The reduction of manpower at the cutting edge in recent years has had a bearing on this.

Public Sector

The public sector is the part of economic and administrative life that deals with the delivery of goods and services by and for the government, whether national, regional or local/ municipal.

Examples of public sector activity range from delivering social security, administering urban planning and organising national defences.

The organization of the public sector (public ownership) can take several forms, including:

- Direct administration funded through taxation; the delivering organisation generally has no specific requirement to meet commercial success criteria, and production decisions are determined by government.
- Publicly owned corporations (in some contexts, especially manufacturing, "State-owned enterprises"); which differ from direct administration in that they have greater commercial freedoms and are expected to operate according to commercial criteria, and production decisions are not generally taken by government (although goals may be set for them by government).
- Partial outsourcing (of the scale many businesses do, e.g. for IT services), is considered a public sector model.

A borderline form is:

- Complete outsourcing or contracting out, with a privately owned corporation delivering the entire service on behalf of government. This may be considered a mixture of private sector operations with public ownership of assets, although in some forms the private sector's control and/ or risk is so great that the service may no longer be considered part of the public sector.

The decision about what are proper matters for the public sector as opposed to the private sector is probably the single most important dividing line among socialist, liberal, conservative, and libertarian political philosophy, with (broadly) socialists preferring greater state involvement, libertarians favouring minimal state involvement, and conservatives and liberals favouring state involvement in some aspects of the society but not others.

Public Services

Public services is a term usually used to mean services provided by government to its citizens, either directly (through the public sector) or by financing private provision of services. The term is associated with a social consensus (usually expressed through democratic elections) that certain services should be available to all, regardless of income. Even where public services are neither publicly provided nor publicly financed, for social and political reasons they are usually subject to regulation going beyond that applying to most economic sectors. Public services is also a course that can be studied at college and/or university. These courses can lead entry in to the: police, ambulance and fire services.

It is also an alternative term for civil service.

Sectors: Public services tend to be those considered so essential to modern life that for moral reasons their universal provision should be guaranteed, and they may be associated with fundamental human rights (such as the right to water). An example of a service which is not generally considered an essential public service is hairdressing.

In modern, developed countries the term public services often includes:

- education
- public transportation
- broadcasting and communications
- electricity and gas
- fire service
- healthcare
- police service
- waste management
- water services

Characteristics: A public service may sometimes have the characteristics of a public good (being non-rivalrous and non-excludable), but most are merit goods, that is, services which may (according to prevailing social norms) be under-provided by the market. In most cases public services are services, i.e. they do not involve manufacturing of goods such as nuts and bolts. They may be provided by local or national monopolies, especially in sectors which are natural monopolies.

They may involve outputs that are hard to attribute to specific individual effort and/or hard to measure in terms of key characteristics such as quality. They often require high levels of training and education. They may attract people with a public service ethos who wish to give something to the wider public or community through their work and are prepared to work harder for less pay as a result. (John Kenneth Galbraith has looked at the role of such "public virtue" in economic growth.)

History: Historically, the widespread provision of public services in developed countries usually began in the late nineteenth century, often with the municipal development of gas and water services. Later, other services such as electricity and healthcare began to be provided by governments. In most developed countries such services are still provided by local or national government, the biggest exceptions being the U.S. and the UK, where private provision is more significant. Nonetheless, such privately-provided public services are often strongly regulated, for example (in the US) by Public Utility Commissions.

In developing countries public services tend to be much less well developed. Water services, for example, may only be available to the wealthy middle class. For political reasons the service is often subsidised, which reduces the finance available for expansion to poorer communities.

Public Ownership

Public ownership (also called government ownership, state ownership or state property) refers to government ownership of any asset, industry, or corporation at any level, national, regional or local (municipal); or, it may refer to common (full-community) non-state ownership. The process of bringing an asset into public ownership is called Nationalization or Municipalization.

A government owned corporation (sometimes state-owned enterprise, SOE) may resemble a not-for-profit corporation as it may not be required to generate a profit; although governments may also use profitable entities they own to support the general budget. SOE's may or may not be expected to operate in a broadly commercial manner and may or may not have to face competitive tendering. The creation of a government-owned corporation (corporatization) from other forms of government ownership may be a precursor to privatization.

Arguments for and Against: For:

- *Public Services*: Some services, such as defence, cannot be provided by the private sector directly-only a government system of taxation can finance them. Others (*merit goods*), such as education, can be under-provided by the private sector (according to social standards concerning access to them).
- *Essential Services*: In the case of an essential service-particularly one on which lives may depend-Nationalization may ensure the continuation of this service regardless of commercial or environmental pressure (saving lives is not always profitable). Furthermore, there may be externalities which mean it is in the interests of all to ensure a good service is available to everyone, even beyond moral concerns.
- *Efficiency*: In natural monopolies, competition is wasteful, and will tend to be eliminated by competitive forces (leading to a private monopoly or oligopoly). A public sector monopoly can be held to account via democratically-elected governments, in a way in which a private monopoly cannot. (A private monopoly may be subject to regulation, but this may be an inefficient way of securing the public interest.)
- *Accountability*: As mentioned above, while a governmental monopoly is nonetheless still a monopoly, it is answerable to the electorate rather than a small group of shareholders. (e.g. if the telephone service is nationalised, voters can bring pressure onto the government to provide better services, and parliament may have the power to sack anyone responsible for a reduction in the quality of service).
- *Consumer Interests*: Public ownership can protect consumer interests in sectors where competition is low, where choices are important but made infrequently, and/or where consumers do not have the expertise to make good decisions (such as in health care).
- *Common Good*: A profitable nationalised industry contributes with its profits directly to the common wealth

of the whole country, rather than to the wealth of a subset of its population.

- *Financial Security*: Public sector institutions have access to finance at government interest rates, which are (almost) always lower than even the most financially secure private sector firms, because the government cannot go bankrupt, which means less risk to the lender.
- *Work Ethic*: Employees may be more inclined to view their work positively if it is directed by a management appointed by a government that they have a say in electing, rather than a management representing a shareholding minority. Also, they may gain intrinisc satisfaction knowing their work is important and essential for society as a whole. There has been discussion of a *public service ethos* which makes public sector workers work harder than they would for a private employer.
- *Equity*: Public ownership can help prevent extreme imbalances of wealth.

Against:

- *Waste*: Government ownership may lead to waste (x-inefficiency) if it proves unable to motivate management and personnel through appropriate incentives, including appropriate pay and threat of redundancy.
- *Consumer Choice*: Public ownership in an industry which could be competitive in private hands may stifle innovation if proper incentives are not provided by the government. Consumer choice may be reduced and there may be no alternative sources-and no catalysts for alternative sources-of goods or services that better meet consumer preferences.
- *Misinvestment/over-investment*: Public ownership of profitable services may lead to "gold-plating" (over-investment in assets) if decisions are driven by engineering ideals and not efficiency concerns.
- *Unprofitable Companies Survive*: Public ownership of a loss-making service or industry (such as flu vaccines)

may inhibit the changes needed to ensure long-term profitability (or permit bankruptcy). This may mean subsidising unnecessary losses indefinitely.

- *Misallocations of Labour and Money*: The government may be inefficient in running production, trading, or service operations, in the sense of causing misallocations of labour and capital, with consequent reductions in the standard of living and economic growth.
- *Accountability*: Accountability to the market may be eliminated, and accountability through government may be an insufficient replacement, particularly if an industry or service does not have a high public profile or if the government is not democratic.
- *Influenced by Politics*: Decision-making in the public sector may be prone to interference from politicians for political or populist reasons. The industry may be overstaffed in order to reduce unemployment; it may be forced to conduct transactions or actions in certain areas in order to win local votes; it may be forced to manipulate its prices in order to control inflation. Of course, some of these measures may be considered positive rather than negative, but if they are not taken properly, in the long run they are likely to be an inefficient way to meet the desired goals.
- Source of Income Sometimes governments are accused for overcharging for products where they hold a monopoly, thus utilising them as an additional source of income, or hidden tax.

GOVERNMENT

A government is a body that has the authority to make and the power to enforce laws within a civil, corporate, religious, academic, or other organization or group. In its broadest sense, "to govern" means to administer or supervise, whether over a state, a set group of people, or a collection of assets. The word *government* is ultimately derived from the Greek (*kybernan*), which means "to steer" or "to control". Typically, "the government" refers to the executive function of the state. In many countries (particularly those having parliamentary systems), the government refers to the executive branch of government or a specifically named executive, such as the Blair government (compare to the administration as in the Bush administration in U.S. usage). In countries using the Westminster system, the party in government will also usually control the legislature.

Forms of Government: Governments are often classified according to the number of people who hold political power.

- In Autocracies one individual holds all the power.
- In Oligarchies political power is held by a small group of individuals who share interests. For example a plutocracy is composed of the wealthiest members of society.
- Democracies are governments where the people as a whole hold political power. It may be exercised by them (direct democracy), or through representatives chosen by them (representative democracy).

The lines between some of the above forms of government can sometimes be ambiguous. For example, during the 19th century, most self-proclaimed "democracies" restricted voting rights to a minority of the population (e.g. property-owning males). This could qualify them as oligarchies rather than democracies· On the other hand, the voting minority was often quite large (20-30% of the population) and its members did not form the compact group with common interests that is the hallmark of most oligarchies. Thus, this form of government occupied a space between democracy and oligarchy as they are understood today.

Ideas about the Origin of Government: There are a wide range of theories about the reasons for establishing governments. The four major ones are briefly described below. Note that they do not always fully oppose each other-it is possible for a person to subscribe to a combination of ideas from two or more of these theories.

Force Theory: Many political philosophies that are opposed to the existence of a government (such as Anarchism, Nihilism, and to a lesser extent Marxism), as well as others, emphasize the historical roots of governments-the fact that governments, along with private property, originated from the authority of warlords and petty despots who took, by force, certain patches of land as their own (and began exercising authority over the people living on that land). Thus, it is argued that governments exist to enforce the will of the strong and oppress the weak, maintaining and protecting the privilege of a ruling class. It states that the government emerged when all the people of an area were brought under the authority of one person or group.

Order and Tradition: The various forms of conservatism, by contrast, generally see the government as a positive force that brings order out of chaos, establishes laws to end the "war of all against all", encourages moral virtue while punishing vice, and respects tradition. Sometimes, in this view, the government is seen as something ordained by a higher power, as in the divine right of kings, which human beings have a duty to obey.

Natural Rights: Natural rights are the basis for the theory of government shared by most branches of liberalism (including libertarianism). In this view, human beings are born with certain *natural rights*, and governments are established strictly for the purpose of protecting those rights. What the *natural rights* actually are is a matter of dispute among liberals; indeed, each branch of liberalism has its own set of rights that it considers to be *natural*, and these rights are sometimes mutually exclusive with the rights supported by other liberals. As a result, there is some debate between natural rights theorists, ranging from modern writers such as Tibor Machan to Enlightenment thinkers such as Locke, Kant, or Jefferson.

Social Contract: One of the most influential theories of government in the past two hundred years has been the social contract, on which modern democracy and most forms of socialism are founded. The social contract theory holds that governments are created by the people in order to provide for collective needs (such as safety from crime, poverty, illiteracy) that cannot be properly satisfied using purely individual means. Governments thus exist for the purpose of serving the needs and wishes of the people, and their relationship with the people is clearly stipulated in a "social contract" (a constitution and a set of laws) which both the government and the people must abide by. If a majority is unhappy, it may change the social contract. If a minority is unhappy, it may persuade the majority to change the contract, or it may opt out of it by emigration or secession. This theory is based on the idea that all men live in a state of nature which is not ideal to perfect harmony. It is also an agreement among the members of an organized society or between the governed and the government defining and limiting the rights and duties of each. Thomas Hobbes, John Locke, Jean-Jacques Rousseau are three of the most famous philosophers of contractarianism. Today, natural rights are the basis for many issues involving the constitution and ones right to privacy under the government.

Governmental Operations: Governments concern themselves with regulating and administering many areas of human activity, such as trade, education, or medicine. Governments also employ different methods to maintain the established order, such as secrecy, police and military forces (particularly under despotism, see also police state), making agreements with other states, and maintaining support within the state. Typical methods of maintaining support and legitimacy include providing the infrastructure for administration, justice, transport, communication, social welfare, etc.; claiming support from deities; providing benefits to elites; providing shops for important posts within the state; limiting the power of the state through laws and constitutions; and appealing to nationalism. Different political ideologies hold different ideas on what the government should or should not do. The modern standard unit of territory is a country. In addition to the meaning used above, the word state can refer either to a government or to its territory. Within a territory, subnational entities may have local governments which do not have the full power of a national government (for example, they will generally lack the authority to declare war or carry out diplomacy).

Size of Government: The scale to which government should exist and operate in the world is a matter of debate. Government spending in developed countries varies considerably but generally makes up between about 30% and 70% of their GDP. One major exception is the United States, where central government spending takes up less than 20% of GDP.

World Government: Some speculate that technological changes such as the Internet and the global English language would bring a World Government into existence. Some consider some governments such as the European Commission as trends towards such a system; however, others do not see this as possible.

PUBLIC COMPANY

A public company is a company owned by the public rather than by relatively few individuals. There are two different meanings for this term.

The first is a company that is owned by stockholders who are members of the general public and trade shares publicly, often through a listing on a stock exchange. The first company to issue shares is thought to be the Dutch East India Company in 1602. Ownership is open to anyone that has the money and inclination to buy shares in the company. It is differentiated from privately held companies where the shares are held by a small group of individuals, who are often members of one or a small group of families or otherwise related individuals, or other companies. The variant of this type of company in the United Kingdom and Ireland is known as a public limited company.

The second is a government-owned corporation. This meaning of a "public company" comes from the tradition of public ownership of assets and interests by and for the people as a whole, and is the less-common meaning in the United States.

"Publicly owned company" can also have either meaning, although in the United Kingdom it will usually refer to ownership by national, regional or local government.

Public versus Private Companies: A public company has several advantages. It is able to raise funds and capital through the sale of stock and convertible bonds. This is the reason why public corporations are so important, historically; prior to their existence, it was very difficult to obtain large amounts of capital for private enterprises. It has the ability to offer stock and stock options to directors, executives, and employees as part of compensation. This is much less advantageous if the company is required to treat stock options as an expense. Large stockholders, typically founders of the company, are able to sell off shares and get cash which they can put to other uses. In contrast, while ownership in a private corporation can also be sold, in part, determining a "fair value" that is acceptable to all parties can be difficult.

The goal of a public company is to enrich the owners of the company (the shareholders). The two ways that it does this is to distribute cash from the companies profits (known as dividends) and/or to reinvest the profits into the company to increase the intrinsic and share value of the company. In particular, since most investors are concerned about "buying low and selling high" the managers must in fact be constantly search for ways to make *more money*, in other words, constantly increasing profits. Besides simply increasing profits, another way to increase the stock price is to attempt to induce investors to pay more for a company's shares relative to the company's profits. Many have theorized that people will pay a higher premium for companies which have more stable profits, this theory has caused companies to diversify and form conglomerates.

A private company has several advantages. It has no requirement to publicly disclose much, if any financial information; such information could be useful to competitors. For example, Form 10-K is an annual report required by the SEC each year that is a comprehensive summary of a company's performance. Private companies do not file form 10-Ks. It is less pressured to "make the numbers"-to meet quarterly projections for sales and profits, and thus in theory able to make decisions that are best in the long-run. It spends less for certified public accountants and other bureaucratic paperwork required of public companies by government regulations. For example, the Sarbanes-Oxley Act in the United States does not apply to private companies. The wealth and income of the owners remains relatively unknown by the public.

The norm is for new companies, which are typically small, to be privately owned. After a number of years, if a company has grown significantly and is profitable, or has promising prospects, there is often an initial public offering and the company becomes public.

Less common, but not unknown, is for a public company to pay cash to its shareholders and become private. This is typically done through a leveraged buyout. Public companies can also become private when purchased by a larger company that is private.

Trading and Valuation: The shares of a public company are traded on a stock exchange. The value or "size" of a public company is called its market capitalization, a term which is often shortened to "market cap". This is calculated as the number of shares outstanding (as opposed to authorized but not necessarily issued) times the price per share. For example, a company with two million shares outstanding and a price per share of $40 would have a market capitalization of $80 million.

Primary Market

The primary market is that part of the capital markets that deals with the issuance of new securities Companies, governments or public sector institutions can obtain funding through the sale of a new stock or bond issue. This is typically done through a syndicate of securities dealers. The process of selling new issues to investors is called underwriting. In the case of a new stock issue, this sale is called an initial public offering (IPO). Dealers earn a commission that is built into the price of the security offering, though it can be found in the prospectus.

Public benefit Corporation

A public benefit corporation is a public corporation chartered by a state designed to perform some public service. A public authority is a type of public benefit corporation that takes on a more bureaucratic role, such as the maintenance of public infrastructure, that often has broad powers to regulate or maintain public property.

Authorities borrow from both municipal corporations law (that is, the laws responsible for the creation of cities, towns, and other forms of local government) and private corporations law. Other public benefit corporations resemble private non-profit organizations, and take on roles that private corporations might otherwise perform. These corporations often operate in heavily regulated industries, such as broadcasting and transportation.

Corporations such as these are often found in common law jurisdictions such as Commonwealth countries, including Canadian provinces and U.S. states.

Origins: Although many associate corporations, sometimes negatively, with private business, corporations in theory began as means to serve public purposes. Corporate theory has its roots in primarily government and religious institutions, where the institution itself is identifiable independently of its membership's mortality. For example, if the Pope dies, the Catholic Church continues to exist, just as it continues to exist as generations pass on and get replaced by new members.

Public benefit corporations likely have their direct roots in mercantile capitalism. In the early days of European exploration and colonization, a government or monarch would sometimes grant a charter to an entity allowing it to incorporate and make potentially risky investments. While certainly not public benefit corporations by today's standards, entities such as the Massachusetts Bay Company, Hudson Bay Company, and the Dutch East India Company arguably are early prototypes of publicly-chartered (in this case, crown-chartered) corporations successfully making risky investments.

History: The first public authority on record is the Port of London Authority, established 1908. According to the Port of London Acts The Authority is a public trust established to "administer, preserve and improve the Port of London." The goal was to create an entity that would be run self-sufficiently like a private company yet remain under the control of the government. The name *Authority* is derived from the founding act of Parliament which repeatedly stated that *"Authority is hereby given..."*

Incorporation and Powers: Public benefit corporations are generally governed by boards of directors, which are appointed, rather than elected, and, internally, reflect bureaucratic forms. The corporation is government-owned and performs a specific, narrow function for the public good.

Public benefit corporations are most often created by statute. In many Commonwealth countries, public benefit corporations continue to receive charters from the British monarchy. In the United States, they receive their charters usually from states, but possibly from the federal government.

Public authorities are usually created with a specific mandate, such as the construction of bridges, mass transit, etc. Unlike departments or ministries of the state, these corporations usually are enabled by statute to raise revenues through bond issues.

PUBLIC FINANCE

Public finance (government finance) is the field of economics that deals with budgeting the revenues and expenditures of a public sector entity, usually government. Governments, like any other legal entity, can take out loans, issue bonds and invest. Based on the taxing authority of the entity, they issue bonds such as tax increment bonds or revenue bonds. A bond issued by a public sector entity may give tax advantages to its owners.

The Economic Basis of Government Activity

Efficiency:

- A model of efficient resource use
- Equity vs efficiency
- Market efficiency conditions
- Market failures
- Pareto efficiency
- Government efficiency-how efficient are governments at obtaining their objectives? how much of their expenditure actually goes to where it is intended? what types of waste exist?
- Scope of government activities-what do governments spend money on? what should governments spend money

on? what can be left to markets? Why governments should be concerned with externalities, public goods.

Externalities and government policy:

- Internalization of externalities
- The Coase Theorem. The Coase theorem is the idea that government, with the power to establish the rights to use resources, can internalize externalities when transaction costs of bargaining are zero.

Public goods:

- The characteristics of
- The demand for pure public goods
- Efficient output of a pure public good
- The free rider problem

Public choice and the political process:

- Arrow's impossibility theorem

Government Expenditures

Income distribution:

- Income distribution-How will these government expenditures influence the incomes of one group relative to another group? Government programs like ?disaster relief? transfer wealth to people that have suffered a loss due to natural disaster. Social security transfers wealth from the young to the old. Engaging in a war transfers wealth to certain sectors of society. Public education transfers wealth to families with children in these schools. Public road construction transfers wealth from people that do not use the roads to those people that do (and to those that build the roads).
- Income Security
- Employment insurance
- Health Care

Financing:

- Income redistribution effects of the various types of taxes and types of borrowing

- Taxation, Prices and Efficiency
    - o Inpact of taxes on market prices and efficiency

Taxes:

- The various types of taxes
- Taxation efficiency
- Taxation fairness
- User fees

Debt:

- Government debt-the effect of previous years borrowing-the cost of servicing the debt-intergenerational consequences
    - o Types of government bonds
    - o Effects on the bond market

Property

Property designates those things that are commonly recognized as being the possessions of a person or group. Important types of property include real property (land), personal property (other physical possessions), and intellectual property (rights over artistic creations, inventions, etc.). A right of ownership is associated with property that establishes the good as being "one's own thing" in relation to other individuals or groups, assuring the owner the right to dispense with the property in a manner he or she sees fit, whether to use or not use, exclude others from using, or to transfer ownership. Some philosophers assert that property rights arise from social convention. Others find origins for them morality or natural law.

Use of the Term: Various scholarly communities (e.g., law, economics, anthropology, sociology) may treat the concept more systematically, but definitions vary within and between fields. Scholars in the social sciences frequently conceive of property as a bundle of rights. They stress that property is not a relationship between people and things, but a relationship between people with *regard to things*.

Private property is sometimes used synonymously with *individual ownership*, but the term may also be used to include collectively-owned property in the form of *corporate ownership*. Both of these are distinct from *public property*, which is that which belongs to a whole community collectively or a state.

General Characteristics: Modern property rights conceive of ownership and possession as belonging to legal individuals, even if the legal individual is not a real person. Thus, corporations, governments and other collective forms of ownership are framed in terms of individual ownership. Exceptions to this pattern include the "commons", which belong to a defined community, and the "public domain", to which access is unlimited.

Property rights are protected in the current laws of states usually found in the form of a Constitution or a Bill of Rights. The fifth amendment to the United States constitution, for example, provides explicitly for the protection of private property against arbitrary seizure by government, providing in part that:

No State shall make or enforce any law which shall abridge the privileges or immunities of citizens of the United States; nor shall any State deprive any person of life, liberty, or property, without due process of law.

Protection is also found in the United Nations Universal Declaration of Human Rights, Article 17, and in the The French Declaration of the Rights of Man and of the Citizen, Article XVII, and in the European Convention on Human Rights (ECHR), Protocol 1.

Property is usually thought of in terms of a bundle of rights as defined and protected by the local sovereignty. Ownership, however, does not necessarily equate with sovereignty. If ownership gave supreme authority it would be sovereignty, not ownership. These are two different concepts.

Traditionally, that bundle of rights includes:

1. control of the use of the property
2. the right to any benefit from the property (examples: mining rights and rent)
3. a right to transfer or sell the property
4. a right to exclude others from the property.

Legal systems have evolved to cover the transactions and disputes which arise over the possession, use, transfer and disposal of property, most particularly involving contracts. Positive law defines such rights, and a judiciary is used to adjudicate and to enforce.

In his classic text, "The Common Law", Oliver Wendell Holmes describes property as having two fundamental aspects. The first is possession, which can be defined as control over a resource based on the practical inability of another to contradict the ends of the possessor. The second is title, which is the expectation that others will recognize rights to control resource, even when it is not in possession. He elaborates the differences between these two concepts, and proposes a history of how they came to be attached to individuals, as opposed to families or entities such as the church.

According to Adam Smith, the expectation of profit from "improving one's stock of capital" rests on private property rights, and the belief that property rights encourage the property holders to develop the property, generate wealth, and efficiently allocate resources based on the operation of the market is central to capitalism. From this evolved the modern conception of property as a right which is enforced by positive law, in the expectation that this would produce more wealth and better standards of living.

Classical Liberals, Libertarians, and Related Traditions: "Just as man can't exist without his body, so no rights can exist without the right to translate one's rights into reality, to think, to work and keep the results, which means: the right of property." (Ayn Rand)

Most thinkers from these traditions subscribe to the labour theory of property. They hold that you own your own life, and it follows that you must own the products of that life, and that those products can be traded in free exchange with others.

"Every man has a property in his own person. This nobody has a right to, but himself." (John Locke)

"Life, liberty, and property do not exist because men have made laws. On the contrary, it was the fact that life, liberty, and property existed beforehand that caused men to make laws in the first place." (Frederic Bastiat) "The reason why men enter into society is the preservation of their property." (John Locke)

- Socialism's fundamental principles are centred on a critique of this concept, stating, among other things, that the cost of defending property is higher than the returns from private property ownership, and that even when property rights encourage the property-holder to develop his property, generate wealth, etc., he will only do so for his own benefit, which may not coincide with the benefit of other people or society at large (and which is argued to go against the interests of non-property-holders).
- Libertarian socialism generally accepts property rights, but with a short abandonment time period. In other words, a person must make (more or less) continuous use of the item or else he loses ownership rights. This is usually referred to as "possession property" or "usufruct." Thus, in this usufruct system, absentee ownership is illegitimate, and workers own the machines they work with. This type of property system has the effect of preventing capitalism.
- Communism argues that only collective ownership through a polity, though not necessarily a state, will assure the minimization of unequal or unjust outcomes and the maximization of benefits, and that therefore all, or almost all, private property should be abolished.

Both communism and some kinds of socialism have also upheld the notion that private property is inherently illegitimate. This argument is centred mainly on the idea that the creation of private property will always benefit one class over another, giving way to domination through the use of this private property. However, some socialists believe in the use of personal property and communists are not opposed to that which is "Hard-won, self-acquired, self-earned" (Communist Manifesto), by members of the proletariat.

Not every person, or entity, with an interest in a given piece of property may be able to exercise all of the rights mentioned a few paragraphs above. For example, as a lessee of a particular piece of property, you may not sell the property, because the tenant is only in possession, and does not have title to transfer. Similarly, while you are a lessee the owner cannot use his or her right to exclude to keep you from the property. (Or, if he or she does you may perhaps be entitled to stop paying rent or perhaps sue to regain access.)

Further, property may be held in a number of forms, e.g. joint ownership, community property, sole ownership, lease, etc. These different types of ownership may complicate an owner's ability to exercise his or her rights unilaterally. For example if two people own a single piece of land as joint tenants, then depending on the law in the jurisdiction, each may have limited recourse for the actions of the other. For example, one of the owners might sell his or her interest in the property to a stranger that the other owner does not particularly like.

Theories of Property: A natural rights definition of property rights was advanced by John Locke. Locke advanced the theory that when one mixes one's labour with nature, one gains ownership of that part of nature with which the labour is mixed.

Anthropology studies the diverse systems of ownership, rights of use and transfer, and possession under the term "theories of property". Western legal theory is based, as mentioned, on the owner of property being a legal individual. However, not all property systems are founded on this basis.

In every culture studied ownership and possession are the subject of custom and regulation, and "law" where the term can meaningfully be applied. Many tribal cultures balance individual ownership with the laws of collective groups: tribes, families, associations and nations. For example the 1839 Cherokee Constitution frames the issue in these terms:

Sec. 2. The lands of the Cherokee Nation shall remain common property; but the improvements made thereon, and in the possession of the citizens respectively who made, or may rightfully be in possession of them: Provided, that the citizens of the Nation possessing exclusive and indefeasible right to their improvements, as expressed in this article, shall possess no right or power to dispose of their improvements, in any manner whatever, to the United States, individual States, or to individual citizens thereof; and that, whenever any citizen shall remove with his effects out of the limits of this Nation, and become a citizen of any other government, all his rights and privileges as a citizen of this Nation shall cease: Provided, nevertheless, That the National Council shall have power to re-admit, by law, to all the rights of citizenship, any such person or persons who may, at any time, desire to return to the Nation, on memorializing the National Council for such readmission.

Communal property systems describe ownership as belonging to the entire social and political unit, while corporate systems describe ownership as being attached to an identifiable group with an identifiable responsible individual. The Roman property law was based on such a corporate system.

Different societies may have different theories of property for differing types of ownership. Pauline Peters argued that property systems are not isolable from the social fabric, and notions of property may not be stated as such, but instead may be framed in negative terms: for example the taboo system among Polynesian peoples.

Types of Property: Most legal systems distinguish different types (immovable property, estate in land, real estate, real property) of property, especially between land and all other forms of property-goods and chattels, movable property or personal property. They often distinguish tangible and intangible property.

One categorization scheme specifies three species of property: land, improvements (immovable man made things) and personal property (movable man made things)

In common law, real property (immovable property) is the combination of interests in land and improvements thereto and personal property is interest in movable property.

Later, with the development of more complex forms of non-tangible property, personal property was divided into tangible property (such as cars, clothing, animals) and intangible or abstract property (e.g. financial instruments such as stocks and bonds, etc.), which includes intellectual property (patents, copyrights, and trademarks).

What can be Property?: The two major justifications given for original property, or homesteading, are effort and scarcity. John Locke emphasized effort, "mixing your labour" with an object, or clearing and cultivating virgin land. Benjamin Tucker preferred to look at the telos of property, i.e. What is the purpose of property? His answer: to solve the scarcity problem. Only when items are relatively scarce with respect to people's desires do they become property. For example, hunter-gatherers did not consider land to be property, since there was no shortage of land. Agrarian societies later made arable land property, as it was scarce. For something to be economically scarce, it must necessarily have the *exclusivity property*-that use by one person excludes others from using it. These two justifications lead to different conclusions on what can be property. Intellectual property-non-corporeal things like ideas, plans, orderings and arrangements (musical compositions, novels, computer programs)-are generally considered valid property to those who support an effort justification, but invalid to those who support a scarcity justification (since they don't have the exclusivity property.) Thus even ardent propertarians may disagree about IP. By either standard, ones body is ones property.

From some anarchist points of view, the validity of property depends on whether the "property right" requires enforcement by the state. Different forms of "property" require different amounts of enforcement: intellectual property requires a great deal of state intervention to enforce, ownership of distant physical property requires quite a lot, ownership of carried objects requires very little, while ownership of one's own body requires absolutely no state intervention.

Many things have existed that did not have an owner, sometimes called the commons. The term "commons," however, is also often used to mean something quite different: "general collective ownership" i.e. common ownership. Also, the same term is sometimes used by statists to mean government-owned property that the general public is allowed to access. Law in all societies has tended to develop towards reducing the number of things not having clear owners. Supporters of property rights argue that this enables better protection of scarce resources, due to the tragedy of the commons, while critics argue that it leads to the exploitation of those resources for personal gain and that it hinders taking advantage of potential network effects. These arguments have differing validity for different types of "property"—things which are not scarce are, for instance, not subject to the tragedy of the commons. Some apparent critics actually are advocating general collective ownership rather than ownerlessness.

Things today which do not have owners include: ideas (except for intellectual property), seawater (which is, however, protected by anti-pollution laws), parts of the seafloor, gasses in Earth's atmosphere, animals in the wild (though there may be restrictions on hunting etc.—and in some legal systems, such as that of New York, they are actually treated as government property), celestial bodies and outer space, and land in Antarctica.

The nature of children under the age of majority is another contested issue here. In ancient societies children were generally considered the property of their parents. Children in most modern societies theoretically own their own bodies—but they are considered incompetent to exercise their rights, and their parents or "guardians" are given most of the actual rights of control over them. Questions regarding the nature of ownership of the body also come up in the issue of abortion.

In many ancient legal systems (e.g. early Roman law), religious sites (e.g. temples) were considered property of the God or gods they were devoted to. However, religious pluralism makes it more convenient to have religious sites owned by the religious body that runs them.

Intellectual property and air (airspace, no-fly zone, pollution laws, which can include tradeable emissions rights) can be property in some senses of the word.

Who can be an Owner?: Ownership laws may vary widely among countries depending on the nature of the property of interest (e.g. firearms, real property, personal property, animals). In some societies only adult men may own property.

In some societies legal entities, such as corporations, trusts, and nations (or governments) own property.

Private Sector

The private sector of a nation's economy consists of all that is outside the state. It includes a variety of entities such as for-profit and non-profit enterprises, corporations, banks (other than central banks), any other non-governmental organizations, as well as individuals not employed by the state. Capitalism revolves primarily around the private sector controlling industry.

Social Sector

Social sector is one of several terms created as alternatives to nonprofit sector and nongovernmental sector. The latter are seen as putting an emphasis on what this sector is not, rather than calling attention to its focus on a social mission. Other terms that have been proposed are voluntary sector, third sector, independent sector and mission-based sector.

Consumer Debt

Consumer debt is consumer credit which is outstanding. In macroeconomic terms, it is debt which is used to fund consumption rather than investment.

Some consider all debt incurred for anything else other than investments unwise, while others believe that consumer credit is beneficial in growing the economy. The difference between perspectives is often a matter of personal values, which can be attributed to widespread social biases. Historically, across many cultures, being in personal debt was considered almost immoral. More recently, an alternative analysis might view consumer debt as a way to increase domestic production. If credit is easily available, the increased demand for consumer goods should cause an increase of overall domestic production. Both domestic and international economists have supported a recent upsurge in South Korean consumer debt, which has helped fuel economic expansion. On the other hand, credit card debt is almost unknown just across the sea in Japan and China, one because of long standing historical biases against personal debt, the other because the economy is still underdeveloped.

Theoretical underpinnings aside, personal debt is on the rise, particularly in the United States.

The most common form of consumer debt is credit card debt, payday loans, and other consumer finance, which are often at higher interest rates than long term secured loans, such as mortgages. Interests rates vary, of course, depending on current economic situation and the financial status of the individual, but 12-15% per annum is not unusual.

Long-term consumer debt is often considered fiscally suboptimal. While some consumer items may be useful investments that justify debt (such as automobiles, which are usually but not always exempted in discussions of *consumer debt*, and business suits), most consumer goods are not. For example, incurring high-interest consumer debt through buying a big-screen television "now", rather than saving for it, can not usually be financially justified by the subjective benefits of having the television early. On the other hand, personal finance advisors like Robert Kiyosaki encourage a more liberal attitude towards taking on debt if it can be leveraged into a small business or real estate. This higher-risk, possibly high-outcome, "personal-finances-as-a-game" attitude runs counter to the traditional mores of rising slowly through the ranks of a company through discipline and hard work, but may have increasingly validity in an age of globalization.

In many countries, the ease with which individuals can accumulate consumer debt beyond their means to repay has paradoxically preciptated a growth industry in debt consolidation and credit counselling.

PRIVATIZATION

Privatization (alternately "denationalization" or "disinvestment") is the transfer of property or responsibility from the public sector (government) to the private sector (business). The term can refer to partial or complete transfer of any property or responsibility held by government. A similar transfer in the opposite direction could be referred to the nationalization or municipalization of some property or responsibility.

The term also has been used to describe an unrelated, nongovernmental interaction involving the buyout, by the majority owner, of all shares of a holding company's stock-privatizing a publicly traded stock.

Types of Privatization: There are three main methods of privatization:

- Share Issue privatization (SIP)-selling shares on the stock market
- Asset Sale privatization-selling the entire firm or part of it to a strategic investor, usually by auction or using *Treuhand* model
- Voucher privatization-shares of ownership are distributed to all citizens, usually for free or at a very low price.

Share issue privatization is the most common type.

Share issue can broaden and deepen domestic capital markets, boosting liquidity and potentially economic growth, but if the capital markets are insufficiently developed it may be difficult to find enough buyers, and transaction costs (e.g. underpricing required) may be higher. For this reason, many some governments elect for listings in the more developed and liquid markets such as Euronext, the London, New York or Hong Kong Stock Exchanges are popular because they are highly developed and sophisticated.

As a result of higher political and currency risk deterring foreign investors, asset sales are more common in developing countries.

Voucher privatization has mainly been used in the transition economies of Central and Eastern Europe-countries such as Russia, Poland and Czechoslovakia (Czech Republic and Slovakia)

Pro-Privatization and Anti-Privatization Arguments

Pro-Privatization: Proponents of privatization believe that private market actors can more efficiently deliver many goods or service than government due to free market competition. In general, over time this will lead to lower prices, improved quality, more choices, less corruption, less red tape, and quicker delivery. Many proponents do not argue that everything should be privatized; the existence of problems such as market failures and natural monopolies may limit this. However, a small minority thinks that everything can be privatized, including the state itself.

The basic economic argument given for privatization is that governments have few incentives to ensure that the enterprises they own are well run. Governments have the *de facto* monopoly to raise money by taxation should revenues be insufficient. As Governments may borrow money more cheaply from the debt markets than private enterprises, they will squeeze out more efficient private companies through this misallocation of resources.

Where governments lack it, it is said that private owners *do* have profit motive. The theory holds that, not only will the enterprise's clients see benefits, but as the privatized enterprise becomes more efficient, the whole economy will benefit. Ideally, privatization propels the establishment of social, organizational and legal infrastructures and institutions that are essential for an effective market economy.

Privatizing a non-profitable company which was state-owned may force the company to raise prices in order to become profitable. However, this would remove the need for the state to provide tax money in order to cover the losses.

A very substantial benefit to share or asset sale privatizations is that bidders compete to offer the state the highest price, creating revenues for the state to redistribute in addition to new tax revenue. Voucher privatisations, on the other hand, would be a genuine return of the assets into the hands of the general population, and create a real sense of participation and inclusion. Vouchers, like all other private property, could then be sold on if preferred.

- *Performance*: State-run industries tend to be bureaucratic. A political government may only be motivated to improve a function when its poor performance becomes politically sensitive, and such an improvement is easily reversed by another regime.

- *Improvements*: Conversely, the government may put off improvements due to political sensitivity and special interests — even in cases of companies that are run well and better serve their customers' needs.
- *Corruption*: A monopolized function is prone to corruption; decisions are made primarily for political reasons, personal gain of the decision-maker (i.e. "graft"), rather than economic ones.
- *Accountability*: Managers of privately owned companies are accountable to their owners/shareholders and to the consumer, and can only exist and thrive where needs are met.
- *Civil Liberty Concerns*: A company controlled by the State may have access to information or assets which may be used against dissidents or any individuals who disagree with their policies.
- *Goals*: A political government tends to run an industry or company for political goals rather than economic ones.
- *Capital*: Privately held companies can more easily raise investment capital in the financial markets, investment decisions are governed by market interest rates. State-owned industries have to compete with demands from other government departments and special interests.
- *Security*: Governments have had the tendency to "bail out" poorly run businesses when, economically, it may be better to let the business fold, often due to the sensitivity of job losses.
- *Lack of Market Discipline*: Poorly managed state companies are insulated from the same discipline as private companies, which could go bankrupt, have their management removed, or be taken over by competitors.
- *Natural Monopolies*: The existence of natural monopolies do not mean that these sectors must be state owned. Governments can enact or are armed with anti-trust legislation and bodies to deal with anti-competitive behaviour of all companies public or private.

- *Concentration of Wealth*: Ownership of and profits from successful enterprises tend to be dispersed and diversified. The availability of more investment vehicles stimulates to capital markets and promotes job creation.
- *Political Influence*: Nationalized industries are prone to interference from politicians for political or populist reasons. Examples include making an industry buy supplies from local producers (when that may be more expensive than buying from abroad), forcing an industry to freeze its prices/fares to satisfy the electorate or control inflation, increasing its staffing to reduce unemployment, or moving its operations to marginal constituencies.
- *Profits*: Private companies make a profit by enticing consumers to buy their products in preference to their competitors'. Private corporations exist to serve exactly the needs of their clients; their clients' propensity to pay is usually correlated with how well they serve the needs. Corporations of different sizes may target different market niches in order to focus on marginal groups and satisfy their demand.

Anti-Privatization: Opponents of privatization dispute the claims concerning the alleged lack of incentive for governments to ensure that the enterprises they own are well run, on the basis of the idea that governments are proxy owners answerable to the people. It is argued that a government which runs nationalized enterprises poorly will lose public support and votes, while a government which runs those enterprises well will gain public support and votes. Thus, democratic governments do have an incentive to maximize efficiency in nationalized companies, due to the pressure of future elections.

Opponents of certain privatizations believe certain parts of the social terrain should remain closed to market forces in order to protect them from the unpredictability and ruthlessness of the market (such as private prisons, basic health care, and basic education). Another view is that some of the utilities which government provides benefit society at large and are indirect and difficult to measure or unable to produce a profit, such as defense. Still another is that natural monopolies are by definition not subject to competition and better administrated by the state.

The controlling ethical issue in the anti-privatization perspective is the need for responsible stewardship of social support missions. Market interactions are all guided by self-interest, and successful actors in a healthy market must be committed to charging the maximum price that the market will bear. Privatization opponents believe that this model is not compatible with government missions for social support, whose primary aim is delivering affordability and quality of service to society.

Many privatization opponents also warn against the practice's inherent tendency toward corruption. As many areas which the government could provide are essentially profitless, the only way private companies could, to any degree, operate them would be through contracts or block payments. In these cases, the private firm's performance in a particular project would be removed from their performance, and embezzlement and dangerous cost cutting measures might be taken to maximize profits.

Some would also point out that privatizing certain functions of government might hamper coordination, and charge firms with specialized and limited capabilities to perform functions which they are not suited for. In rebuilding a war torn nation's infrastructure, for example, a private firm would, in order to provide security, either have to hire security, which would be both necessarily limited and complicate their functions, or coordinate with government, which, due to a lack of command structure shared between firm and government, might be difficult. A government agency, on the other hand, would have the entire military of a nation to draw upon for security, whose chain of command is clearly defined. Opponents would say that this is a false assertion: numerous books refer to poor organisation between government departments (for example the Hurricane Katrina incident).

Furthermore, opponents of privatization argue that it is undesirable to transfer state-owned assets into private hands for the following reasons:

- *Performance*: A democratically elected government is accountable to the people through a legislature, Congress or Parliament, and is motivated to safeguarding the assets of the nation. The profit motive may be subordinated to social objectives.
- *Improvements*: the government is motivated to performance improvements as well run businesses contribute to the State's revenues.
- *Corruption*: Government ministers and Civil servants are bound to uphold the highest ethical standards, and standards of probity are guaranteed through codes of conduct and declarations of interest. However, the selling process could lack transparency, allowing the purchaser and civil servants controlling the sale to gain personally.
- *Accountability*: The public does not have any control or oversight of private companies.
- *Civil Liberty Concerns*: A democratically elected government is accountable to the people through Parliament, and can intervene when civil liberties are threatened.
- *Goals*: The government may seek use state companies as instruments to further social goals for the benefit of the nation as a whole.
- *Capital*: Governments can raise money in the financial markets most cheaply to re-lend to State-owned enterprises.
- *Lack of Market Discipline*: Governments have chosen to keep certain companies/industries under public ownership because of their strategic importance or sensitive nature.
- *Cuts in Essential Services:* If a government-owned company providing an essential service (such as water supply) to all citizens is privatized, its new owner(s) could lead to the abandoning of the social obligation to those who are less able to pay, or to regions where this service is unprofitable.
- *Natural Monopolies*: Privatization will not result in true competition if a natural monopoly exists.

- *Concentration of Wealth*: Profits from successful enterprises end up in private, often foreign, hands instead of being available for the common good.
- *Political Influence*: Governments may more easily exert pressure on state-owned firms to help implementing Government policy.
- *Downsizing*: Private companies often face a conflict between profitability and service levels, and could over-react to short-term events. A state-owned company might have a longer-term view, and thus be less likely to cut back on maintenance or staff costs, training etc., to stem short term losses.
- *Profiteering*: Private companies do not have any goal other than to maximize profits. A private company will serve the needs of those who are most willing (and able) to pay, as opposed to the needs of the majority, and are thus anti-democratic.

Outcomes: Nellis and Kikeri have shown that in competitive industries with well-informed consumers, privatization consistently improves efficiency. Such efficiency gains mean a one-off increase in GDP, but through improved incentives to innovate and reduce costs also tend to raise the rate of economic growth. The type of industries to which this generally applies include manufacturing and retailing. Although typically there are social costs associated with these efficiency gains' many economists argue that these can be dealt with by appropriate government support through redistribution and perhaps retraining.

In sectors that are natural monopolies or public services, the results of privatization are much more mixed, as a private monopoly behaves much the same as a public one in liberal economic theory. In general, if the performance of an existing public sector operation is sufficiently bad, privatization (or threat thereof) has been known to improve matters. Indeed, Megginson & Netter showed that the greatest gains from privatization are achieved in the pre-privatization period as reforms are made to prepare for the transfer to private hands. Changes may include, inter alia, the imposition of related reforms such as greater transparency and accountability of management, improved internal controls, regulatory systems, and better financing, rather than privatization itself.

Regarding political corruption, it is a controversial issue whether the size of the public sector per se results in corruption. The Nordic countries have low corruption but large public sectors. However, these countries score high on the Ease of Doing Business Index, due to good and often simple regulations, and for political rights and civil liberites, showing high government accountability and transparency.

Also regarding corruption, the sales themselves give a large opportunity for grand corruption. Privatizations in Russia and Latin America were accompanied by large scale corruption during the sale of the state owned companies. Those with political connections unfairly gained large wealth, which has discredited privatization in these regions. While media have reported widely the grand corruption that accompanied the sales, studies have argued that in addition to increased operating efficiency, daily petty corruption is, or would be, larger without privatization, and that corruption is more prevalent in non-privatized sectors. Furthermore, there is evidence to suggest that extralegal and unofficial activities are more prevalent in countries that privatized less.

Alternatives to Privatization

Municipalization: Transferring control of a nationalized business to municipal government is an alternative sometimes proposed to privatization.

Sub-contracting: It is possible that national services may sub-contract or out-source functions to private enterprises. A notable example of this is in the United Kingdom, where many municipalities have contracted out their garbage collection or administration of parking fines by tender to private companies.

In addition, the British government is debating the possibility of involving the private sector more in the workings of the NHS, principally by referring patients to private surgeries to ease the load on existing NHS human resources, and covering the cost of this.

Part Ownership: An enterprise may be privatized, with a number of shares in the company being retained by the state. This is a particularly notable phenomenon in Germany, where the state owns around a third of Deutsche Telekom. As of 2005, the state of North Rhine-Westphalia is also planning to buy shares in the energy company E.ON in an attempt to control spiralling costs.

Whilst partial privatization could be an alternative, it is more often a stepping stone to full privatization. It can offer the business a smoother transition period during which it can gradually adjust to market competition. Some state-owned companies are so large that there is the risk of sucking liquidity from the rest of the market, even in the most liquid marketplaces, and thus must be sold off bit by bit. The first *tranche* of a multi-step privatization would also in the first instance establish a valuation for the enterprise to mitigate complaints of under-pricing.

Notable Privatizations: Privatization programmes have been undertaken in many countries across the world, falling into three major groups. The first is privatization programmes conducted by transition economies in Central and Eastern Europe after 1989 in the process of instituting a market economy. The second is privatization programmes carried out in developing countries under the influence of international financial institutions such as the World Bank and IMF. The third is privatization programmes carried out by developed country governments, the most comprehensive probably being those of New Zealand and the United Kingdom in the 1980s and 1990s.

Privatization *has* been notably successful in telecommunications in Europe because genuine competition has arisen: the former state-owned enterprises lost their monopolies due to legislation and technological change, competitors entered the market, and prices for broadband access and telephone calls fell dramatically. Some examples of failed privatizations of natural monopolies may be the rail privatization in the UK and in telecommunications in Mexico; in both countries, public disaffection has led to government intervention. Another notable example of this is Thames Water.

British Rail is an example of privatization program that has been deemed a failure. The track-owning company has been effectively repossessed by the British government, and many of the train-running companies are at risk of having their concession removed on the grounds that they fail to provide adequate services. One of them, Connex, actually had its franchise cut short in June 2003 by the government for what the Strategic Rail Authority called "poor financial management." In this case Stephen Byers (then Secretary of State for Transport) decided to call in administrators with regard to Railtrack (the infrastructure company created in 1993 and privatised in 1996) and transferring the infrastructure to the new Private Company Limited by Guarantee, Network Rail (a not for profit private company with no shareholders), Train Operation remains in the hands of private operators with franchises awarded by the Department for Transport (except for Merseyrail the franchise of which is awarded by Merseyside Passenger Transport Executive).

There are various precedents in history which some would claim as examples in which improper privatization, or the failure of government to conduct certain functions, caused various complications.

1. In the 18th Century, military functions such as maintaining forts and garrisons along the African coast were, in effect, privatized to the East India Company, with parliament obliged to pay 13,000 pounds a year to support the East India Company in this end. However, this being somewhat of a government monopoly itself, it cannot said to be a perfect counter to privatization. The East India Company proceeded to shirk various expenses, most notably in the maintenance of fortifications. In one case, a shipment of inferior bricks sent to repair the walls of one fortification were of such low quality that it became necessary to rebuild the entire wall from its foundation.
2. Prior to the great depression, various state governments and the Hoover administration attempted to provide relief through private firms like the Red Cross. However, due to their limited capabilities, the firms were often

unable to provide for the various functions that people required, and could only provide them in specific areas besides. Also, because they depended on limited resources (even with occasional payments from the government) they would usually be unable to provide them for very long.

3. During World War Two, the Truman Commission uncovered various instances in which contracts given out to various private firms to provide various military materials fostered considerable profiteering which often resulted in inadequate weapons and equipment being sent to the front.
4. In the reconstruction of Iraq, the government decided to contract out many different reconstruction functions to private firms. Shortly thereafter, those firms have been accused of cutting corners and being generally ineffective in reconstructing the country. Halliburton, in particular, was accused of, among other things, skimping on the cost of providing meals to soldiers. Various other complaints include the lagging reconstruction of water and electricity utilities, and providing defective equipment to soldiers.
5. Many, such as Dick Polman of *The Philadelphia Inquirer*, noted that prior to Hurricane Katrina, the government had "privatized many of FEMA's basic functions". The uncoordinated action between private emergency relief agencies, as well as the military (which would often turn back relief trucks) resulting in the poor response to the storm that many would claim was a result of this privatization.

NATIONALIZATION

Nationalization is the act of transferring assets into public ownership. It usually refers to the transfer of private assets, but may also mean assets owned by other levels of government, such as municipalities. The opposite of nationalization is usually privatization, but may also be municipalization. A renationalization occurs when assets are nationalized after a previous privatization. Nationalizations are distinguished from property redistributions in that in the former case, the government retains control of the property after acquisition.

Some nationalizations take place when a government seizes criminal property. For example, the French government seized Renault because its owners had collaborated with Nazi Germany.

Compensation: A key issue in nationalization is whether the private owner is properly compensated for the value of the institution. The most controversial nationalizations are those where no compensation or an amount unreasonably below the likely market value of the nationalized assets is paid, and are known as expropriations. Many nationalizations through expropriation have come after revolutions.

The traditional Western stance on compensation was expressed by United States Secretary of State Cordell Hull, during the 1938 Mexican nationalization of the petroleum industry, that compensation should be "prompt, effective and adequate." According to this view, the nationalizing state is obligated under international law to pay the deprived party the full value of the property taken. The opposing position has been taken mainly by developing countries, claiming that the question of compensation should be left entirely up to the sovereign state, in line with the Calvo Doctrine. Communist states have held that no compensation is due, based on communist notions of private property.

In 1962, the United Nations General Assembly adopted Resolution 1803, "Permanent Sovereignty over National Resources," which states that in the event of nationalization, the owner "shall be paid appropriate compensation in accordance with international law." In doing so, the UN rejected both the traditional Calvo-doctrinist view and the Communist view. The term "appropriate compensation" represents a compromise between the traditional views, taking into account the need of developing countries to pursue reform even without the ability to pay full compensation, and the Western concern for protection of private property.

When nationalizing a large business, the cost of compensation is so great that many legal nationalizations have happened when firms of national importance run close to bankruptcy and can be acquired by the government for little or no money. A classic example is the UK nationalization of the British Leyland Motor Corporation. At other times, governments have considered it important to gain control of institutions of strategic economic importance, such as banks or railways, or of important industries struggling economically. The case of Rolls-Royce plc, nationalized in 1971, is an interesting blend of these two arguments. This policy was sometimes known as ensuring government control of the "commanding heights" of the economy, to enable it to manage the economy better in terms of long-term development and medium-term stability. The extent of this policy declined in the 1980s and 1990s as governments increasingly privatized industries that had been nationalized, replacing their strategic economic influence with use of the tax system and of interest rates.

Nonetheless, national and local governments have seen the advantage of keeping key strategic assets in institutions that are not strongly profit-driven and can raise funds outside the public-sector constraints, but still retain some public accountability. Examples from the last five years in the United Kingdom include the vesting of the British railway infrastructure firm Railtrack in the not-for-profit company Network Rail, and the divestment of much council housing stock to "arms-length management companies," often with mutual status.

MUNICIPALIZATION

Municipalization is the transfer of corporations or other assets to municipal ownership. The transfer may be from private ownership (usually by purchase) or from other levels of government. It is the opposite of privatization and is different from nationalization.

Services: There have been two main waves of municipalization in developed countries. The first took place in the late nineteenth and early twentieth century, when municipalities in many developed countries acquired local private providers of a range of public services. The driving reason in most cases was the failure of private providers to sufficiently expand service provision outside wealthy parts of urban areas.

The second wave took place in the early 1990s, when after the end of the communist states in eastern Europe state-owned companies in many public service sectors were broken up and transferred to municipal control. This was typical in sectors such as water, waste management and public transport, although not in electricity and natural gas.

Such regional companies either remained under municipal control, or were privatized. Privatization was done variously: by selling them to investors, by giving a concession or a management contract. Examples include the water sector in the Czech Republic, over half of which has been privatized.

Governments: In the U.S., municipalization often refers to incorporation of an entire county into its municipalities, leaving no unincorporated areas. This generally ends *de facto* the county's own home rule, which in most states allows it to act as the municipal service provider in those unincorporated areas. The county is left offering only those services mandated of it by the state constitution, which are generally only extensions of state government like courts and sheriff departments. As with utilities, the county's assets usually end up being distributed among the cities, though this is less likely if the process is gradual rather than all at once.

One example of municipalization is the Sacramento Municipal Utilities District, or SMUD, of Sacramento, California. In another, larger example, Fulton County, Georgia, which includes the city of Atlanta, is currently undergoing full municipalization. For a more complete discussion of this process in the Fulton County context, see the "Politics" section of the Fulton County article.

Regulation

A regulation is a legal restriction promulgated by government administrative agencies through rulemaking supported by a threat of sanction or a fine. This administrative law or regulatory law is in contrast to statutory or case law. Regulation mandated by the government or state attempts to produce outcomes which might not otherwise occur, produce or prevent outcomes in different places to what might otherwise occur, or produce or prevent outcomes in different timescales than would otherwise occur. Common examples of regulation include attempts to control market entries, prices, wages, pollution effects, employment for certain people in certain industries, standards of production for certain goods and services. The economics of imposing or removing regulations relating to markets is analysed in regulatory economics.

Regulation as a Legal Term: A *regulation* as a legal term is a rule created by an administration or administrative agency or body that interprets the statutes setting out the agency's purpose and powers, or the circumstances of applying the statute.

A *regulation* is a form of secondary legislation which is used to implement a primary piece of legislation appropriately, or to take account of particular circumstances or factors emerging during the gradual implementation of, or during the period of, a primary piece of legislation.

Other forms of secondary legislation are *statutory instruments, statutory orders, by-laws* and *rules*. Some of these (but not all of them) need to be referred back before being implemented, to the primary legislative process.

Types of Regulation: Regulations, like any other coercive action, have costs for some and benefits for others. Efficient regulations may only be said to exist where the total benefits to some people exceed the total costs to others. Regulation are justified using various reasons and therefore can be classified in several broad categories:

- Market failures-regulation due to inefficiency. Intervention due to a classical economics argument to market failure.
  - Risk of monopoly
  - Collective action, or public good
  - Inadequate information
  - Unseen externalities
- Collective desires-regulation about collective desires or considered judgements on the part of a significant segments of society

- Diverse experiences-regulation with a view of eliminating or enhancing opportunities for the formation of diverse preferences and beliefs
- Social subordination-regulation aimed to increase or reduce social subordination of various social groups
- Endogenous preferences-regulation's purpose is to affect the development of certain preferences on an aggregate level
- Irreversibility-regulation that deals with the problem of irreversibility – the problem in which a certain type of conduct from current generations results in outcomes from which future generations may not recover from at all.
- Interest group transfers-regulation that results from efforts by self-interest groups to redistribute wealth in their favour, which may disguise itself as one or more of the justifications above.

Public Broadcasting

Public broadcasting is a form of public service broadcasting (PSB) intended to serve the diverse needs of the listening public. Except for the United States, it has traditionally been the dominant form of broadcasting in much of the world.

It is a system in which radio, television, and potentially other electronic media outlets receive some or all of their funding from the public. The broadcasters' funds can come directly from individuals through voluntary donations, licence fees, or indirectly as state subsidies that originated as taxes. Many public broadcasters supplement this with contributions from corporations, in return for underwriting spots. While these announcements resemble traditional advertisements on commercial broadcasting stations, there are usually limitations, such as a prohibition of making product claims, stating prices, or providing an incentive to buy.

Commercial broadcasting now occurs in many countries around the world, and the number of countries with only public broadcasting has declined substantially. The mass media marketplace is tremendously competitive, and as such, it can be difficult for a public service broadcaster to survive amongst commercial interests. This may become even more of an issue with the increased number of channels that digital broadcasting provides.

Defining Public Broadcasting: There is no standard definition of what public broadcasting is exactly, although a number of official bodies have attempted to pick out the key characteristics. Public service broadcasters generally transmit programming that aims to improve society by informing viewers. In contrast, the aim of commercial outlets is to provide popular shows that attract an audience—therefore leading to higher prices when advertising is sold. For this reason, the ideals of public broadcasting are often incompatible with commercial goals. Of course, public broadcasters also strive to entertain their viewers, but they can still come across as being overly paternalistic in nature.

The Broadcasting Research Unit lists the following as major goals or characteristics of a public broadcaster: 1 *Geographic universality* — The stations' broadcasts are available nationwide, with no exception. This criterion is failed by Five in the UK, which a substantial minority of the population cannot receive. Generally, the "nationwide" criterion is satisfied by either having member stations across the country (as is the case with PBS in the United States) or, as is the case with most other public broadcasters around the world, the broadcaster owning sufficient transmitters to broadcast nationwide.

Some of these definition points may not be acceptable everywhere. For example in the United States public broadcasting may see part of its mission to bring in foreign shows, e.g. shows from the CBC/Radio-Canada or the BBC.

An alternative model for implementing public service media exists, known as Citizen Media. As it relates to broadcasting, this generally means a radio or television outlet which has some sort of public access, that is, most or much of the programming is created by members of the public which receives the programming. This can be in the form of community radio, campus radio, and public access television, although the latter is not a form of over-the-air broadcasting, as it is only available on cable television systems.

Advantages and Disadvantages: Public broadcasters receive all or a substantial part of their funding from government sources, either from the general tax revenues or from licence fees. Since public broadcasters do not rely on advertising as a source of revenue to the same degree as commercial broadcasters, this allows public broadcasters to air programs that are less saleable to the mass market, such as public affairs shows, documentaries, and educational programs. The fact that public broadcasters do not chase ratings in the same way as commercial broadcasters often leads to the criticism that they are unresponsive to what their viewers want.

Additionally, public broadcasting facilitates the implementation of cultural policy (an industrial policy and investment policy for culture). Some examples include:

- The Canadian government is committed to official bilingualism (English and French). As a result, the public broadcaster, the CBC employs translators and journalists who speak both official languages and it encourages production of cross-cultural material. Quebec separatists argue that this is also a policy of cultural imperialism and assimilation.
- In the UK, the BBC supports multiculturalism and diversity, in part by using on-screen commentators and hosts of different ethnic origins.
- In New Zealand, the public broadcasting system provides support to Aboriginal (Maori) broadcasting, as a way to improve the opportunities and maintain the cultural heritage of these New Zealanders.

Critics of public broadcasting systems argue that this implementation of cultural policy imposes the values of the public broadcaster on the populace. However, it can also be argued that commercial broadcasting has a bias for certain values or cultural forms, such as pop culture, militarism, culture bias, and consumerism.

Public broadcasting, and also some pirate broadcasting, provides a counterweight to the commercial media. Advocates of deliberative democracy, argue that public broadcasting helps to maintain modern technological democracies. At the same time, public broadcasting systems have also been used by dictators and totalitarian governments to spread hatred and incite genocide. However, in theory in "western democracies" public broadcasting is not beholden to political parties, or the government of the day. This is especially true where the broadcaster is funded by television licence fees and so, theoretically, not dependent on the government for any of its funding.

Implementation of Public Broadcasting around the World: The model, established in the 1920s, of the British Broadcasting Corporation – an organization widely trusted, even by citizens of the Axis Powers during World War II – was widely emulated throughout Europe, the British Empire, and later the Commonwealth. The public broadcasters in a number of countries are basically an application of the model used in Britain.

Modern public broadcasting is often a mixed commercial model. For example, the CBC has always relied on a subsidy from general revenues of the government. However, more recently CBC television has started taking advertising. This means they must compete with commercial broadcasting. Some argue that this dilutes their mandate as truly public broadcasters, who have no commercial bias to distort their presentation. The rest of this section looks at some specific implementations of public broadcasting around the world.

2

Information Systems for Public Sector Management

As in many countries, public sector reform in India has consisted of five main components: increased efficiency, decentralisation, increased accountability, improved resource management, and marketisation. 'Information age reform' means delivering these ongoing reform components with a more overt role for information and with greater use of information technology. A review of global experience suggests that information age reform has great potential to improve public administration and other components of the public sector.

However, the Indian reality – like that for many developing countries – has been more problematic, with many failures of such reform; failures that can be described as total, partial or failures of sustainability and replication. The explanation for such failure lies partly in the approach to reform adopted by senior public officials. A 'four Is' model of approaches is described: the pre-information age approach of 'ignore', and the information age approaches of 'isolate', 'idolise' and 'integrate'. Analysis of Indian cases suggests it is the last approach that is most likely to deliver reform objectives; yet it remains the least commonly-adopted. Changes are therefore required in current strategies for public administration training and the management of change. Such findings will hold true for many other developing countries.

The Reform Agenda

Public sector reform is, if generally defined, change within public sector organisations that seeks to improve their performance. As such, reform can be seen as an ongoing process in India since the inception several centuries ago of institutions that we now label 'public sector'. However, reform is typically defined more narrowly. It is often associated with the ideology of the 'New Right' towards the public sector; an ideology that grew up especially from the 1970s and which sought particular types of change in the way the public sector was run. This ideology has, albeit slowly and by 'fits and starts', increasingly begun to shape the agenda for change in the Indian public sector.

What constitutes the public sector reform agenda in India? There has been no consistent menu of elements but typical components – driven by the global agenda of new public management – include those listed below (Bhattacharaya, 1996; Maheshwari, 1996; Sengupta, 1995; Singh, 1996).

- *Increased Efficiency*: improving the input:output ratio within the public sector. The rationale of such reforms is to address the large size of public sector expenditure and/or the inefficiency of many of its processes.
- *Decentralisation*: the transfer of decision making to lower, more localised levels of the public sector. The rationale of such reforms is to reduce the costs of centralised decision making, and to create more flexible and responsive decision making.
- *Increased Accountability*: making public sector staff more accountable for their decisions and actions. The rationale of such reforms is to increase the pressure on staff to perform well, to make them more responsive to recipient groups, and to reduce inefficient or corrupt practices.
- *Improved Resource Management*: increasing the effective use of human, financial and other resources. The rationale of such reforms is clear from their definition. It often includes a refocusing of the way the performance of these resources is planned, measured and managed.
- *Marketisation*: increasing the use of market forces to cover relationships within the public sector, relationships between citizens ('consumers') and the public sector, and relationships and boundaries between public and

private sector. The rationale of such reforms is that market relations will drive costs down and increase efficiency and/or effectiveness of service delivery.

There has been much criticism of the components listed: of what they seek to achieve in theory, and of what they do and do not achieve in practice. In this paper, we are not going to participate in that particular debate because that is not our purpose. These components will be taken as a given; as initiatives that are being evermore widely undertaken or imposed. For increasing numbers of Indian public servants, the issue is not the rights and wrongs of reform, but how best to implement reform initiatives in which they find themselves involved.

The Information Age

Almost simultaneous with the development of a reform agenda, there has been a growing sense in India of a real or impending 'information age'. The roots of ideas about a new 'information age' – treated here as synonymous with emergence of an 'information economy', 'information society' or 'post-industrial society' – are invariably traced back to the work of writers such as Daniel Bell, Fritz Machlup, Yuji Masuda and Alvin Toffler (e.g. Bell, 1974; Machlup, 1962; Masuda, 1983; Toffler, 1980). Through analysis of extant trends, they described a vision of a new world paradigm that was already coming into existence and that would increasingly develop. General features of this new paradigm include a domination of services over other economic sectors, niche instead of mass markets, and the emergence of a 'post-bureaucratic' form of organisation.

The early, and optimistic, writings about the information age have been much criticised. Critics argue:

- That things have not changed as much as predicted. Peasant farmers – who, with their families, form a major proportion of the world's population – continue to live and work much as they have ever done. They have yet to appreciate the pleasures of surfing the Net or teleworking. Even in the high citadels of the new world, shifts in working patterns and social life may be tangible and important, but they are not yet revolutionary. A modified criticism is therefore that change has been, and will be, a very uneven process that creates inequalities.

- That, when things do change, there will be problems as well as benefits. The information age may be marked by higher living standards but also by unemployment, insecurity, electronic surveillance and alienation.
- That the technology focus of information age writing distracts us from the human, social and political factors which explain – and therefore ultimately determine – what happens in our world.

There is a great deal of validity in these criticisms, but what they do not deny is that – albeit slowly and unevenly, for better or worse – there are identifiable information age trends. Thus, while the concept of an information age retains a large measure of hyperbole, it does serve to highlight important trends that are shaping the world in which we live.

It is certain that they have begun to shape the economic and political context in India.

Whilst many see the 1970s as something of a 'lost decade' for India in computing terms, the country more than made up in the 1980s. The 1984—87 period in office of 'Rajiv and his computer boys' marked a defining moment during which India's image and activity as a global software player really began to take off, and during which a clear link was made between computing and reform of Indian public administration.

Although information technology (IT) has never since been so heavily-championed at such a high level in government, the catalytic actions of the mid-1980s set loose two specific, related and seemingly unstoppable information age trends in India:

- The increasing importance of information, including the increasing visibility and value of information systems.
- The increasing use of information technology.

Defining IT and IS: *Information technology* can be defined as computing and telecommunications technologies that provide automatic means of handling information. IT is therefore taken here to represent equipment: both the tangible hardware and the intangible software. A computer linked to other computers on a local area network represents one example of IT.

Information systems (IS) can be defined as systems of human and technical components that accept, store, process, output and transmit information. They may be based on any combination of human endeavours, paper-based methods and IT. A financial information system of staff and computers that gathers data and processes it into reports used for managerial decision making represents one example of an IS.

Thus:

- IT on its own does not do anything useful; in order to do anything, it must become part of an information system.
- Information systems do not necessarily involve computers and telecommunications equipment.
- Even when they do, information systems are much more than just IT because they involve people and their actions.

For the public sector in India, this means that one can therefore see a trend of 'information age reform' that combines the existing reform agenda with the promise of the information age. Indeed, from humble beginnings in the Indian Statistical Institute in 1956, government expenditure on IT has grown to average more than US$350m per annum by the late 1990s (*Dataquest*, 1998).

Information age reform is therefore a growing reality for India which means two things that are different from traditional reform:

- First, a much greater (i.e. more overt) role for information and information systems in the processes of change in the public sector.
- Second, a much greater (i.e. more widely employed) role for information technology in the processes of change in the public sector.

THE PROMISE OF INFORMATION AGE

Reform: There is great potential for these trends of information age reform to bring significant benefits to India because government has been, and still remains, the single largest collector, user, holder and producer of information. Information is a central resource for all staff levels and for all activities: 'In pursuing the democratic/political processes, in managing resources, executing functions, measuring performance and in service delivery, information is the basic ingredient' (Isaac-Henry, 1997, p.132) The work of government is thus very information-intensive, and four main types of formal information are identifiable:

- *Information to Support Internal Management*: This includes information about staff for personnel management, and information about budgets and accounts for financial management. Like the other three types of information, it can be used for everything from day-to-day operational implementation up to long-term policy analysis and planning.
- *Information to Support Public Administration and Regulation*: This includes information that records the details of the main 'entities' in India: people, business enterprises, buildings, land plots, imports/exports, etc. It is used for a variety of purposes such as legal, judicial and fiscal.
- *Information to Support Public Services*: Examples include education (e.g. school staff records), health (e.g. patient records), transport (e.g. passenger reservation information) and public utilities (e.g. customer billing information).
- *Information Made Publicly Available*: This includes:
  - Information government wishes to disseminate such as press releases, consultation papers, details of policies, laws and regulations, and details of benefits and entitlements.
  - Information government collects that it may make available, such as demographic or economic statistics.
  - Information government is required to supply such as audited accounts, internal policy documents and correspondence, and responses to requests from politicians or journalists or citizens.

Given this information-intensity, changes in information systems must be an essential part of all reform initiatives in India, and changes in information technology will also have a great potential. In theory, everything that IT can do could be done by some other means. In practice, its ability to increase the speed and/or reduce the cost of information tasks mean it can do things that would not otherwise be contemplated. IT therefore can bring change and has three basic change potentials within reform:

- *Supplant*: automate existing human-executed processes which involve accepting, storing, processing, outputting or transmitting information. For example, the automation of existing clerical functions.
- *Support*: assist existing human-executed processes. For example, assisting existing processes of government decision making, communication, and decision implementation. (This can also be seen as a potential to *empower* if IT assists the activity of citizens outside government.)
- *Innovate*: create new IT-executed processes or support new human-executed processes. For example, creating new methods of public service delivery. IT can bring five main benefits to the reform process. In practice, these are not neatly differentiated but they can be summarised as:
- *Cheaper*: producing the same outputs at lower total cost.
- *More*: producing more outputs at the same total cost.
- *Quicker*: producing the same outputs at the same total cost in less time.
- *Better*: producing the same outputs at the same total cost in the same time, but to a higher quality standard.
- *For the First Time*: producing new outputs.

The first three represent efficiency gains for the public sector; the last two represent effectiveness gains. Of course, these are the direct and objective benefits. IT can bring many others such as better staff motivation, greater political control, or an improved public image for the organisation (with Indian Railways being a case in point for all three of these indirect benefits).

IT is therefore seen to have a great potential to contribute to reform (Traunmuller and Lenk 1996), with this potential being illustrated by the following examples from around the world:

- *Increased Efficiency*: IT's role in increasing efficiency has been described above, mainly relating to its 'supplant' role. In the US, the Lawrence Livermore National Laboratory developed a World Wide Web-based system to reduce the cost and increase the speed of parts procurement (Gebauer and Schad, 1998).
- *Decentralisation*: IT can provide support for more efficient and effective decision making at decentralised locations and create new information flows that incorporate those locations. In Ireland, the Department of Social Welfare created more than a dozen computerised applications in order to support the decentralisation of responsibilities from Dublin to outlying offices (Cooney and O'Flaherty, 1996).
- *Increased Accountability*: IT can create new accountability information and can deliver accountability information to new recipients, providing for more efficient or effective accountability. In the US, 'collusion detection software' was developed and applied to root out impropriety in bids and contract awards for supply of public school milk (Anthes, 1993).
- *Improved Resource Management*: IT can create new performance information and deliver it to decision makers, providing more effective managerial control over government resources. In Malaysia, government development authorities collaborated to develop a computerised system to facilitate land resource management (Raman and Yap, 1996).
- *Marketisation*: IT can supply the new information necessary for the establishment of market relations,

and can also form the conduit for delivery of new forms of public service. 'In Spain and Portugal, smart cards are issued to people to claim unemployment benefit at kiosks, and to check on job vacancies and training opportunities.' (Gosling, 1997, p.69).

INDIAN REALITIES OF INFORMATION AGE

Reform: Globally, then, new information systems and new information technology are both supporting and driving forward the process of public sector reform. But what of India? Has the country unleashed the power of information age reform, or does the potential still lie mainly dormant?

Objective reporting of information age reform cases in India (and elsewhere) is rare.

Many reports are written from a 'rose-tinted' viewpoint by those with a vested interested in the reform initiative. Their glowing and uncritical claims of success frequently bear little relation to reality. Nonetheless, reliable cases can be found and one can place these into three categories.

Success: Computerisation of the Indian Railways' Passenger Reservation System may be branded a success (Heeks, 1996a). Not only did it significantly increase the efficiency of the reservation process, but it also reduced corruption (though did not eliminate it), increased rail staff morale, and improved the quality of customer service. Beyond these reform components, it also gave Indian Railways (and India more widely) a more modern image, and it helped to build information age capabilities within the country.

Sadly, this case remains almost a lone beacon in India which 'seems to stand out as a solitary example of success.' (Bhatnagar, 1997, p.5).

Open Verdict: A few ongoing information age reform projects have yet to fall clearly into the categories of either success or failure. Perhaps the best-known of these is CRISP, the Computerised Rural Information Systems Project. When initially analysed, after some five years of operation, this appeared to have made little impact and to be heading for failure (Madon, 1993). Subsequent analysis, however, revealed 'sparks of life' within the project, with some computers being used to support analytical management decision making, thereby enabling decentralisation and improved delivery of assistance (Madon and Sahay, 1996).

Failure: By far the largest category of reports – both from the formal literature and from the dozens of Indian public servants trained each year by the author – is that of failure. There are no cast-iron statistics on this and there are unlikely ever to be. Nonetheless, based on the available evidence, one can state with some degree of certainty that the majority of information age reform initiatives in India end in failure. This may be the *total failure* of an initiative never implemented or in which a new system is implemented but immediately abandoned; the *partial failure* of an initiative in which major goals are unattained or in which there are significant undesirable outcomes; the *sustainability failure* of an initiative that succeeds initially but then fails after a year or so; or the *replication failure* of an initiative that succeeds in one place but cannot be repeated elsewhere.

Formally-reported examples include the following:

- The Director of Adult Education in the National Literacy Mission Authority was smitten by the potential of IT to improve the management of literacy programmes (Jain, 1994). Having seen a software firm's demonstration, and despite glaring technical and data constraints that were obvious to any neutral observer, he commissioned a complex executive information system (EIS) that soon fell squarely into the 'total failure' category.
- Part of the Income Tax Department's tax system was computerised. The project ran into difficulties due to political antagonisms between various groups; notably between regional tax commissioners and the central tax board, and between management and unions. As a result, only parts of the information system and only a sub-set of intended process reforms became operational and even these were resisted by staff. There was therefore only very limited achievement of reform objectives (Singh, 1990).

- A computerised decision support system (DSS) was created for the Narmada Irrigation Project Authority (Rama Rao, 1990). The system was initially used to increase efficiency by helping engineers save time in their cost estimations of canal engineering work. However, the system was never properly used for its main intended purpose: the production of improved canal design. Upon retirement of the Chief Engineer who had championed use of the DSS, even the estimation use was discontinued.
- A computerised management information system was developed in Surendranagar district, Gujarat state, to demonstrate the feasibility of providing computer support to planning and monitoring tasks at the district level, thereby enabling decentralisation (Bhatnagar, 1992). Although the system proved useful, it was never adopted elsewhere because other district officers had a 'not invented here' mentality that rejected innovations made by anyone other than themselves.

UNDERSTANDING INFORMATION AGE REFORM FAILURE IN THE INDIAN

Context: One is naturally drawn to analyse why failure should be so prevalent in India. There are almost as many explanations for failure as there are information systems. However, one key factor that emerges again and again from case study analysis is the attitude and actions of senior public officials, both politicians and managers (Gupta, 1996; Bhatnagar, 1997; Peterson, 1998). Based on discussions with such officials and their subordinates, and a review of relevant cases, we can create a 'four Is' model of different approaches to information age reform that appear over time, as described below.

The 'Ignore' Approach: In this case, public officials are ignorant about IT and information systems. They therefore do not include consideration of either in their plans for reform. IT expenditure is minimal or non-existent. This approach does not constitute information age reform and will therefore not form a major focus of this paper. Nevertheless, this approach is still found in many – perhaps even most – Indian public sector organisations. This is sometimes even so when computers are present for, in some cases, those computers remain unused and merely act as costly 'executive paperweights'.

The 'Isolate' Approach: In this approach, public officials remain computer-illiterate and lack an understanding of information's role. They nevertheless are aware of IT and its potential. Investment in IT is therefore included in reform plans but is seen as the separate responsibility of 'computer experts'. It is mainly associated with automation and some (often spurious or concocted) idea that efficiency gains will result. For other reform agendas, it is added as an afterthought and is not linked in any systematic way to the process of reform. This, nonetheless, represents the first step on the path of information age reform.

Both the early years of the CRISP project and the Indian Income Tax project cited above are examples of the isolate approach. In these cases, the introduction of computers was seen as the responsibility of technical staff rather than being something in which mainstream managers should become involved. As a result, huge investments made very little, if any, contribution to reform agendas in these Indian public sector organisations.

This approach should not be seen as some historical aberration for it can still be found. The recent Asian Development Bank-supported project for restructuring of Gujarat's financial sector provides an example:

'Yet when it comes to computerisation, the cart has been put before the horse. There is a separate allocation for computerisation ... The type of hardware and its allocation to various tax collection agencies has already been decided. It was envisaged that the process of computerisation would be completed even before the thinking on financial sector reform made any headway.' (Bhatnagar, 1997, p.8)

The 'Idolise' Approach: In this approach, public officials have become semi-literate. They use computers and are over-aware of IT's potential. They believe that IT can transform the business of government (or at least transform their own career/ political prospects if they are seen to initiate a high-profile IT project). They are dimly aware that information is something important. The public sector becomes awash with IT-driven reform projects which place technology at the heart of the change process.

This approach has recently leapt to prominence thanks to N. Chandrababu Naidu, Chief Minister of Andhra Pradesh state. In 1997, he launched a high-profile project – the LEAP21 (Leadership and Excellence in Andhra Pradesh in the twenty-first century) initiative – that exactly fits the idolise description. This initiative aims to use IT as a main lever in the creation of better government in Andhra Pradesh and, more generally, 'focuses ... on using Information Technology as a strategic tool for improving the quality of life for the people of Andhra Pradesh.' (Naidu, 1997, p.1).

The jury currently remains out on LEAP21. Chief Minister Naidu's intention of using state promotional interventions to support the development of the IT industry and IT technological capabilities is based on sound historical precedent (Heeks, 1996b).

However, his hopes of driving public sector reform with IT are not. There is a long history of failure to deliver reform objectives via technology-driven projects, of which the literacy EIS case cited above is but one example (Kraemer *et al.*, 1981; Davies, 1997).

Even where technology-centred projects initially appear to succeed in delivering reform objectives, Bhatnagar (1997) warns that they may not be sustainable or replicable since they so often depend on a single 'idolising' figurehead. When that senior official transfers to a new post, the project often collapses; when other organisations try to copy, failure ensues because the originator's drive or skills are lacking; and copying rarely takes place because 'a replication will never attract the same attention as a first time use' (Bhatnagar, 1997, p.6). In all situations, the cause is the lack of the original IT-focused champion.

Examples of these sustainability and replication failures from India include the canal design and district administration cases cited above, and another DSS used to support improved planning of resource usage in two zonal railways which was never used in other zones (Ramani, 1994). With LEAP21 so focused on Naidu himself, prospects are limited for the sustainability and replication of any successes it may fortuitously achieve.

The 'Integrate' Approach: In this approach, public officials have become information-literate. They recognise information as a key organisational resource that is central to all government functions. IT is relegated to a secondary role: it is seen as a valuable means to achieve certain reform ends, not as an end in itself. The reengineering of information systems and the introduction of IT are now fully integrated into the process of organisational change, driven by reform objectives.

The integrated approach therefore places information in the driving seat, relegating technology to an important but enabling role. In very simple terms, we can see four main steps in initiation of this approach:

1. Acceptance by key stakeholders of the need for reform.
2. Identification and communication of an agenda for reform.
3. Identification of the new and/or reengineered information systems requirements of this reform agenda.
4. Identification of the role, if any, that information technology has to play in meeting these requirements.

The successful computerisation of passenger reservations on Indian Railways can be seen to have followed this route. The need for reform of reservations was understood since at least the mid-1970s, with an agenda of modernisation widely discussed and the need for reengineering of systems to escape the old 'one-train-per-clerk' situation widely accepted (Jain and Raghuram 1992). Information technology was then identified as the servant of this pre-existing reform agenda, not as the master of reform.

Despite undeniable hiccups, this project was kept on track thanks to a vision of efficiency, accountability and customer service objectives that was shared by key stakeholders, not held by just one champion. As a result, technology solutions were shaped to fit reform objectives rather than vice versa, as is so often the case in examples of the idolise approach.

However, other examples of the integrated approach hardly exist in India. Approaches and chronologies remain unevenly distributed in India, but Bhatnagar (1997) sees much of the public sector still struggling to move away from the ignore stage. If anything, it seems likely to move on to 'idolise', as exemplified by the LEAP21 initiative, rather than 'integrate'.

INDIA AND THE INFORMATION AGE

As the world enters the information age, success of nations—as of individuals—depends on the exploitation of knowledge and innovation of ideas. In business and industry, the focus is shifting to computers and software. The marketplace itself is changing with the advent of the World Wide Web. New technologies could either increase the gap between the rich and the poor nations or, if harnessed properly, they could provide the means for the poor nations to catch up with the developed ones.

The central significance of information in the modern world was pointed out in the 1920s by the philosopher, Richard von Mises, who argued that a command system of the kind envisioned by the Marxists would eventually collapse in a sea of files, because its high officers, no matter how efficient or competent, could never deal with the flood of information being generated. The Soviets endured only so long as the strength of the State rested on just a few big, aggregated industrial projects. By the early 80s, with the increasing importance of computer and information technology, the writing was on the wall. The Soviets tried to control access to telephones and electronic mail, but to no avail.

The recent onion-price crisis in India, which decided the result of an election, was the result of a similar information overload. The failure of the onion crop in 1997 had not been factored in the decisions of the ministry and so India was exporting onions even as the local prices were skyrocketing. When import and export of commodities is controlled by a single authority, it is quite unlikely that all the implications of the decisions will be anticipated.

It is also being recognized that information cannot be looked at objectively, in isolation, since it is interpreted by a culture. A mediating class must transform ideas into a form that would be meaningful in the receptive culture. This is brought out most clearly in the new book by Janine R. Wedel, Collision and Collusion: The Strange Case of Western Aid to Eastern Europe 1989-1998 (St. Martin's Press). She argues that it is wrong to consider information and aid as being delivered by a transmission belt. In reality, information and even material aid is more like a series of chemical reactions, "transformed by the agendas, interests, and interactions" of the donors and the recipients—often with unexpected results. The failure to recognize these details is the explanation why, despite more than $80-billion in aid, Eastern Europe's transition to free economies has been relatively unsuccessful.

In this essay, I take a brief look at the Indian situation from the perspective of information to analyze and suggest prescriptions.

The last fifty years in India were a twilight age of transition from the imperial British Raj. Not just the ideology of divide-and-rule, dressed up in the phraseology of "identity politics", but also pervasive bureaucratic controls remain. The Indian system was born of the Raj but nursed on the milk of the socialist ideology. A modern system of government is yet to emerge.

The bureaucratic controls go beyond industry's license-raj, including, as they do, the regulation of religion to the extent that many temples are run by government-appointed boards. But more than physical control of organizations, what characterized the old dispensation was its subtle control of the media. The reason why India persisted with socialism for nearly half a century is because ideas were not freely debated. Even now emotive calls for economic nationalism emanate not only from the left, but also from the right.

Information technology works best when individuals work within an open system where initiatives are encouraged, where ideas and information are allowed to travel freely. In a bureaucratic system, information technology can become an instrument of oppression. Since Indian administration remains overly bureaucratized, India will reap full benefits of information technology only with basic reforms.

India's self-image has been principally moulded by colonial and orientalist constructs. The basic argument, devised by the Indologists of the 19th century, is racist: Indians are the descendents of invaders who, in order to control the population, devised a complex, caste-based social organization. Perceiving themselves at the bottom of the racial totem-pole, Indians developed an acute sense of inferiority, which they tried to mitigate by seeking approval from Western "masters" for their acts of self-transformation. The Indian intellectual was a participant in a symbolic theatre where to demonstrate allegiance to the new ideas was paramount.

Anthropologists no longer believe in the 19th century idea of pure races. That there is nothing wrong with the Indian has been proved by the enormous success individual Indians have had as scientists, engineers, businessmen, and other professionals around the world. It is also being realized that a self-definition in terms of any neat ideological categories is simplistic and useless. The search for a true identity has been made difficult by the fact that the public discourse is still dominated by an elite in whose opinion the question of identity was settled by the indologists of the last century! By freezing its self-definition either to the prescriptions of the schoolbooks or to a mythic past, the Indian finds himself shackled to false histories.

The economic policies of the Nehruvian system were based on the logic that India's poverty was primarily from the loss of its raw materials to the factories in Britain. This led to a closed economic system ruled with strong central controls. It took several decades to learn that progress is a result not just of resources but information and commerce.

If the Indian polity is to make more than just a few symbolic changes, it must recognize the centrality of the issue of free ideas. It is common for Indian politicians to instigate the banning of books, films, and plays because such controversies provide political advantage. But sanctity of free speech is more important than the inconvenience it may bring from time to time. In order to take these issues out of the ambit of political discourse,

Article 30 of the Constitution, that has led to much sectarian disaffection, must be amended so that it does not discriminate on the basis of religion or community.

New Ideas: There is a mistaken belief that if only there was less corruption India would be on the way to rapid progress. But what is needed in not just the reform of old institutions but the creation of new ones to deal with the problems of urban decay, poverty, infrastructure, environment, and resource development. Corruption should be eliminated but new ideas are also needed.

Corruption in India cannot be fought just by getting a fresh set of people who have clean pasts. Indian corruption is systemic, because there is no proper framework of checks and balances. Without such a framework, anyone in authority will soon be stealing and cheating.

Two hopeful things that have emerged out of India in the last few years are the activism of the high courts and the Election Commission. But the oversight by these institutions just scratches the surface of the problems.

The legal system is a great mess. Laws to deal with the regulation of civic issues in a modern city have not even been drafted. No wonder Indian cities are the most polluted and filthy in the world; the buildings are run down and the roads are pot-holed.

Perceptive observers have said that India's independence is still only in name. Democracy has not yet percolated down to levels below that of the parliament and the state legislatures. The British ruled India through its bureaucracy, which has only strengthened itself in the last five decades. The system was meant to hold down a potentially rebellious populace by increasing their dependence on the instruments of the state; it wasn't meant to facilitate material progress.

The Administrative System: The phrase that the "IAS is the iron-frame of India" has been repeated so often that the service has become a blind spot of public debate. The IAS culture, mimicked by other bureaucracies in India, is responsible for much is what is wrong with the India state.

The IAS culture has no place for innovation and reform. Promotions are determined by seniority and not by ability or performance. The postings expect that the officer will manage to keep the organization running without any thought given to the goals of the organization. The administrators are themselves so loath to take responsibility that the decisions are normally based on the note on the files which starts up at the level of the office clerk.

The rules are byzantine; using common-sense could lead any officer into trouble. The administrative review systems and the legal systems are dysfunctional so a really honest officer could spend a lifetime clearing his name. To be safe, officers just go along with the recommendations that arise from the bottom of the hierarchy.

Ironically, it is the corrupt who are decisive. Just the making of a decision may be worth a large bribe. In government purchases, a certain percentage goes as bribe to the purchasing officer which is shared by other officers. For the honest, the most prudent thing to do is to look the other way, and forgo one's share. Officials and ministers are known to have amassed fortunes worth hundreds of millions of rupees.

Corruption pervades all levels of life in the twin forms of bribes and extortion. It is even effecting the manner in which technology is used. For example, most people illingly get their long-distance telephoning privileges revoked so that the telephone exchange staff will not put someone else's phone charges on the bill. The other way to ensure there are no bogus charges is to pay protection money to the lineman.

Investments: India needs enormous resources to build its infrastructure. Why don't the NRIs, who are patriotic and also perhaps the richest community in the world, invest? Simply because the laws in India don't guarantee that their investments will be secure. If one owns land and property, squatters can occupy it and there is no real recourse in the courts. The lower courts are so corrupt that one cannot be sure that contracts will be legally enforceable. It is easy to get the consideration of a case delayed by giving a bribe. The judge may be honest but what oversight is there of the clerks in the courts?

In the purchase and sale of real estate, half or more of the transaction is made in cash. To cleanse this cancer in the economy should be one of the highest priorities of the government. Such cleansing will attract large new investments which will lift the economy.

Reforms: Here are some other structural reforms that are absolutely essential at this time:

- Restructure and scale down the IAS system. Let each district elect its administrating bodies and let they be given financial authority. The district administration should directly receive an outlay from the state according to some clear rules.
- Provide authority to the states, districts, and cities to levy taxes if so voted by the citizens.
- Build a wall between the affairs of the state and religion. The state should get out of the business of management of temples and mosques and stop subsidies to religious schools and pilgrimages.
- Reform tort law so that the bureaucracy is held accountable for its errors in matters of civil law.
- Develop a system of oversight at all levels, in all operations. Use sting operations to nab corrupt ministers and officials.

Rather than deal with substantive issues, the Indian polity continues to be enthralled with the theatre of symbols. The complexity of the old religious ritual is nothing compared to this theatre. In this theatre, as in any other, posturing counts for more than convictions.

Where are the energies of the polity concentrated? On quotas, smaller states, swadeshi! The issue of quota for women is degenerating into further quotas within this for women of different castes. Once this is granted, would quotas for religious affiliation be far behind? Lacking vision, the politicians merely address the symptoms, and not the systemic problems of governance and social justice.

Inevitably, India is opening up to increasing use of information technology. But it remains stuck in the colonial paradigm of the Raj where, instead of grants and concessions to this Maharaja or that, problems are being "solved" by quotas and new administrative arrangements. No thought is being given to changes that will facilitate information becoming the vehicle for transformation of attitudes and structures. Wanting these systemic reforms, it appears that India will remain ill-equipped to deal with the challenges and opportunities of the information age.

Acquisitive Mimesis in the Theories of Reflexive Globalization and the Politics of Human Rights

First, a word concerning the title of my presentation. It is not out of any voguish reason that I use the term mimesis, rather than imitation. Certainly, it was Gabriel Tarde (1895) who first reminded us that the "tendency towards imitation is a main drive behind both creation and the development of social institutions, legal and other" (Stone, 1966: 481). But it is Rene Girad's corpus which educates us into the more complex notion of mimesis and relationship between mimesis on the one hand and violence, victimage and truth of the sacred on the other (1978, 1986). He has made it possible for us to think that social theory and thought, too, may become objects of mimetic desire, of acquisitive mimesis (where "two mimetic rivals attempt to wrest from one another an object because they designate it desirable to one another") and even about the phenomenon of mimetic "contagion."

Contemporary social theorizing concerning 'reflexive' globalization provides an exciting spectacle of acquisitive mimesis at work. It also enacts its own distinctive order of victimage by means of emistemic violence, exposing to doubt the anti foundationalist discourse celebrating Stanley Fish's maxim: Theory has no consequences (1989).

'Reflexive' globalization provides an exciting ongoing conversation "brilliant stuff" as Lash himself would describe it (1994:203) among social and cultural theorists of the North, often modestly placed at the service of the creation of a global sociology (Robertson, 1992) or "undoing culture" (that is 'globalizing cultural complexity': Featherstone, 1995), reflective globalization theorizing is, in reality, addressed to the task of construction of future histories of humankind. The point of departure for theoretical sketches is not provided by the mad integrity of a Nietesche who after all constructed nihilism as a way of writing the future history of Europe. 'Reflexive' globalization thinkers address the future of the world as a whole, with varying degrees of "pessoptimism." And the path followed is that of philosophical anthropology, sedimented by [-but going beyond] discursive traditions of 'modernity' and 'post-modernism." The debris of thought traditions of the North provides the raw materials for doing this kind of philosophical anthropology. Its other distinctive, indeed constitutive, feature is the deployment of enormously suggestive (seductive) power of anecdotal narrativism, unburdened by any rigors of method in assembling global social facts.

To take just one example, we hear Arguably, the workings of power, politics and ideologies in these new transnational flows of capital, people, commodities, information and culture are generating a cyberspace/telesphere that is coextensive with, but different from, first nature in biosphere and second, nature in the industrial technosphere. This new 'third nature' of cyberspatial/televisual information glocality fuses the local and the global in new everyday life-worlds. And it is the hyperreal estate of these glocal territories which anchors many social struggles, political organizations, economic conceptions and cultural creolizations in most regions of the existing capitalist world system (Luke, 1995: 91 emphasis added).

The tentativeness of this prologue (marked by italicized words) is soon dissolved in the heavy text which follows. It is not necessary in talking about 'cyberspatiality' to acknowledge the fact that only about 15 million people have access to Internet (that is, little over the population of the capital city of India!) or Canada has more telephone connections (approximate 27 million) than many a developing country put together or further that the televisual information glocality is available to those who have access to electricity (aside from other resources), a fortune yet to visit millions of impoverished people in the Third world whose governments proclaim, over and over again, five year rural electrification plans ! Much more could be said in this vein but I will desist.

Of course, such 'facts' can be quickly countered by other 'facts'-Rambo's "larger-than-life-heroes" being applauded by "remote villagers in rural Burma" only "days after they hit the screens of Wisconsin" (Iyer, 1989: 12, quoted in Featherstone, 1995: 116) or Paul Theroux's The Happy Islands of Oceania where people narrate to him the latest developments in Gulf War they'd heard on the Radio or and people in the tiny island of Savo (Solomon islands group) where a single generator video made Rambo a folk-hero. For Featherstone all this talk produces at least a reflexive anxiety "such accounts are by now legion yet how are we to read them?" (p.116) and suggests that "we should not be too hasty in dispensing with theories of social relations [of power domination-] altogether" (p.125). But haste for prognosis lies at the heart of reflexive globalization theories.

Reflexive globaliztion theorists' penchant for disregarding or transcending social facts makes its discourse essentially poetic, at time lyrical, in its imagery. The prophetic mode of contemporary theory-construction is more assured of future facts about glocalizing neo-world order in which agency will becáme even more autonomous of the structures and reflexivity will prefigure as well as transfigure things now hidden from view. Hidden only, I should add, partially from view because mimetic rivalry over conceptions should as 'reflexivity', 'risk', 'trust', 'culture', 'glocality', 'flows', 'hyperralitization', 'liminality' already indicate, via trajectories of imaginative social theory, the shape of things to come. Thus, for example, we now hear of 'reflexive subjects', 'reflexive accumulation', 'reflexive' consumption where "global economies of sign and space" become the only 'reality' there is, or that is worth talking about (Lash & Urry, 1994). Perhaps, we should adapt Girad's notion of acquisitive mimesis to 'reflexive' mimesis.

But let me as a mere lawperson (significantly, law and human rights have very little resonance in theoretical sketches and skirmishes of reflexive globalization narratives) not rush in, in this vein, where angels used to fear to tread ! Instead, let me look at result, consequences, implications of some of these narratives recalling Kerl Lewellyn's memorable counsel to first-semester law students at Chicago; his doyen of American legal realism used to ask the class not to look at what judges say but rather to look at what they do with what they say ! Perhaps, this hermeneutical jurisprudential maxim may be usefully extended to theories of, and about, reflexive globalization.

At the heart of conviction about 'open-ended' 'fluid' 'up-for-grab' notions of globalization (Robertson, 1992) the germ of social Darwinism gnaws, it does not display itself as outrageously as in Jacques Attali (1990) who elaborates the 'thesis' that the North is the millienial winner, the South the millenial loser. Attali boldly declares that Latin American countries represent a situation of 'terminal poverty'. Africa is a 'lost continent' and baring a few, Asian nations are millenial losers. We find much more refined versions of this kind of approach in contemporary globalization narratives, prominently for example, in Scott Lash and John Urry's recent proclamation of 'reflexivity winners' and 'reflexivity losers' (1994), the latter being the denizens of 'dead zones' or 'wild zones' of underclasses living in ghettos, a marker of exclusion from "information and communication structures' (Lash, 1995: 132). Lash and Urry are refreshing in their candor in asking: "what can reflexive production and consumption mean to a single mother in a Chicago ghetto?" (p.143). Nothing, as far my close reading can tell, excepting that the reflexivity losers are situated (interpellated) in the "wider zones of disorganized capitalist landscape," that is in their "exclusion from civil society itself." The zones are 'wild' or 'dead' as "spaces characterized by a deficit of economic, cultural and social regulation" (p.8). Students of histories of pauperism will know (as from the beginning of Elizabethan poor law system) that 'wild' or 'dead' zones can also be created by regulation-surplus as well! That apart, after this gesture of acknowledgment of 'underclass', at the heart of modern economies of signs and space, the caravan moves on to its proper exotic destinations. The trace of empathy proves barren, after all.

Another large example of Social Darwinism implicit, of almost innate epistemic violence of reflexive globalization theories, comes from no less thinker than Anthony Giddens who is sensitive to fashioning 'dialogic democracy' as the only alternative to violence (1994: 105-107), sensitive, too, to acknowledge that "liberal democracy is not the end of history in the political sphere" nor is "capitalist production in the domain of economic relations" (p.104). Yet, at the end of it all, Giddens is able to speak of the "possibility of the emergence of a post-scarcity order" in which "the drive to continuous accumulation has become weakened or dissolved" partly as a result of the "well-known contradictions of abundance" (p.195). Conscious of the difficulties that the problematique of mass impoverishment in the Third World immediately posses Gidden's grandly concludes that the post-scarcity order "is far from something that only has relevance to the economically advances sectors of the globe" in the sense that the "affluent have a great deal to learn from the poor: and the West from other cultures which in the past it has simply threatened with extinction" (p.196 emphasis added).

It is, of course, not Giddens' fault that I read his brilliant analysis of 'detraditionalization' 'reflexivity' and 'trust' around the same time I chanced to read War & Hunger (1994), a hauntingly contemporary account of planned acts of creation of "conflict-famines" where food (access to food as a basic need and to resource for agricultural productivity) is used as a weapons-system in insurgency and counter-insurgency operations, in wars throughout Africa (and, one may add, the rest of the Third World, including the New Third World emerging as a result of downfall of the Soviet Union). Even when conditions of belligerency abate, the presence of active land mines (estimated to be in the order of 18 to 30 million in most war-zones of Africa) continues to aggravate recovery and rehabilitation.

Among other things, reading of this account made me feel strongly about the violence of past tense in Gidden's italicized sentence quoted above (re: other cultures which the West has "in the past threatened with extinction.") Directly by aggressive intervention, or indirectly by complicity with rebels or incumbents, and/or by formal and informal profiteering by armament supplies as well by acts of diplomatic management, and at times out right usurpation, of legitimate roles, functions and missions of the United Nations system, destruction proceeds in infinitely complex ways. Indeed, the production of "complex emergencies" in the South, a conscious 'reflexive' foreign policy project in the era of cold war continues even now as a central concern in the varieties of versions of pax Americana. Given the dynamics of the 'new military world order' (which Giddens himself introduced in the discourse on contemporary globalization: 1990), it should at least be clear that the emergence of past-scarcity order in the North is causally correlated to manufacturing of conflict-famines in the South.

In addition, the prophetic notion that past-scarcity order, though Northern in origin but marking an incipient global order, proceeds on a theory of international social learning ("the affluent have a great deal to learn from the poor") stands problematized by the manufacturing of "complex situations", including the militarization of ethnicities embedded in the new international military order. The logic of this order as concerns the South consists in production of an order of super-scarcity. The 'learning' does occur but not in the direction of the production of any post-scarcity world order.

The situation is the same when we turn to the dimension of the international economic order. One has to just turn to the 'rationality' of the accomplishments of the WTO 1994 regime or of the US omnibus super-301 legislation providing an arsenal of first strike weapons of trade retaliation for the protection and promotion of the very sectors of production of "informational goods" imbricated with "reflexive" production. The "reflexive" agency of people in struggle against new economic regimes of "free trade" was successfully overridden by the hegemony-or rather dominance without hegemony-of the 'globalizing' regimes of the North. Most of 'reflexive' globalization conversation naturalized global economic, trade, capital, commodities and peoples' flows instead of problematizing these. It is this formation of mentalite which remains, as it were, a necessary, perhaps even sufficient, condition for the intellectual production of reflexive globalization, the prophecy concerning the emergence of a world "post-scarcity order" being among its notorious examples.

It is also mightily curious that for theorists of 'reflexive gloabalization' the world of international diplomacy and the products it so regularly sprouts, is largely non-existent or irrelevant. In the older ways of doing social theory the global 'facts' would have been accorded the status, at least, of Durkhemian social facts. The prophetic discursivity of reflexive globalization passes by the entire happening of the U.N. Social Summit on Development (Copenhagen, 1995) whose Declaration and Plan of Action proceed on the candid acknowledgment of the relentless global social facts of mass impoverishment, destitution and deprivation rampant, especially out not only there in the Third World-a world, incidentally, for which according to Giddens that naming is no longer "appropriate", together with the "idea of 'development studies'" which has lost its "cogency" (1994:188.) Similarly, reflexive globalization theorists pass by the labours of society of states and international civil society exemplifies by the U.N. Conference on Population and Development (Cairo, 1993) and the U.N. Fourth World Conference on Women (Beijing, 1995). It requires no great imagination to see espy similar fate awaiting the human labours of the World Summit on Habitat due to take place in Istanbul (June, 1996). One's ambivalence concerning the behaviours of states within contexts of high-minded international diplomacy or of vibrancy and urgency with which groups of 'reflexive' NGOs participate, with a matching degree of Utopian realism-one's assessment of the intent and impact of such praxiological formations can only be meaningfully articulated when such global social facts are in the first place acknowledged by 'reflexive' theorizing on globalization. But for the prophetic 'reflexivity' discourse, cast in the mode of philosophical anthropology, such facts count for little or nothing, despite the celebration of such themes as the 'decentering' of the nation-state.

The constitution of "we-ness" in reflexive globalization theorizing remains ineluctably parochial and Eurocentric and therefore social-Darwinistic. It would take me for afield to archive all the illustrations. But a couple of examples should suffice. Writing in 1995 on the heroic and everyday life. Mike Featherstone (1995, 59-71) does not even mention once Mohandas Karamchand Gandhi, Nelson Mandela, Martin Luther King Jr. or Aung San Suu Kyi. The discourse is 'peoples' with Weber, Baudrillard, Horkheimer and Andorno, Nietesczhe, Simmel, Bauman and Heller. The 'we-ness' of reflective globalization narratives centres upon construction of social reality of Northern sociological thinkers and thought. And everyday heroism, too, does not appear in narratives of workers in struggle, women fighting patriarchy in lived lives, Pakistani child leader brutally assassinated for articulating struggle against bonded labour, indigenous peoples' struggling to conserve biodiversity but out of the cult of "mythic hero images of Superman and Rambo types as well pastisches and parodies of the whole heroic tradition such as the film, Monthy Python and the Holy Grail (1975) and various blends of both such as are found in Indiana Jones films." (p.67) Overconcentration of the 'mediascapes' or celleuioid realities cancels in theories of cultural globalization the embodied traditions of resistance, struggle and heroism in everyday life of the South. Here, alienated reflexivity functions to form visions of globalization which obliterate by refusing even to name the only heroes who would were in the past, and remain new and for the future, the arch-practitioners of emanicipative deglobalization.

Similarly, in articulating a gigantomachy between 'tribalism' and 'globalism' via the prism of McDonaldization of the world (named Mcworld, adding to the property of goodwill in the registered trade mark!) B.R. Berber in an article entitled 'Jihad v. Mcworld' (1992)-certified by no less than Ronald Robertson from whom I quote (1995: 25) as a "widely disseminated" statement-posits tensions between a "Mcworld of homogenizing globalization versus a Jihad World of particularizing 'leabonization.'" These are metaphors run wild for the destitute, starving, millions of human beings for whom the McWorld does not exist or for the 'reflexive' Leabenese subjects, mercilessly exposed to a series of violent disembeddings and reembeddings in a 'structure' from which they have supposedly won enclaves of 'autonomy'. While contesting some of Berber's thesis, Robertson lends his-both cognitive and aesthetic-authority to Berber's violent musing on how the creation of Mcworld signifies the realization of "the Enlightenment dream of universal rational society" in a remarkable degree. Perhaps, (though it does not really matter any more!) a more weighty labour of thought would have been provided by the lamented Walter Rodney's poignant text How Europe Underdeveloped Africa (1983). But, aside from the Dead White Males, the conversation on reflexive globalization is uniquely self-referential denying even a modest acknowledgment to thought and voice from the South, unless of course they are 'nomads', 'structured' hybrids or diasporic intellectuals. The discursive "we-ness" of contemporary globalization narratives barely conceals the exclusion of "reflexivity losers." The difference, this time round, being that among those excluded are labourers of thought within the growing "underclass" in a globalizing world, including practitioners of political thought from Nehru to Nyrere. Ghettoization of thought, in a world supposedly bursting with information access, is remarkably symptomatic of glocalizing theories about "reflexive globalization!"

The foregoing commendation on the current genre of globalization theorizing would have accomplished its task well if it were to persuade some eminent Northern thinkers to be more inclusive of the rest of the world in their labours of thought. Let me now move to my second thematic: politics of rights in the context of India, returning at the end of my presentation to Ulrich Beck's fecund notion of the reinvention of politics.

In focusing on law, constitution and rights I derive some comfort from Georges Guruvitch (1942) who said, memorably, that too little sociology leads us away from law and much sociology returns us to it. The founders and forerunners of modern social theory richly illustrate the truth of this dictum. The relation between societal complexity and legal evolution (Durkheim), the emphasis on constitutions and laws as necessities of class struggles (Marx) and the dialectic relationship between economic development and legal rationality (Weber) furnished salient dimensions of understanding societies. This tradition of taking law seriously persisted well till Parsons (who at one point described law, with language, as an "evolutionary universal". The lack of serious social/cultural theory interest in law in the narratives of reflexive globalization is understandable as an aspect of epistemological break with the older traditions of social reflexivity.

As and when, reflexive globalization theorists turn to law and rights, they are more likely than not to have recourse to the contemporary outpourings of critical legal studies, deconstructive jurisprudence, critical race theory, postmodernist perspectives on law and state. For these discourses, too, while providing sites for sustained iterrogations of traditions of western/capitalist legality remain, on the whole, in a state of well-bred amnesia of crises and contradictions in the construction of rights, legality and justice in the South.

Undoubtedly, the Indian formation of juristic thought provides us with many an inaugurator of new discursivity on law, rights and justice; M.K.Gandhi, Babasahed, Ambedkar and Jai Prakash Narayan among them. In particular, well ahead of John Rawls, and contemporary debate between 'liberalism' and 'communitarianism', Ambedkar persciently developed a critique of liberal legality (Baxi, 1995). But this is a theme by itself. Gandhi's discursive and political praxis creating collisions between the truth of people's law formations and imperial state law informations, his creative siting of duty of civil disobedience within the values of British legality and his unceasing search for commingling ethic of human rights with human responsibilities provides splendid examples of reflexivity so far not available in narratives of reflexive globalization. But it would take me for afield to explore these patterns of inaugural discursivity. It is indubitable that the Gandhi-Ambedkar conflicted legacies of thought and action made possible distinct points of departure in the construction of post-colonial legality just as Jai Prakash Narain notions of Total Revolution based substantially on a critique of the constitutional model, summoning people including the police, para-military and armed forces of India to disobey manifestly unjust laws and orders and calling for people's participation in administration of justice laid firm basis (after the brief but cruel authoritarian interlude of the Emergency of 1975-1977) for a new Indian jurisprudence, especially through the agency of judicial activism. The full narrative of the histories of those formations is beyond the scope of this paper. But the importance of Indian constitutional thought and development cannot be overstated, even in terms of invention of politics.

Just as the South African interim constitution marks a watershed in the history of constitutionalism on the eve of the Third Millennium, the Indian Constitution marked the first major break with the world (Western) constitutionalism. And it served as a model for most South Asian and Third World constitutions. The discontinuities with the inherited tradition of constitutionalism are perhaps more critical (these certainly have been so in the last two decades of the Constitution at work) than continuities. The Indian Constitution's remarkable persona manifests itself in massive normative assault against dominant institutions of civil society. In a society marked by millennial conception of hierarchical equality, the Constitution proclaims all citizens as free and equal. For a society almost irredeemably patriarchal in character, the Constitution asserts values and rights of gender equality casting (since 1976) an obligation by way of citizenship on all to renounce practices derogatory of women. In contrast to the Hindu society's valorization of 'purity' and 'pollution', Article 17 of the Constitution prohibits, as a matter of fundamental right, the notion and practice of "untouchability". Through Article 23, a fundamental right against exploitation, the Constitution outlaws bonded labour, beggar, and other forms of servitude in a society slow to emerge from semifeudal relations of agrarian production. Proclaiming a charter of rights to conscience and religion, the constitution mandates reform of Hindu religion. In these, and many related vital respects, the constitution declares a war on social practices and beliefs deeply rooted in Indian society and culture. The symbolic significance of all these normative aspirations is immense, even when sonorous words written on parchment do not by themselves transform material social relations. But, as development since its adoption have shown these texts of justice and rights has helped to energize state action, to defeudalize public discourse on power, to sustain momentous scope for rigorous redirection of the Indian future. The constitution provides basis as much for legitimation of power as for its delegitimation.

To this inaugural dimension of Indian constitutionalism must be added the departures its theory of rights marks in terms of the classical liberal theory of human rights. This occurs in a least five distinct ways.

First, the Indian constitution is practically unique in the annals of world constitutionalism in recognizing basic human needs as human rights, whose progressive realization is a constitutional obligation of the state. Formulated as Directive Principles of State Policy, unenforceable in principle by courts (but now being gradually enforced by activist jurisprudence), the Constitution of India anticipates by two decades the bifurcation of international human rights conventions into the International Covenant on Civil and Political Rights and the sister covenant on Social, Economic and Cultural Rights.

Second, the fundamental rights are subject to limitations (reasonable restrictions) placed by legislation, subject to judicial review.

Third, and perhaps most critical, the constitution does not merely conceive of human rights as a corpus of constraints on state power but also addresses them to institutions in civil society (notably through constitutional outlawry of untouchability and semi-slavery); what is more, the constitution creates offenses (a task normally assigned to criminal law) in the part enunciating fundamental rights and overrides federal principles by providing on obligation on Parliament to enact further suitable legislation.

Fourth, the constitution provides not just for affirmative action programmes for the scheduled castes, scheduled tribes and other backward classes but also provides for a scheme of reservation of seats in state legislatures and Parliament providing secure modes of access to political power and principle now extended to grassroots governance in villages and cities, extending the reservation to women, by the commonly known as Panchayati Raj amendment to the constitution.

Fifth, the fifth and the sixth schedules to the constitution provide for autonomy to Hill District Councils, such that they have the power not merely to declare that the state law is inapplicable but also the Federal law may not operate in the indigenous areas.

The Indian constitutionalism extends conceptions of rights, innovatively, to civil society, embraces social and economic rights, provides of rights to political participation for the "weaker" sections of society, and reconfigurates 'positive' and 'negative' liberties. The Namibia, and one in the making in

Eriteria build on but also transcend the Indian modelling of civil liberties and peoples' rights.

We see in Indian constitution is texturing of rights notion an invention of tradition (cf. E.Hobsbawn, 1983). The nearest in the classical Hindu jural tradition equivalents were notions of adhikar (which conflates 'rights' with 'power') and hak (which is more akin to legally enforceable claim). While sustained research is needed in varieties of rajdharma (the dharma of the ruler, the king) and the imperative of respecting lokadhikar (rights of the people but usually conceived of a rights of communities personified). It is clear that these did not anticipate any major elements of modern conceptions of human rights. In this sense, the invention of tradition, contra Giddens, does not result in the "evacuation" of any tradition (1994: 95-96) or any tautology in the sense that "all traditions... are invented." All the same, both in intention and historic impact the constitutional enunciations serve the role of what he describes as "detraditionalization."

The notion of detraditionalization apparently does not extend at a global level to modes of production of knowledges of dominant ideologies or entrenched paradigms of governance and rights. It is altogether natural, therefore, that the question is not even posed, how through the nationalist struggle and the accomplishment of constitutional enunciation, as to how the Indian conceptions of rights developed both through the nationalist struggle and accomplishment of constitutional enunciation, may have affected the dominant paradigms. But there is reason for saying that contemporary conceptions of self-determination, freedom from social discrimination, and notions of just freedom were distinctively Indian contributions.

When Lokmanya Tilak dared to say in the twenties that "swaraj is my birthright and I shall have it" he was not situating himself within the Indian traditions or the high colonial versions of the rule of law. Radically incomprehensible to the ruling ideology, this motto propelled, as it were, the nationalist movement to a high attitude. Equally important, it contributed to a ferment of thought which fifty years later achieved for the peoples' of the world an enunciation of the right to self-determination under international law. Mohandas Gandhi's heroic protest at early forms of apartheid was an attempt to detraditionalize colonial legal liberalism and yielded, under the leadership of the Third World, again a century later, the Convention on the Elimination of Racial Discrimination. Ambedkar's notions of justice as emancipation-not just freedom but just freedom-certainly anticipated with remarkable originality the current crises of (Northern) theories about justice.

Perhaps, my attempt to bring all this back to the context of reflexive globalization may be assimilated merely to "global babble" explained, elegantly by Mike Featherstone as a process where "the rest are increasingly speaking back to the West" (1995:13). Once you reduce old and complex cultures and civilizations to the 'periphery' it is but natural, even though arrogant, to reduce voices from these as "babble', inviting would-be discursivity partners to worry about the progressive hearing impairment on the other side! The task then is how to glocalize the theorists of globalization!

The story of development of Indian constitutionalism in its formative years has often been told. The narrative centres upon the conflict between a hegemonic executive which relied on charismatic leadership and symbolic capital of nationalist struggle and a judiciary construing legalism as an ethical value summoning interpretative fidelity. The first two decades marked the ascendancy of executive power over definitions of individual rights (especially the fundamental right to property) and more importantly in the assertion of sovereignty of Parliament over the issue of amendment to the Constitution. This is not the time or place to revisit the narrative. But it should be sufficient to say that the conceptions of postcolonial legality which emerged on both sides-legislature executive and the judiciary-did not mark any discursive rupture with the dominant metaphors of colonial legal liberalism.

The incipient break occurs in 1967-1969 and a more fully fledged discontinuity establishes itself, in momentous ways, in 1973. Both these moments result in even more, and relatively irreversible discontinuity with the past, since the 80s. All these three moments amount to the reinvention of rights and of politics of human rights. We will need to dwell, howsoever briefly on each.

The first moment of incipient discontinuity registers an interrogation of the paradigm of executive hegemony over the nature and fate of human rights enshrined in the constitution. The Supreme Court accepts yet another abridgement of property rights by the Seventeenth Amendment, but not without raising the germinal question whether fundamental rights may be construed as "playthings of power." Two years later the Supreme Court, in an anxious and deeply divided articulation, ruled that Parliament's power to amend the constitution does not extend to abrogation of fundamental rights. This was the first historic step towards the discipling of a hegemonic and dominant executive power in the title of protection and promotion of human rights and gesture of autonomization of adjudicatory power of the state from legislative/executive realms.

Faced with an incredible reassertion of Parliament's power to amend and even repeal the constitution, on the basis of liberal majoritarian 'democratic' principles, the Supreme Court in the second moment in 1973 concedes. Parliamentary supremacy to amend all parts of the constitution but denies the power to repeal it and subjects this power to the judicially enunciated doctrine of the basic structure of the constitution. Amendatory power cannot take away the essential features of the constitution named as 'rule of law,' 'equality before the law,' 'democracy,' 'socialism,' 'secularism,' 'federalism' and above all the powers of judicial review, reducing to pale historical significance the celebration of Marbury v. Madison.

And exercising this power in the heyday of emergency, it declares unconstitutional an amendment enacted by Indira Gandhi. Ineluctably, the basic structure is what the Judges at any time say it is but peoples' rights are placed now on a more secure footing within the discipline of articulate legal contention, judicial tradition and emergent constitutional cultures.

The detraditionalization of the dominant cosmopolitan traditions of legal liberalism proceeds apace in the third moment, through the post-emergency cathartic growth of judicial engagement with the violations of the democratic rights of the Indian people. These news structures of engagement begin with a public acknowledgment of judicial failure, and the shame of it, during the brief interlude of Emergency unconstitutional governance. In the first phase, a radical democratization of access to courts takes place by privileging people's letters to Judges (the epistolgry jurisdiction) as legitimate vehicles of raising the issues of rights violation. The historic shift takes place in throwing overboard the restricted colonial legal liberalism's notions of standing (now any citizen may write letters complaining about violations of rights of other citizens by way of public interest). And the process matures (with initial distortions and waywardness) to a partnership between civil society and the adjudicatory powers of the state aimed at combating governmental lawlessness.

This moment marks a remarkable disjunction in the project of centralized unity of state power. The adjudicatory power no more seeks to recombine itself with legislative and executive power, but rather sets itself up in active tension, even contradiction, with it. And it does so with the title of protection and promotion of human rights, rule of law and democraticity of governance. The break with colonial/post-colonial traditions of liberal legality stands inaugurated, making the entire discourse on the legitimacy of judicial review power (with its well known celebration of judicial role as being 'antimajoritarian' and therefore 'undemocratic', still robustly alive in Anglo-American juristic traditions) somewhat irrelevant, and even archaic, to the nature and career of democratic development in India. And within a decade the unique Indian innovation of expansive judicial review resonates in Pakistan, Bangladesh and Nepal. The genre takes a life of its own. Regardless of the well-bred cultivated ignorance or indifference by the first 'world' theorists of democracy, legality and rights, the media, the academia, social action and political groups, human rights activists, ecological and feminist action groups, indigenous and unorganized rural labour associations forge an ever-increasing people-judiciary partnership. Not merely is the repertoire of procedural jurisprudence renovated but a whole new array of people's rights are judicially created and enforced. Thus, the previously categorized unenforceable human rights (directive principles of state policy) are converted into enforceable human rights of life and liberty: the right to shelter, privacy, dignity, health, primary education and literacy, environment. Both micro-and macro-fascism of power now stands subject to strict judicial invigilation. The Supreme Court, and the High Courts, supervise and monitor public administration and state institutions (psychiatric, juvenile, women's homes, jails, 'correctional' centres and related custodial institutions). As one privileged to initiate the potential for judicial activism, I have narrated this story often enough (Baxi, 1989). It is naturally not to be expected that even such a mightly activist judiciary can perform tasks of governance. There are backslidings, factures, of governance. (the Bhopal settlement being archetype).

But there is no manner of doubt that judicial activism has, on the whole, succeeded in making state a little more ethical, power increasingly accountable and governance little more just. In a globalizing Indian economy judicial activism is harnessed by peoples' group to interrogate the headlong and heedless policies of liberalization especially denationalization, disinvestment, deregulation. The extension of judicial activism in this arena has led to a programme for its structural adjustment (Baxi, 1996). But the institutionalized processes of social action litigation are more resilient. By treating immunity from corruption as the most basic of peoples' human rights, the Supreme Court has now captured (in recent months) the commanding heights of redirection of the Indian polity and captured peoples' imagination as the only site available for accomplishing the tasks of redemocratization of India.

This brief but accurately adulatory account of Indian juristic and judicial development (which in many ways continues to nourish similar developments in Asia and Africa) will, I hope interest the projects on regional worlds as well as theorists of "reflexive" globalization. I now wish to return to Ulrich Beck's splendid notions of the "reinvention of politics" in the context of my understanding of the Indian development.

Beck, of course, addresses a wholly Northern scenario but the conceptual apparatuses he erects have a wider resonance, especially the distinction between "rule-directed" and "rule-altering" politics. The former, even with its potential for creativity and non-conformivity, "operates within the rule system of industrial and welfare state society in the nation-state" or "simple modernity" system. In contrast, the latter "meta" or "super-politics" aims at "politics of politics" confronting the inevitable questions concerning the "switching of the rule system" and "what system of rules one should switch to" (1994: 35). Not that these distinctions are wholly hermetically sealed compartments: "both types of politics overlap, mingle and interfere with each other" (p.36). A related distinction is "provided by official politics (rule-directed) and "reflexive" politics ("rule-altering"). To this distinction we must add Beck's notion of "sub-politics" which differs from politics on the following dimensions:

- *Agency:* in sub-politics "agents outside the political as corporatist system are allowed to appear on the stage of social design" or the "shaping society from below"
- *Organization:* institutionality of "sub-politics:" shaping of its power resistance capabilities and "potential for strategic action"
    - o *Policy:* organization of "sub-policy" in terms of arenas of social action
    - o *Dynamics:* both in the sense of internal and external dynamics (that is internal conflicts of power/leadership; patterns of networking, coalition-building, democraticity; coptability and corruptability)
- *Outcomes:* "viewed from above" results of "loss of implementation power, the shrinkage and minimization of politics:" viewed from below "the mobilization of means of the constitutional state against one another" entailing often a "general relative paralysis" of both official and sub-politics (pp.22-23).

What does then the reinvention of politics through these processes lead to? In the face of despair on the project of "transformation from a national economy of self-destruction to a global and democratic world civilization" the reinvention of politics would proceed at least on a "consensus that the present obsolescent institutions will be unable to achieve these goals under any circumstances" (p.37). In this sense reflexive politics "does not mean just the invention" it also means "the clearing out of the political" (p.41).

I here expounded Beck's conceptual framework at some length (and even then in a schematic form) with a view to make mediation on the politics of human rights in the dominant mode of McWorldism and social Darwinism preeminent in the outpousings of "reflexive" globalization. Insofar as the latter provide any space for human rights, it is wholly assimilationist. Put another way, reflexive globalization theories heavily suggest that it is the globalizing processes which provide conditions constitutive of autonomy, reflexivity, pluralism, diversity and global institutionalization of human rights (Robertson, 1992). Such almost causal celebration of the emancipative potential of contemporary globalization is historically frivolous though indeologically potent (Baxi 1966).

It also violates the canon of reflexive globalization theorizing of increasing relative autonomy of agency vis-à-vis the structure. In contrast, Ulrich Beck's perspectives besides being forthful to this canon suggest the potential of politics as a terrain for peoples' deglobalizing/deglocalizing power of praxis.

In terms of Beck's scheme the politics of human rights is both sub-and super-politics being, by definition, rule-altering. Of course, at each level of historical circumstance, condition and complexity, this politics will remain as strong as the integrity which actors bring to it. Given, however, the unleashing of forces production (cybernetics, biotechnology) and new social global relations of production (including McDonaldization, 'hyperrealization' diaspora and "flows"—for the latter see (Appadurai 1991)) "integrity" becomes profoundly problematic. Its reservation demands allegiance to the "reason" of human rights amidst the "unreason" of globalization (Baxi, 1996).

At the same time, even Ulrich Beck reverts to embed the politics for human rights to the "process of modernization", "political modernization disempowers and unbinds politics and politicized society" (1992: 194, emphasis deleted). How do we relate the inaugural historic struggles of Indian peoples for freedom from the colonial rule of these fertile productivity attributes of "processes of modernization?"

The struggle was not merely an example of "sub-politics" but constitutes the site of "meta-" or "super-" politics. It is aimed not merely to transform the grundnorm (to evoke—Hans Kelsen) of the Indian governance but the grundnorm of the international social/imperial governance. It is possible to say that "freedom" being the Other of "colonialism" the latter caused or contributed to the attainment of the former. But this surely trivializes agency, reducing agency merely to the states of pertinent effect of structures of colonial globalization. It also suggests that all struggles against colonialism/imperialism derive their innate and historic strength from the tradition of classical western liberalism. A mere look at Mahatma Gandhi's corpus will show how misleading such assumptions are.

But Beck is profoundly correct when he says that constitutional rights "are hinges for a decentralization of politics with long-term amplification effects" and that basic "rights with universalistic validity claim" provide a "generally directed process" for political development (1992: 105).

His metaphor of the "judge's potential verdict with an omnipresence in the political system" (p.197) could have been better illustrated with reference to Indian, and South Asian, developments than those in the North. The "living law" (or the peoples' law, to evoke Eugene Ehrlich) increasingly pulsates in judicial enunciation than in the moribund acts of legislature and administrative public policy in India.

If theories of "reflexive" globalization were sufficiently 'reflexive' not merely would notions about the reinvention of politics will be world-historically enriched but also the parochialism of juridical and judicial production of legality and rights in the North will be sufficiently problematized.

A more inclusive constitution of "we-ness" will also make theory incline itself to address how the fantastically exponential process of new forces of production (biotechnology, cybernetics, telecommunications) and the new social relations of global production (the neo-colonial division of labour, including sexual division of labour; "Mcdonaldization," "creolization," structural hybridizations in production of "liminality" etc.) impact on the politics of human rights.

Already, there is in place the emergent paradigm of trade-related human rights (celebrating the human rights of aggregates of capital and technology) conflicted with human rights paradigms, the former conflating free trade and structural adjustment fusing it with social development and the latter siting resistance through empowerment of individual human being and historically disadvantaged groups to reinvent politics. If the enslaving morality of trade-related human rights find its high platform in GATT, NAFTA, APEC and ASEAN, for example, the emancipative morality of human rights articulates itself through enunciation of motto: "Women's Rights are Human Rights", the charter of rights of the world indigenous peoples, the Rio Convention on Biodiversity, and the U.N. Decade on Human Rights Education.

The tasks of grasping the totality the new forces of global production and the emerging global relations of production have been essayed already by activist imagination of globalization theory labelled "reflexive" human subjects, who have asserted the 'reason' of human rights against the 'unreason' of globalization. (Baxi, 1996) Their praxis is certainly worthy of inscription on the agendum of reflexive globalization theorists.

3

Administrative Discretion and Representative Bureaucracy

INTRODUCTION

Much has been said about the public service lately. Most of the time, the opinions tend to be negative. Wasteful, inefficient, arrogant, unresponsive, impersonal, autocratic, and undemocratic are among the harsher criticisms thrown at the bureaucracy. Yet, despite these criticisms, the public service plays essential roles in implementing and enforcing government policies. Many people whose lives have been affected by government agencies though a variety of policies in areas such as income redistribution, environmental protection, crime prevention, and health care management realize the importance of those agencies. However, when government becomes too big and too powerful, it poses a threat to democracy. Thus, when Kingsley (1944) started to argue that the civil service needed to be representative in order to be responsive, he basically introduced a new concept of representation that was previously a domain in the study of political systems. Ever since his conception of "representative bureaucracy," a plethora of scholars and practitioners has argued the need for a diverse bureaucratic workforce that reflects the population it serves. According to these scholars, representative bureaucracy enhances its legitimacy in a democratic political system.

A shift in philosophy from avoidance to acceptance of the reality that bureaucracy would continue to generate power in the policy-making process fostered the demand for a more representative bureaucracy. Rourke (1978) contends that although a powerful bureaucracy threatens the "traditional freedoms of democratic society, the bureaucratic power can be used to protect and extend those freedoms." The idea of representative bureaucracy was further highlighted by Marini (1971), who points out that "we were reminded of relevance, social problems, personal morality, innovation, clients, the evils of hierarchy and bureaucracy." In other words, bureaucracy has power and thus needs to be included in the scheme of representation and social justice.

Representative bureaucracy has now become essential in a democratic political system. Riggs (1970) asserts that representation in all forms of government is critical to the stability of that government. He points to the rise of public rebellion in various countries as a consequence of the failure to have an equitable representation in the political dimensions of government and its administration.

He maintains that there is a "need for diverse elements in a population to be adequately represented in order for a government to command their loyalty as a legitimate expression of common welfare" (1970: 570).

The concept of affirmative action in the bureaucracy is essentially an attempt to broaden the social composition of the bureaucracy to reflect that of the whole population, especially from certain under-represented groups such as women and African Americans (Kernaghan and Siegel 1989). The idea that a diverse workforce will better enhance customers' demands is also gaining momentum in the private sector. Kiel (1994) believes that an organization that is reflective of its population will have a better understanding of its clients' needs. Similarly, Dresang (1974) agrees that an organization that mirrors society allows it to serve as "an index of openness and access." Furthermore, a large number of private organizations have considered employment diversity to be a good business strategy (Howes 1993). Howes argues that affirmative action has now become a prerequisite for future success or even survival for any organization.

Building upon this foundation, I intend to explore this issue in greater detail, especially as it pertains to Malaysian bureaucracy. The first part of this article explores the theory of representative bureaucracy, highlighting previous empirical studies that explore the transition from descriptive representation to substantive representation in government agencies. The second part explores the concept of administrative discretion and highlights how individuals' perceptions of the discretion influence the formation of a representative role.

The final section explores the hypothesis that individual administrators who perceive themselves as advocators of certain groups prefer policy outcomes that are more responsive to the interests of women and minorities than those of their colleagues.

THE THEORY

A general consensus maintains that the mere existence of various institutions of public accountability is not enough; they have to be effective in protecting the interests of the public. This is because the quality of governance is determined not by the objective perceptions of a few experts but by the net impact of government policies on the well-being of its citizens (Shah 1996; Huther and Shah 1998). The quality of governance is thus enhanced by closely matching government services with citizen preferences, as well as by moving government closer to the people it is supposed to serve, something that ensures greater accountability of the public service. In recent years concern has proliferated about the consequences of governance and misgovernance (Kaufman, Kraay, and Zoido-Lobaton 1999). For example, a few empirical studies have demonstrated the link between accountability and performance.

Wade (1994) finds that when irrigation officials in India and Korea face more local pressure, they tend to perform better than traditional arrangements that insulate them from political pressure. In addition, Isham, Narayan, and Pritchett (1995) reveal that aid-financed rural water supply projects performed much better with greater participation from their beneficiaries. A wealth of crosscountry indicators of various aspects of governance now strongly suggests that good governance improves government accountability to citizens and enhances the quality of public services (Kaufmann, Kraay, and Zoido-Lobaton 2000).

These concerns have certainly renewed interest in protecting democratic values as they pertain to control of government agencies. The growth of public agencies has forced theorists and practitioners to revisit bureaucratic paradigms such as fairness, representation, participation, accountability, responsiveness, political neutrality, efficiency, rationality, and expertise. Yet, the very nature of public administration poses problems to accommodating these values. For example, bureaucracy consists of appointed public officials and has a tendency to rely on expertise and knowledge over accountability, participation, and democratic control (Weber 1968; Mosher 1968). In addition, bureaucrats' lack of accountability at the ballot box, as well as various civil service regulations that insulate them from political pressure, further compound the fear that bureaucratic power comes at the expense of public interest (Krislov and Rosenbloom 1981).

Hence, the essence of traditional public administration that tends to be rigid, rule-bound, centralized, insular, self-protective, and profoundly antidemocratic has often collided with the contemporary paradigm of bureaucracy that "allows qualified voters an efficient instrument through which the will of the people may be expressed; makes officers both responsive and responsible;" and ensures the common welfare (Lynn 2001). Thus, a critical question in the field of public administration is whether or not these bureaucratic characteristics are legitimate in terms of democratic principles. In this regard, David Rosenbloom (1993) opines that the legitimacy of bureaucracy occurs when bureaucratic policy making is subject to direct popular control. If bureaucracy is isolated from public accountability, then bureaucracy can in no way be responsive to public interests and desires. As a result, we are faced with the persistent problem of how best to ensure bureaucratic responsiveness and accountability to the public.

Representative theory initially emerged during the Greek civilization.

Aristotle first mentioned the importance of representation of different classes of society in government (Vietri 1981). Book III of the *Politics* is always regarded as the foundation of political science in the West. The *polis*, the supreme form of community for Aristotle, is the best community, because it enables rational men to participate in the political process. However, Aristotle also believes that class conflict between the rich and the poor is inevitable in all societies.

This conflict always poses a threat of instability, violence, and revolution. Hence, blending the class interests in government by supporting political equality avoids conflicts and at the same time increases legitimate sovereign authority. The writings of Karl Marx and Max Weber also contribute to the development of representative bureaucracy. The elimination of class-biased bureaucracy and the emergence of classless administrative systems came about because of Marx's fear of the danger of dominant bureaucracy. Likewise, Weber's rational-legal approach allowed unrepresented groups to seek access to government. For example, the procedures of merit-based appointment increased the democratic potential of all groups to join the civil service (Krislov 1967).

However, the contemporary intellectual roots of the idea of representative bureaucracy can be traced to J. Donald Kingsley. Kingsley's comprehensive analysis of the British civil service revealed a pattern of administrative arrangements that reflected the character of the social structure of the nation.

In his view, because the middle class dominated British society, it was inevitable that the composition of the bureaucracy was largely middle class (Kingsley 1944). Since Kingsley's discovery of the term, the concept of representative bureaucracy has been widely interpreted and debated.

David Levithan (1946) was the first to propose that representative bureaucracy be integrated into the American civil service. He contended that representative bureaucracy could act as an internal control on the behaviours of administrators and hence could promote democratic values. Following Levithan, Long (1952: 813) espoused a more extreme form of representative bureaucracy. He suggested that Given the seemingly inevitable growth in the power of the bureaucracy through administrative discretion and administrative law, it is of critical importance that the bureaucracy be both representative and democratic in composition and ethos.

In essence, Long believed that a representative bureaucracy enhanced the democratization of the American civil service by promoting the interests and demands of the people it represented. Building upon this theory, Van Riper (1958) argued that an "open public service" was necessary so that the American public service consisted of a reasonable cross-section of the population by occupation, class, and geography.

To create a representative bureaucracy, he argued, government should accelerate the upward mobility of women and minority administrators through an equal opportunity system. He was basically the first American scholar to emphasize social characteristics as part of the representative concept. Meanwhile, Subramaniam (1967) suggested that representative bureaucracy is an organization "in which every economic class, caste, region, or religion in a country is represented in exact proportion to its number in the population." Krislov (1967, 1974) also argued that American bureaucracy should be representative in its social composition. He posited several advantages of having a diverse workforce:

> The most obvious is the simple representational notion that all social groups have a right to political participation and to influence. The second one can be labelled the functional aspect; the wider the range of talents, types, and regional and family contacts found in a bureaucracy, the more likely it is to be able to fulfil its functions, with respect to both internal efficiency and social setting.
>
> Bureaucracies also symbolize values and power realities and are thus representational in both a political and an analytic sense. Therefore, finally social conduct and future behaviour in a society may be channelled and encouraged through the mere constitution of the bureaucracy (1974: 64).

However, even after 2 decades during which representative bureaucracy became a concept of considerable importance as an explanatory tool in the discussions of the American civil service, its concepts, meanings, and applicability remained ambiguous and underdeveloped. As a result of this confusion, Mosher (1968: 14–15) attempted to clarify the concept of representativeness by introducing the passive and active form of representation.

Mosher advocated the form of passive representation because the passive (or descriptive) meaning of representativeness concerns the origins of individuals and the degree to which, collectively, they mirror the whole society.

> It may be statistically measured in terms of locality or origin... and its nature (rural, urban, suburban), previous occupations, father's occupation, education, family income, family social class, sex, race, religion. A public service... which is broadly representative of all categories of the population in these respects, may be thought of as satisfying Lincoln's prescription of government "by the people" in a limited sense.

Mosher believed that passive representation was important because it signified democratic values such as open service, equal opportunity, social mobility, and participatory management. Kranz (1976) further expanded the concept of representation by emphasizing the idea of proportional representation. For example, he pointed out that a bureaucracy is representative if the ratio of a particular group in an agency equals that of the group's percentage in the population. He argued that a representative bureaucracy was desirable for economic, social, and political justifications in such a way that bureaucracy was not only providing essential services but also was becoming a source of jobs, as well as "a potential form of significant group representation" (Kranz 1976: 135). He reiterated that the public sector was the preferred avenue for women and minority grievances, since it offered them greater employment opportunities.

Thompson (1976) illustrated three different forms of bureaucratic representation that could increase bureaucratic responsiveness to particular groups and advocate their interests in the policy outputs. First, he underlined the importance of demographic representation in the civil service, which would reflect certain characteristics of the population. Secondly, he emphasized the attitudinal representation in which citizens' values and beliefs must be proportionately represented among public administrators. Finally, he argued for substantive representation, such that the actual behaviour of bureaucrats should benefit intended social groups. In addition, Krislov and Rosenbloom (1981) were interested in integrating bureaucratic power into democratic government. In a similar manner to Thompson's, they also proposed three types of representation: representation by personnel (diverse workforce), representation by agencies (agencies promote specific groups' interests), and representation through citizen participation (citizens have greater access to decision-making processes). These representation models have indeed been part of administrative reforms aimed at increasing greater accountability and responsiveness. In short, the different versions of representation clearly emphasize the new perspective of the role of representative bureaucracy within the context of democratic theory.

A representative bureaucracy that broadly reflects the values, interests, aspirations, and desires of the general public has a legitimate position in a democratic country. Administrators who come from various demographic backgrounds will initially be much more sensitive to the issues and interests of their own groups and thus be able to make policy decisions that reflect those interests. However, individual administrators normally go through socialization processes that influence their values, beliefs, attitudes, and behaviours. These socialization experiences in turn shape the way they perceive their work roles as well as their policy decisions. Thus, different socialization experiences will produce different perceptions of work roles and different bureaucratic decisions. This means that administrators who first come into the civil service with specific values and beliefs might not be able to hold on to those values and beliefs anymore. The organizational values and beliefs will now be more likely to shape their attitudes and behaviour.

ADMINISTRATIVE DISCRETION AND REPRESENTATIVE BUREAUCRACY

The essential role of government bureaucracy in formulating and implementing public policies makes it a central player in a democratic nation. Bureaucratic actions basically constitute what government chooses to do or not to do. The original politics/administration dichotomy has clearly faded because of the increasing importance of civil servants in the policy-making processes. Scholars of public administration have long recognized that bureaucracy has now become the centre of political power and authority. It has a direct impact upon the population because of its role in the decisionmaking and implementation processes (Weber 1968; Peters 1988; Thompson 1961; Lenin 1969; Kingsley 1944; Herring 1936; Appleby 1949; Wright 1974–75; Sutherland 1993; Kaufman 1954, 1978; Friedrich 1978; Finer 1978).

However, the degree of administrative discretion required to implement public policy stands in stark contrast to the democratic government requirement of popular sovereignty. As a result, the delegation of policy-making authority to government agencies raises a serious dilemma in democratic societies. On the one hand, bureaucratic discretion is essential because lawmakers cannot foresee all possible circumstances surrounding the application and execution of public laws. On the other hand, their lack of accountability to political pressure further constrains the ability of legislatures to control bureaucratic behaviour (Meier 1993a; Mosher 1982; Redford 1969; Ripley and Franklin 1991; Rourke 1992). Consequently, bureaucrats are often called upon to make judgments based on their experiences, expertise, and intuition, rather than in the interest of the public (Warmsley et al. 1990).

In addition, a serious concern arises that certain agencies of government seem to develop a special relationship with special private interests, the very interests they are supposed to regulate, again suggesting the inability of public agencies to ensure bureaucratic responsiveness and accountability to the public. Lowi (1969) argues that the exercise of discretion tends to neglect the larger public interest. As a result, he proposes a "juridical democracy" that enlists detailed legislative action designed to eliminate discretion. In addition to specific legislation and greater legislative review of administrative actions, other proposals have suggested increasing public accountability. Cooper (1982) discusses various roles, obligations, and objective responsibilities that limit the boundaries of administrative actions. Gawthrop's (1984) system theory is a mechanism used to redesign organizational structures to achieve bureaucratic responsiveness. Ziegler and Tucker (1978) argue that efficiency and responsiveness can only be maintained when policy initiative rests with the elected representative. Furthermore, economics-based approaches have also contributed to the search for democratic accountability. The principal-agent model that is widely used in economics, management, and sociology (Levinthal 1988; Zucker 1987) has become a powerful new tool for assessing bureaucratic responsiveness. This model stipulates that the principals (executive and legislative) design incentives and sanctions to control administrators' behaviour so that the behaviour is always in conformity with the policy preferences of the principals (Wood and Waterman 1993).

Finer (1972) has also argued for greater legislative control and increased supervision of administrative activities as a means of controlling bureaucrats. Fearing that bureaucrats' views become the dominant view of society, he recommends that legislatures engage in detailed supervision of government agencies. Recent theoretical and empirical studies (Ferejohn and Shipan 1990; Carpenter 1996; Hamilton and Schroeder 1994; Wood and Waterman 1993, 1994) have all highlighted the utilization of mechanisms such as administrative procedures, appointments, budgets, and oversight hearings to enhance bureaucratic responsiveness in public agencies. Other empirical studies even indicate that many public administrators believe that elected officials should exercise some degree of dominance over them (Green 1982; Gruber 1987).

Finally, the growing influence of the democratic accountability model on administrative theories brings forth the argument for a representative bureaucracy. Proponents of representative bureaucracy argue that bureaucratic decisions reflect the general will of the population if bureaucratic composition shares similar characteristics of the population, such as geographical locations (Denhardt 1992), social classes (Kingsley 1944), and race or gender (Krislov 1974). Van Riper (1958) argues that the concept of representative bureaucracy offers a positive perspective on the theory of administrative responsibility.

Others argue that the representative nature of bureaucracy makes it potentially responsive to the needs and interests of the population (Long 1952; Meier 1993a; Saltzstein 1985, 1992). A bureaucracy that consists of people from diverse backgrounds can certainly influence policy preferences to be in sync with the interests and demands of the groups they represent.

VARIOUS MODELS

Stakeholders' Role Expectations

The focus of this variable is to examine administrators' perceptions of what significant others perceive their role should be. With such a focus, the aim is to demonstrate that an administrator defines his or her role with reference to others. For example, role theorists infer that a certain behaviour will follow a particular position. (For a further discussion of role theory, see Gross, Mason and McEachern 1958: 12; Conway and Feigert 1972: 124-125; and Linton 1945.) Individuals' attitudes are thus a reflection of the attitudes held by the group with which he or she associates. Michael Dawson (1994) calls this attachment being "one of us." He defines this notion of linked fate as the degree to which particular groups believe that their own self-interests are linked to the interests of others. As a result, the role itself is formed by the expectations of significant others and the expectation that the administrator attaches to it.

For example, when administrators perceive that the community of minorities and women expect them to represent women's and minority interests, they are more likely to accept this role (Kahn et al. 1964). However, when an administrator perceives that other actors have different expectations of how he or she will behave in this position, the clash of incompatible expectations leads to role conflict. For instance, political leaders expect the administrator to represent their interests and take sides on policy matters. On the other hand, the administrator also feels that his supervisors expect him to be neutral and efficient in carrying out his tasks. As a result of these different expectations, a public administrator often experiences intra-role conflict. It is generally true that administrators may have to deal with outside actors in carrying out their duties. The role expectations of other actors may significantly alter administrators' own perceptions concerning work roles. Actors such as politicians, the general public, superiors, professional associations, women and minority colleagues, and women and the minority community possess different political agendas. Most likely, the role expectations of these actors often do not coincide with the administrators' perceptions of organizational goals.

As a result, administrators must find ways to reconcile these different expectations with their own goals and commitments. For example, literature on representative bureaucracy reveals that minority and women administrators will often advocate policies that cater to the interests of their groups if other actors in the policy-making process hold such expectations for them. Likewise, administrators will tend to follow traditional bureaucratic roles if they perceive that other actors expect them to adhere to bureaucratic norms and practices (Martinez [1991] and Murray et al. [1994]). Thus, *administrators who* perceive that other important actors in the policy environment expect them to represent women's and minority interests are more likely to assume the role of women's *and minority advocates and hence have policy preferences that reflect this role.*

Women and Minority Role Acceptance: The perception of role orientations is central to this study. Selden (1997: 117) defines roles as "sets of expected behaviours to be performed by a person occupying a particular position." (For further discussion of role orientations, please see Kahn, Wolfe, Quinn, and Snoek [1964], Turner [1956], and Widmer [1993].) Role expectations are demands conveyed by significant others expressed either formally or informally. However, these expectations are not as important as individuals' own perceptions of what is expected of them (Kahn et al. 1964, Turner 1956). This is because according to Kahn et al. (1964: 16), "It is the received role, however, which is the immediate influence on... behaviour and the immediate source of... motivation to role performance." As a result, despite multiple role expectations, administrators may ultimately decide which role orientations they will meet.

Several scholars have examined organizational and environmental conditions that influence the role orientations of public administrators (McClain and Karnig 1988, Henderson 1988, Martinez 1991, and Murray et al. 1994). Although the expectations vary from one significant actor to another, Selden (1997) identifies two most common expectations: representative role orientation and traditional role orientation. The emphasis on the representative functions of bureaucracy was first codified in the "new public administration" school of thought, which essentially dismisses the old Wilsonian tradition that public administration is a value-free practice (Waldo 1971; Marini 1971).

The landmark Minnowbrook conference of public administration professionals in 1968 was the earliest indication that the voices for inclusion had started to gain prominence in the administrative arena. Frederikson (1971), one of the proponents of this school, argues that bureaucracy has to be included in the scheme of representation and social justice. Similarly, Riggs (1970: 570) points out that there is a "need for diverse elements in a population to be adequately represented in order for a government to command their loyalty as a legitimate expression of common welfare." As a result, the idea of representative bureaucracy is not only to create a civil service that is more reflective of its population, but also to strive to make policies that promote the interests of historically disadvantaged groups such as women and minorities. Mosher's (1982) prescription for passive and active representation is reflective of his position that it is simply not enough to have a diverse workforce. Instead, public administrators should also advocate public policies that advance the interests and wishes of disadvantaged groups. Thus, when administrators perceive their role as advocates of women's or minority groups, they are more likely to pursue policy preferences that benefit women's and minority interests.

Therefore, *administrators who assume the role of minority and women's role advocate are likely to prefer policies that advance the interest of women and minority groups.*

Traditional Role Acceptance: The traditional bureaucratic roles emphasize economy, neutrality, rationality, meritocracy, and efficiency (Ingraham and Ban 1986). Traditional role orientation is based on the principle of merit and neutral competence. To this end, Kaufman (1956: 1,060) emphatically argues that public administrators need to "do the work of the government expertly, and to do it according to explicit, objective standards rather than personal or party or other obligations and loyalties." While neutral competence is important, the ultimate objective is efficiency in administration (Denhardt and deLeon 1993). Dahl (1947: 2) concurs that, "the doctrine of efficiency runs like a half-visible thread through the fabric of public administration literature as a dominant goal." Similarly, Frederickson (1971: 311) asserts that the classic definition of public administration has always been "the efficient, economical, and coordinated" delivery of public services.

More recent observations of public administration also underline the fact that economy and efficiency continue to remain the central values among public administrators (Ingraham and Ban 1986). As a result, it is believed that administrators who accept the traditional bureaucratic role orientation will be less inclined to conceive their role orientation representing any particular group. Specifically, *administrators who assume traditional roles are not likely to engage in behaviours that support the interests of women and minorities.*

Control Variables: I also include two control variables in this model: the ethnicity and the gender of the administrator. Since organizational socialization experiences may lead administrators to accept representative role orientation, a control variable of ethnicity is included to determine whether it has any effect on policy preferences (Selden 1997; Selden et al. 1998). In addition, a control variable of gender is included because scholars examining the role of women in government tend to argue that women administrators often have a "heightened awareness of feminist issues [that] often give[s] them a better feel for the problems women encounter, making them especially adept at recognizing when policy solutions fail to account for women's unique needs" (Dolan 2000: 514). Thus, it is reasonable to assume that gender may have an additional impact on administrators' policy preferences.

Methodology

The Research Setting: The focus of the empirical research conducted in this article is the federal ministries in Kuala Lumpur. Since the focal point of the research is the discretionary power of bureaucracy, it was imperative that only higher civil servants be selected. They ranged from officers in the managerial and professional group to top managerial positions such as secretary general, undersecretaries, their deputies and assistants, and directors of departments.

The selection of higher civil servants in the study also resonates with the argument by Meier and Stewart (1992) that public administrators who are the subjects of the analysis must first have a significant amount of discretion in the decision-making process. Second, the decisions must have important implications for the groups being represented, and third, the administrators can be associated directly with the decisions they make. Because these assumptions clearly fit the characteristics of higher civil servants, they are appropriately selected in this study.

Data Collection: Data for this study were collected in Malaysia during October 2002 and July 2003. Two main sources were i) government documents, official reports, and national statistics data of Malaysia and ii) survey questionnaires from a sample of Malaysian higher civil servants from Group A (management and professional and upper management) drawn from 12 federal ministries: the Ministries of Domestic Trade and Consumer Affairs, Women and Family Development, National Unity and Social Development, Youth and Sports, Agriculture, Transport, Works, Home Affairs, Primary Industry, Finance, Energy, Communications, and Multimedia and Human Resources.

The survey was self-administered. I personally distributed the questionnaires to a top-ranking civil servant in each ministry, who then randomly distributed the questionnaires to the officials in the ministry. I specified the time for collecting back the questionnaires and even extended the time when the responses were poor.

All of the ministries I surveyed are located in Kuala Lumpur and Putrajaya. The number of questionnaires was distributed based upon the number of Group A officials, as well as the requested number from the relevant ministries. I distributed 545 questionnaires and recovered 205 completed questionnaires, about 37%.

Findings and Discussions: Overall, the variables included in the model account for 34% of the variation found in the policy preferences favoring women's and minority interests.

Perhaps most crucial, administrators who perceive their role as that of an advocate of women and minority interests are significantly more likely to prefer policy decisions that advance the interests of women and minorities (beta =.45).

Second, although it does not attain statistical significance, the traditional role perception variable is related negatively to policy preferences favouring women and minorities, suggesting that acceptance of traditional role orientation does not further women's and minority interests.

Third, as hypothesized, role expectation of other actors has a significant impact on policy preferences favouring women's and minority interests. The positive relationship between perceived role expectations and policy preferences indicates that the more administrators perceive that other actors expect them to advocate women's and minority interests, the more likely it is that they will choose policy decisions that benefit women's and minority interests.

The control variables introduced into the model do not remove the significant influence of women's and minority representative role acceptance and role expectations of other actors. Because administrators' perceptions of their roles have been shown to be influenced by organizational socialization, control variables were included to examine whether differences in policy preferences exist between minority administrators and Malay administrator and between administrators of different genders (Selden 1997). The findings indicate that even when gender and ethnicity are controlled statistically, perceived role expectations and the advocacy representative role accepted by administrators affect administrators' policy preferences.

Conclusion: The findings of this study further enhance the understanding of the concept of representative bureaucracy. Krislov (1974) was the first scholar to argue that examining the descriptive representation alone was of limited usefulness. This is because descriptive characteristics of administrators offer little evidence that they will represent the interests of people who are of similar backgrounds. As such, the study to understand how descriptive representation can be translated into substantive representation becomes much more pertinent among representative bureaucracy scholars.

By exploring the relationship between role perceptions and policy preferences, this study is able to provide evidence of the linkage between descriptive representation and substantive representation. Despite the importance of ethnicity to administrators' role perceptions and policy preferences, this study strongly suggests that administrators who perceive their role as advocates of women and minorities are more inclined to prefer policy decisions that benefit women and the minority community. Most important, the research also suggests conditions that translate descriptive representation into substantive representation. The data analyzed indicate that role expectations of others and role acceptance significantly influence the degree to which Malaysian administrators engage in substantive representation of women's and minority interests.

4

Deliberate Democracy and Electoral Fallacy

INTRODUCTION

The problem of strengthening democratic institutions in a time of transition to globalization has become a problem of sustaining democracy in grassroots institutions. Electoral processes in the third world countries are not strengthening them, as the dominant corporate interests have discovered means of turning them into farce. The governments adopt regulatory changes to democratize institutions by throwing them open to elections, but elections alone do not bring democracy. Democratic ideals have to be reinvestigated in the light of freedom and justice to citizens and not just to the assumed monolith of civil society. "All of a sudden, an electoral system arises in a country so the government can get some aid, credits or most-favoured-nation trading status," writes Terry. "I call this electoralism; that is, having the procedures of democracy without deeper internal roots" (Terry 1986: 9).

The process of growth and development toward urbanization and market expansion has subdued or silenced institutions that magnify people's voices. In globalizing cities, the radicalism of civil society movements has become blunted, since elected politicians defeat them after they are elected. Thus, *panchayats* (councils) and municipal bodies have become arenas of corporate warfare. A corporate-friendly candidate in the panchayat helps the multinational seize village resources like land, wetlands, and cheap labour. Similarly, a corporate backed municipal councilor helps in the distribution of land and infrastructure services like electricity, water, and road construction for shopping malls, plush apartments, and casinos without providing housing for the uprooted slum dwellers. Most of the development policies show an inclination for assisting big business companies rather than implementing programs for poverty eradication or information dissemination to their constituencies. In the absence of institutions of accountability and transparency, they become vulnerable to the control of land mafias and private urbanizers.

The second part of this paper attempts to show how the coexistence of mushrooming activist people's organizations and regulatory changes blunts democracy in local institutions. It becomes imperative to explain at this point that deliberate democracy fails to prevent electoral fallacy in globalizing cities, but it trains citizens to band together to set up smart institutions that combine the functions of citizen as a unit of governance and as a consumer in democratic systems. These organizations are composed of intelligent, aware, and professionally trained people forming the "epistemic community" of local government, which sets the direction and the speed of reform processes. Evidence from the case study of Gurgaon, in Haryana State, which is an example of a globalizing city in the middle of a largely rural and traditionally governed state, helps to substantiate the above hypothesis.

The last part of this paper sets out a model of governance based upon quantum physics. This model elaborates the process in which photons of energy move from people, communities, and their relationship to their ecosystem, in a way that not only accelerates participation and deliberation in local institutions but also reduces the element of public choice and thereby electoral fallacy.

But, when an ecosystem is stressed and community spaces shrink, people do not contribute to this social dynamism. Their local deliberative bodies shrink and community spaces are reduced. This situation strengthens market fundamentalism and new institutionalism in policy deliberations in higher legislative bodies.

The last part of this paper sets out a model of governance based upon quantum physics. This model elaborates the process in which photons of energy move from people, communities, and their relationship to their ecosystem, in a way that not only accelerates participation and deliberation in local institutions but also reduces the element of public choice and thereby electoral fallacy.

But, when an ecosystem is stressed and community spaces shrink, people do not contribute to this social dynamism. Their local deliberative bodies shrink and community spaces are reduced. This situation strengthens market fundamentalism and new institutionalism in policy deliberations in higher legislative bodies.

Methodology: The study is built around three indicators: changes in the regulatory mechanism, land acquisition, and development programs that compensate for the land that they lose to global companies in exchange for other opportunities. These indicators are accepted as fundamental to the assessment of deliberative bodies that help clear people's access to benefits of globalization. Other factors, such as that of service delivery improvements, which include variables like speed, cost of transactions, and corruption in public offices, are treated as spillovers from the previous indicators. Democratic institutions are taken as dependent variables of global investments, i.e., foreign direct investment (FDI) and foreign institutional investment.

The research methods for this study are largely based upon interactive research in which participation in governance networks and implementation strategies for micro-level policy interventions is the prime source of information. Municipal bodies and several secondary autonomous structures, such as district industrial centres, urban development authorities, and boards, are trying to implement reforms to gain greater marketization of public services and infrastructure expansion. The catalytic push through the introduction of information technology systems in the district is also treated as complementary to the processes that reduce the gap between "private" and "public" spaces of citizens. The primary reliance is upon data about visibly shrinking community spaces and questionnaires put before respondents from the village. The target groups are divided into two groups: landowners and those who are landless but are animal rearers and cattle grazers and thus are land dependent. The second stage is an exploration into the objective data available from state and local government offices. This helps in the objective and dispassionate comparison of data. Data has also been acquired from the Punjab, Haryana and Delhi Chamber of Commerce to understand the relative position of Gurgaon not only in terms of Haryana, its home state, but also in terms of Delhi, which witnesses cautious globalization and relies more on synergistic partnership with people.

The primary purpose of this paper is not to criticize the process of reforms that open the Indian economy to global competition and to entrepreneurial discovery [Austrian model], but to suggest that because of the limited use of public choice, a missed link impinges upon the democratic functioning of institutions. Data collection is mainly through secondary sources, which are derived from media reports, nongovernment organization (NGO) research, and state government reports on panchayat and city administration.

The study attempts to conflate the socially woeful and structurally xenomorphic gap between transaction cost and agency theory, on the one hand, with that of the critical theory model used by Riggs in Comparative Administrative Group (CAG) analysis, on the other. The theory of transaction cost (Williamson 1964) and agency analysis (Moe 1997) are used along with a more rigorous use of interpretive method (Walsham 1993) to understand the flow of information in a governance network, which influences the process of aggregation and consolidation in society and among service recipients in a city. The interpretive method is indispensable to fill the gap between charged society and nonavailability of any data to show people's increased participation in government programs.

This also helps to generate an improved understanding of the linkages of democratic institutions to the anthropological and cultural factors in a society rather than to the state regulatory mechanism leading toward decentralized and accountable administration. Thus the apt remark that "the modern liberal democratic state goes the furthest in trying to accommodate cultural identities within it. The structures it must necessarily institute to be able to do so constitute the challenge of our times" (Gupta 2000).

The trade alignments of transitional economies like India are posing grave disjunctions between the demands of citizenship and those of their cultural identities. Movements against the state in the form of bureaucracy bashing had been in existence prior to the turbulent refusal of communities to implant megaprojects on their land in the early 1980s. The state failed to prevent either the marginalization of communities or the breakup of their social fabric, which became in itself an embedded fact of most government development policies.

This has made intermediate institutions an important aspect of discourse on deliberate democracy. As Gupta (2000) observes, this led to recall of sentiments and structures of the past; it has also strengthened the demand for empowering intermediate institutions that will realize the promise of constitutional democracies. However, this study also recognizes the emergence of a civil society movement resonating with rigor the moral sentiments provoked due to the exclusion of groups with weak consolidation.

To explain that the process of decentralization and people's participation in globalizing cities has followed the pattern that suits the ruling political party more than people's demand for service delivery improvements, some of the crucial administrative decisions have been analyzed within local parameters.

This reveals their impact upon voting patterns of various communities and the marginalization of electorally weaker sections of society. Considering the speed with which these changes are taking place and the difficulties faced by a researcher in obtaining data, the study has largely depended upon local media and information through resident welfare associations, local activist groups, and small-scale industry associations.

DELIBERATE DEMOCRACY AND GLOBALIZATION

John Stuart Mill upholds the values of "direct face to face democracy."

The secret ballot system, according to him, erodes the very idea of democracy by letting citizens vote on the basis of "interest, pleasure or caprice" (1991: 227). The problem of electoral fallacy, which is defining the degree of democratic deliberation in Gurgaon, is the enormous gap that has occurred between the representative and the represented. This is understood through an explanation of the democratic processes in any place. The first important stage of democracy is "elections"; the second is "institutional democracy," which is an official effort between the elections; and the third is the process of sustaining these efforts by strengthening deliberative bodies of citizens.

The first stage is a short and regulated system functioning within the framework of the country's law and constitution. The second is the process of putting those many norms and values of society in place through a gradual and incremental process of adaptation and implementation.

The third involves a sincere effort to give a voice to every citizen. Since every citizen has a cultural, linguistic, or occupational bonding through innumerable informal groups that act as "steam release" communes, the task of sustaining democracy would mean that these groups may not be allowed to wilt. However, the first stage becomes visually very imposing, just like the hero of a blockbuster film whose gigantic publicity hides the enormous efforts of the whole studio team which led the film to this glory. Representative democracy has placed elections on the highest pedestal of insurance against despotism, as it bridges gaps between various policies and makes them more coherent and mutually consistent.

Thus representation that originated as an instrument of democracy has now become bigger than democracy itself. Groups that are politically better consolidated have a natural advantage over others and can appropriate state resources as they want. Being a "vote bank," they become the preferred choice of the elected representative. Such nexuses manufactured through the democratic process share state resources in a way that shrinks and reduces institutional spaces that provide for open deliberations on policy issues. Thus, deliberate democracy converts into a hush-hush democracy governed by the state's ability to bring about amendments to their composition, procedures, and life span. Globalizing cities have witnessed the subjection of their local bodies to many regulatory changes brought about by the demand for efficiency, economy, and speed.

Thus, although deliberation is a process of enabling citizens to make a rational choice about the political system they desire, this process is vested with institutions that reflect the core of electoral fallacies, such as the parliament, state legislatures, or local bodies in urban and rural areas.

Marginalization of deliberate democracy leads to at least one very important aspect that sustains democratic states, which is its substantive aspect. F. W. Riggs had studied this aspect in the early days when he was working in the CAG. Its important feature, which tends to be crucial to transitional societies, is *reciprocity*. The relevance of Riggs's ecological framework and its consistent applicability to Indian analytical studies is due to his normative understanding of community institutions and their embedded rationality, which form the core of bureaucratic institutions. He rejected the functional argument of Almond's systems approach, and he indicated those variables where inputs did not lead to predictable outputs, and thus policy slippages remained unexplained.

To Riggs goes the credit of liberating public administration theory from the US federal experience and suggesting a model based upon the cultural argument and providing an explanation of community relationships and administrative diversities, despite the fact that his path-breaking effort to reach a general theory of administration was left off half way with the early and premature demise of the CAG.

Recognizing the futility of theoretical efforts to implant Western models into India, Riggs wrote, "We may expect that a model which throws light on administrative realities in one setting may simply obscure the facts in another situation" (Riggs 1960: 225–242). He illustrated this in an interesting discussion on the issue of land revenues, addressing whether they should be classified as "taxes" or "rents." Since this dichotomy assumes the existence of a market system (which it was not), he drew on a study by Walter C. Neale (1957) to prove the fact that it was "neither" (1957: 218–235). Neale mentions that the system prevailing in the Indian village could be called "reciprocative" and "redistributive," in which every occupational group (barbers, washermen, carpenters, etc.) performed its traditional duties for other members in the village without direct compensation. The cultivator at harvest time would distribute shares from his crop to all of them as well as to the Rajah, who also reciprocated by distributing it to his officials in the court and himself. This entails a highly specialized system of activities and exchange without reliance on markets, price mechanisms, or demand-supply forces.

Globalization has once again thrown open to debate a very pertinent question about the need for marketizing such a specialized network embedded in traditional society. Riggs (1960) further suggests that marketizing might inadvertently lead to a transformation of society by replacing or eliminating the existing benign structures. This carries the theoretical argument about the prevalence of "substantive" economics, which contrasts with the formal market system and provides a way for community members to interact with their natural and social environment in such a manner that they are able to satisfy their material needs even in times of scarcity. This is an adequate explanation about India's subsistence economy, in which a large number of rural poor are capable of surviving simply due to the availability of biomass resources (like natural produce from land, wetlands, village forests) free of any cost. When developing countries like India undergo "debt servicing," these biomass resources are subsidized for industries, as a result of which poor people lose access to them.

Thus an economic system prevails without having a formal economic structure, and an administrative system prevails without in any way having the rationally justifiable administrative model. Riggs's study suggests that an administrative system may function without having a bureau just as an economic system can work without a market. "One may discover, of course, that what exists is not at all a bad thing" (Riggs 1960: 227). Reciprocity is at the core of "deliberate democracy" (Gutmann and Thompson 2003). Deliberation ensures cooperation and reciprocity prevents the majority from overlooking or sidelining the particular systems that regulate fairness in small communities. "Reciprocity is to justice in political ethics what replication is to truth in scientific ethics" (Gutmann and Thompson 2003: 35). Replication in scientific research requires public demonstration and strengthens truth; similarly with reciprocity, which justifies a law through public deliberation. In doing so, some substantive principles like cultural freedom, moral values, and access to opportunities other than the formalistic and procedural ones play a dominant role. By insulating legal processes from substantive democratic systems, the deliberative element of democratic governance is affected, as a result of which it is unable to face the moral and political challenges of globalization.

Russell Hardin's "street level epistemology" (Hardin 2003: 165), or a theory of knowledge of ordinary persons, is another defense of substantive factors that provide fundamental structures to the democratic framework ("street level epistemology is the subjective account of knowledge, not a public account" [2003: 165]). This knowledge is about usefulness, trust, and free interaction of people in a social system that is not generated by outside, exogenous forces but from within the system itself and therefore prioritizes social justice and normative values in democratic governance.

Globalizing cities are a result of exogenous pulls based upon justifications of a kind that increase FDI in the region. Consequently, the political regimes adopted the mode of legitimizing this transition from the protectionist economy to a liberal economy on the basis of free and fair elections rather than deliberations on the substantive modes of governance. This flawed conception of democracy privileges elections over other dimensions of democracy and ignores the degree to which multiparty elections (even if they are competitive and uncertain in outcome) may exclude significant portions of the population from contesting for power or advancing and defending their interests, or may leave significant arenas of decision making beyond the control of elected officials (Terry 1986: 9–36).

This has in fact increased the hold of formal properties of governance over substantial features that consolidate societies and help democratic aggregation. Communities have become more vulnerable than ever before to the dominant interests that lubricate the procedural machinery of elections. The extent of political repression of weaker communities, marginalized groups, and the rural poor are issues that the modern liberal state tries to answer through the electoral process rather than invoking issues of substantive justice in law and governance. Fung and Wright (2003: 3) argue that the apparent decline of state capacity to govern democratically has helped the "right of the political spectrum" to escalate its attack on the very idea of the affirmative state. As they further write, "deregulation, privatization, reduction of social services, and curtailments of state spending have been the watch words, rather than participation, greater responsiveness, more creative and effective forms of democratic state intervention" (2003: 4).

A strong critique of new institutionalism in administrative practices has come from critical theorists. Habermas, in *Between Facts and Norms* (1992), carried a very strong emphasis on participation and what he prefers to call "discourse democracy." This democracy emerges from those critical realities of society that solidify through participation in formal and informal forums rather than in electoral politics. Cultural presuppositions about traditional communities can model a process of informal logic that would test validity claims and design a framework of democratic participation. Social actions are regarded as the reproduction and transformation of practices and structures that are relatively enduring and exist prior to the individual. Even Riggs's advancement of the theory from *Prismatic Society Revisited* (1973) to *Applied Prismatics* (1978) was an intensive search for frameworks of ethnicities and interethnic processes and problems that continue to remain relevant for Indian administration. Kothari (1991) and Dipankar Gupta (2000) are forthrightly suspicious of the homogenization process and suggest revival of civil society institutions based upon traditions of mutuality and togetherness.

The present period of advancement calls for strengthening constitutional democracy by reviving modern rational-legal intermediate institutions, such as the institutions of local governance like the municipality, panchayat, or judiciary, or the corporate structure of the economy. It is this aspect that an affirmative state, rather than a retreating one, is more empowered to take cognizance of. The support for the affirmative state has declined in the recent years of advancing globalization because the capacity to mobilize community-guided movements has also declined. This feature manifests itself in a more pronounced manner in globalizing cities, because of their ability to draw people from all regions of the world as a technical support work force or as unorganized lowwage labourers. Thomas and Heller (2003: 77), in their case study on decentralized planning in the Indian state of Kerala, assert, "A fiercely competitive political party system grafted onto a highly unequal and fragmented social structure has privileged narrow and opportunistic interest politics over more encompassing forms of representation." Thus, politics has been reduced to a zero-sum scramble for public resources (Thomas and Heller 2003: 77). To use Karl Polanyi's metaphor, these regions of the country have become "satanic mills" of the poor, where all people's movements freeze. This also suggests the growth of a shadow governance system, as elaborated in Strange's *The Retreat of the State* (1996), in which transnational diplomacy between national mafias has found it easier to operate economic enterprises. In globalizing cities, it is the "land mafia" that is a more visible and tangible variant on the political scene, though actual data about their influence may take more time to emerge in research.

REFORMS IN LOCAL GOVERNANCE SHRINK DELIBERATION SPACES

The purpose of this paper is to explore whether reforms are shrinking the arena of deliberate democracy and subordinating institutions of social deliberation to demands of the new market. Reforms undertaken at the local governance level, which affect the acquisition of village resources for infrastructure development and urbanization processes, have raised serious problems. Public administration is subjected to theoretical tensions to understand it in the background of the spirit of constitutional democracy and demands of new markets. Rosenbloom (1982: 54) suggests that the trinity of values that arrive from traditional professionalism in public administration such as efficiency, effectiveness, and economy should never be allowed to displace discursiveness and deliberations about public policies in society, or prevent autonomy of communities and the idea of common good. Long (1976: 21) also argues that we must not "substitute a market with consumers for a polity with citizens." This has, however, not been the case in globalizing cities.

Indian democracy rests upon a substratum of villages composed of communities that are ethnically, linguistically, and culturally very diversified. Yet one factor that links them into a nation is the agriculture cycle of the *Rabi* and *Kharif* cropping seasons. Since life revolves round it, their community institutions also revolve round it. Sir Henry Cotton in his book *New India or India in Transition* (1886) states that even the British House of Commons Report of 1812, during the peak of colonial occupation of India, carried observations about the self-supportive governance system prevailing in Indian villages. Villages have been constantly pressured by state authorities to dispense with their land and forests which, being arid types, are generally treated as wastelands under centrally sponsored schemes for land regeneration such as the Drought Prone Area Programme or Desert Development Programme. The penultimate value attached to village governance in the Constitution gets derailed due to the lopsided and exotic reforms being carried toward marketization of local governance. This has prevented the growth of participatory bureaucracy and emboldened the rule of dominant caste mafias in rural areas.

Panchayats were sacrosanct to villages in India even before they were constitutionally recognized in the 73rd Constitutional Amendment Act of 1992. This amendment was a new milestone in the democratic evolution of India, since it finally recognized this innate capacity of Indian governance. It was a landmark in the direction of decentralized decision making. Panchayati Raj Institutions (PRIs), which are the rural governance structures, and municipal bodies (urban structures) ensured people's participation in planning, decision making, implementation, and delivery. This paper takes up the reforms undertaken by globalizing cities to facilitate speedy infrastructure development and FDI investments. It would also work on the logic that reforms have to reflect people's habits and value systems and for that reason they also have to originate from people, since administrative practices can not divert from established habits and norms of society.

The element of deliberation embedded in local institutions gets weakened right from the preparation of the Master Plan prepared for the city, as it is a plan for city expansion and urbanization over agricultural lands. It is mandatory for every city to prepare a development plan. This is generally called a Master Plan, which sets in motion the task of land acquisition for development purposes in accordance with the prospective problems that the city may encounter as it grows. The problem begins when the core component of development—that is, "land"—is the scarcest commodity within the municipal limits. So this land has to be acquired from the surrounding villages. Thus, agricultural fields, land under panchayats, and village community resources such as ponds, wells, village forests, and watershed areas, which are cherished as the common property of all village inhabitants, suddenly become commodities to be sold in the market.

This process of acquiring land from villages has been going on for a long time, but as administrators from three development offices in Gurgaon reveal, earlier they were being acquired for laying a railway line, a road, an electric line, or an industry that in many ways compensated villages for the loss of land through the ethical argument of capacity development. In the present times, globalization pushes multinationals into the market, as a result of which the government acquires land and passes it to the developer, who finally becomes the major beneficiary. This is evident in the statistics on foodgrain production in Gurgaon, which has declined as a percentage of the gross value of agricultural output at current prices from 71.02% in 1970–71 to 49.01% in 2001–2002 (Government of Haryana 2004: 768).

Even the land use pattern of the state of Haryana suggests that the area under forests has been drastically reduced, from 4.62% in 1980–81 to a mere 1% in 2004. (Statistical Abstracts of Haryana 1980–81 2004) and therefore the percentage of Gurgaon's forest area to the total geographical area of the district is a pathetically low 2.56%. (Forest Department, Haryana 2004: 332).

These factors are seen in the process of people's contribution to the developmental process and their participation in state programs. The Community Development statistics of Haryana (2004: 346–347) reveal that people's contribution to the community development programs in Haryana, which rose from Rs. 648.19 in 1967 to Rs. 763.44 in 1981, show a sharp downturn in the globalizing period to a mere Rs. 75.00 in 2002–03.

A startling revelation here is that the less globalized industrial states have more working population, for the simple reason that these small states offer more diversified and community-based options available to every class of citizen, whereas the globalizing townships are straightline trajectories to urbanized middle-class growth, marginalizing the rural poor. This is adding to the burgeoning numbers of unemployed people in Haryana. Statistics from the Haryana Director of Employment show that the number of unemployed persons has almost doubled, from 486,706 in 1985 to 802,581 in 2002. Even though the market has opened up, the state capacity for placement has decreased from 17,253 persons in 1985 to 4,764 in 2002.

In the early era of liberalization, most of the state governments did not have the money to compensate villagers for their acquired land. This anomaly was partly rectified in 1996 when Government of India's Urban Development Plans Formulation and Implementation (UDPFI) rationalized the problems of land acquisition so that the benefits of adequate compensation go straight to the owner and the predictability of development programs for the city are also assured.

UDPFI defined "transfer of development rights" as the development right to transfer the potential of a plot designated for a public purpose in a plan, expressed in terms of total permissible built space calculated on the basis of Floor Space Index or Floor Area Ratio allowable for that plot, for utilization by the owner himself or by way of transfer by him to someone else from the present location to a specified area in the plan, as additional built up space over and above the permissible limit in lieu of compensation for the surrender of the concerned plot free from all encumbrances to the planning and Development Authority.

This system recharged the real estate developers and thus the total land cost flows from the developer to the landowner. The process was accelerated when the Government stated in

November 2003 that it would permit 100% FDI, on a case-to-case basis, in the development of integrated townships. This would permit FDI in housing, commercial premises, hotels, resorts, city-and regional-level urban infrastructure facilities such as roads and bridges, and mass rapid transport systems. Two Malaysian companies, Feedback Integrated Infrastructure Development Corporation and IJM Infrastructure Ltd., have already entered into agreement to develop townships at Gurgaon and in Kukatpally in Hyderabad. According to the 2004 Global Retail Development Index by A. T. Kearney, India ranks second in the world when it comes to opportunities in the organized retail business—even higher than the People's Republic of China, which is ranked third. Investment in retail real estate yields 13–16% per year. This system lies behind the rapid growth of some of the previously sleepy and slogging townships. Reforms that have reduced bureaucracy and liberalized laws have also helped the generation of private facilitators from local areas who help in land acquisitions by suppressing the local communitarian voices.

The developments mentioned above have made rural areas and their local bodies such as panchayats vulnerable to the pressures of real estate developers. The role of panchayats in protecting and generating income for the poor landless, animal-rearing tribes and *dalits* (groups of communities which have remained socioeconomically backward for reasons of social discrimination due to caste factors) in the village by protecting most of their resources such as land, water bodies, and forests, including the common property resources, has decreased and mostly subsided. This, however, would not mean that panchayats have acted as responsible and honest guardians of village's common areas, but they score better in traditional face-to-face accountability forums within their communities than the new structures created through exogenous pulls of the new market regimes. The Planning Commission has also noticed this lacuna of planning, in which the higher administrative bodies of the country have failed to relate people's problems to their policies. The *Report of the Task Force on Panchayats*, constituted in 2001 under the Chairmanship of K. B. Saxena, had pointed out certain grave factors that prevented people's access to the planning process. "It is observed that a number of Ministries of the Central Government have not taken any concrete steps to integrate PRIs in their strategy of planning and implementation of various programmes which essentially fall in their jurisdiction" (2001: 1).

This problem has also been exacerbated due to the direct access by some NGOs to relevant ministries. The shocking fact uncovered in the report is that "PRIs do not really this strategy of implementation and in fact there is not even a conceptual recognition of it. NGOs are operating in areas and on subjects which belong to the PRIs and therefore are expected to work in tandem with them (2001: 1). The report further admits that since ministries undertake internationally funded projects, they tend to implement them directly, without any involvement of PRIs. The Ministry of Rural Development has failed to bridge this gap. Its 2001 Annual Report (2001: 5) listed 232,278 panchayats at the village level, 6,022 at the intermediate level, and 535 at the district level.

These panchayats were being managed by 29.2 million elected representatives at all levels, of whom one third were women. Ironically, this huge deliberative framework has been ignored in the process of planning, and the NGO-led decentralization has brought in experts who are delinked from the anthropological history of that region.

This paper mainly looks into the process of globalization and FDI investment in Bangalore and Gurgaon. The selection of these townships is due to their physically distinct nature. Bangalore is the largest cosmopolitan area of urban India, besides being a major software producer in India. Gurgaon has taken to that status quite recently and both the cities are called the "Silicon Valley of India." Bangalore has always been an urban, literate society, whereas Gurgaon has been a rural and traditionally a caste-dominated township, despite its proximity to the capital city Delhi. It would be interesting to begin from the panchayats of the capital city "Delhi," where the panchayati raj continues to be suspended by the state government and no effective steps have been taken to revive PRIs. Much of the illegal activity of land mafias continues over this juridically overlapping area of governance, also called the "lal dora land." The Delhi Development Authority controls most of the development of land. Bangalore had also set up the Bangalore Development Authority in 1976 as a successor to the erstwhile City Improvement Trust Board. The Bangalore Agenda Task Force is a recent creation to act as a catalyst in realizing the city's potential. Gurgaon has the Haryana Urban Development Authority, which till 1996 was acquiring land and then giving it to Haryana State Industrial development Corporation for demarcating plots for development activities. It is a paradox that in these cities no specific body has arisen to look into these irregularities of globalization-led land acquisition from rural communities. This has helped the state government acquire the benefit of centralizing city plans including financial flows.

It is imperative to study the process of development and urbanization in globalizing areas and seek ways to measure the democratic deficit of such townships. The most important administrative and political strategy is that of acquiring land from adjoining villages. It involves a number of interrelated measures. First comes the most essential ingredient, a developer-friendly *legal framework,* which ensures that land can be easily bought and sold. Second is the administration-friendly *procedures and regulations* to ensure the development of land at an affordable cost. The third measure is that of a legitimacy in which the *land taxation* system is designed to promote equity and efficiency in land use. This process also includes an installation of a *transparent and corruption free local administration,* which may not really push reforms to improve people's access to these measures.

MODEL OF GURGAON

To understand the shrinking deliberative power of panchayats in Gurgaon, it is important to assess their status since the beginning of global marketization in the early 1990s. In the 1991 census, Gurgaon had 688 inhabited villages, which increased to 700 in the 2001 census because of the explosive increase of 44.64% in its population; but the number of so called "uninhabited villages" mentioned in the Director of Census Operations records fell from 42 in 1991 to 26 in 2001. This is reflected in the creation of a new town in Gurgaon district: the number of towns increased from 11 to 12 during this period.

These so-called uninhabited villages were the grazing grounds of cattle-and sheep-rearing rural inhabitants, who gained little out of a global spread of business process outsourcing companies. Gurgaon being a district with a dominant rural population, the workforce largely arrived from cities outside Gurgaon. The massive housing and construction boom that followed took place on the land acquired from villages.

The District Town and Country Planner (TCP) claims that the controlled areas that fall at the rural-urban fringes are real centres of planning for further industrialization. In Gurgaon alone it comprises something like one third of the total land in the district, out of which only 9.5% of the areas are urban, thereby leaving more than 90% of the state's area free from any of the controls of Acts enforced by the Government. There has been a substantial amount of infrastructure mismanagement, since the Municipal Committee and the panchayats are not obliged to function within this area and the TCP cannot undertake work without an officially declared plan for that area. They may more reasonably be termed as the "areas of diluted governance." The land purchased within the controlled areas needs a change of land use (CLU) Certificate from the District TCP, which the land purchased outside the controlled areas does not require. Since the industrial townships have not been able to develop plots, these industries have started buying plots directly from the farmers and managing to obtain CLU certificates from the Directorate of Town and Country Planning. This process was guided by a colonial legal system defined under the Land Acquisition Act of 1894. In 1995, on 9 February, the government constituted a committee comprising the following officers as a process to decentralize the power hereby concentrated in the Divisional Commissioner's office:

- Divisional Commissioner as the Chair,
- Deputy Commissioner as the Member Secretary,
- Representative of the Concerned Member Department, and
- District Revenue Officer as the concerned Member.

This also restricted the District Commissioner's discretion to determine the market price of land, not on the basis of

5 years' sale average but only on the basis of 1 year's sale average. Section 5A of this New Land Acquisition Act of 1995 also enabled the landowner to refer to the court under Sec. 18 of the Act. At the peak of this globalizing exercise in Gurgaon, another amendment was undertaken on 8 September 2003. Into Section 22 of the Punjab Scheduled Roads and Controlled Areas Restriction of Unregulated Development Act 1963, after clause (a), an amendment (aa) clause was added to increase the "*abadi deh* areas" [inhabited areas around the village] and reduce the controlled areas where numerous restrictions on construction activities apply. The explanation for the amendment given in the statement of objects and reasons by the TCP Minister of Haryana was the need to exempt construction activity in abadi deh areas.

Parallel to liberalizing the process of laws related to ceilings on agricultural land acquisition and disposal of surplus area has also been a systemic restraining of the decision-making autonomy of local bodies. The 73rd Panchayat (Amendment) Act 1992 had given a constitutional status to panchayats and the Haryana Panchayati Raj Act 1994 had adopted this provision for better administration of rural areas. With the globalization of the market, certain amendments were made to the state act that raise questions about the democratic imperative of these local bodies. Three provisions may be mentioned here. First, the Act of 1994 says that "If the whole of the *sabha* area is included in a municipality or a cantonment, the Gram Panchayat shall cease to exist and the assets and liabilities of it shall vest in the municipality or cantonment as the case may be" (Part II, 7). Taking their cue from this, the developers constructed urban areas on village lands and thus were given the benefit of not having any taxation regime like that of cities. But the price for this anomaly is extremely high, as these villages are at the verge of extermination by real estate developers in business here, such as DLF City, Unitech City, Ansal City, or Ardee City. These areas, exempted from the restrictions imposed by the 1963 Act mentioned above, have not been included in the Municipal Council of Gurgaon for fear of losing a vote bank, since their inclusion into a municipality would mean their subjection to a taxation system on property and land transfer deeds. But besides this tax exemption, these residents of multinational corporation-led urban areas also become entitled to vote in panchayat elections without being physically residents of the villages, historically or emotionally.

This is a total turnaround to the very idea of panchayats as a system of selfgoverning institutions for village communities, as recognized by the

Constitution of India (Article 243 G). The urban voters almost outnumber the rural communities living in these village areas, who have lost their land and occupations, as well as access to their community governance systems.

Second is the series of amendments to the 1994 Act that have systematically weakened the checks and balances system embedded in the Act. Part II Art 8 (2b) of the Act, which provided for six to 20 *panches* (representatives) from wards in a panchayat area in the manner prescribed so that the despotism of the *sarpanch* (headman) could be restrained, has been omitted (*vide* Haryana Act No. 10 of 1999). This has abolished the power of the panches to call a special meeting with notice to the sarpanch and has also led to the Haryana Act No. 14 of 2003, in which the obligation upon the panchayats for having a circle supervisor from among the existing *gram sachivs* (village secretaries at the local body) to supervise the work of *gram vikas sahayaks* (village development volunteers) was substituted.

The third concern is that such measures becoming common in India also raises questions of constitutional propriety. In a case pending in Haryana High Court against a major colonizer in this area, DLF Ltd., and a few other minor developers, it has been recognized that a clear violation of Articles 243X and 243W exists, read with Schedule 12, in which the developer was to undertake the responsibility of maintenance under agreement between DLF and the District TCP. The contesting Resident Welfare Association of urban settlers charges it as the "Biggest Land Scam in the Country." People's awakening has led to the demise of the regime of former Chief Minister of the state, Om Prakash Chautala, and his sons in the last Assembly elections of 2004, who were instrumental in importing an uncontested rule of colonizers and land mafias in the district of Gurgaon (*Amar Ujala* 2003).

MODEL OF BANGALORE

The Bangalore Development Authority (BDA) came into existence in 1976 as a successor to the erstwhile City Improvement Trust Board. The BDA does not have a parallel in Gurgaon. Even rural panchayats have undergone a systematic trimming through gradual amendments, but the presence of an alert and educated citizenry in Bangalore as a buffer has prevented the state government from colonizing citizens' lives through big corporate builders.

The *gram sabhas* (village bodies) were constituted in the 1983 Act and the first elections to panchayats were held in 1987. But in 1992, these local bodies were superceded and administrators were appointed. In 1993, following the Constitution 73rd Amendment Act, the Karnataka Panchayat Raj Act was passed, but still these local bodies could not emerge as deliberative institutions.

They have been fund-starved since their inception, and the newly created post of the Chief Executive Officer (CEO), who retains most of the powers, is not under the control of local panchayats. This Act has since been amended six times. The Nayak Committee, which was appointed in 1997, tried to debureaucratize these bodies by transferring many functions back to the panchayats. Inbanathan's (2000) study on these local bodies in Karnataka records an observation that, although panchayats are provided the opportunity for the widest section of rural society to participate in local governance, social conditions ensure that only a section of the village people actually acquire and wield power.

The rise of development authorities has also been a serious threat to flourishing local economies. The Master Plan for Bangalore was drawn to promote "urban renewal" under the Mega Cities program, similar to the cyber city program of Gurgaon. Though this brought megamalls and multistoried apartments, yet the local economies got blocked. The BDA has also demolished small enterprise-centred commercial areas to recover land that was finally allocated to higher-income groups.

Procedures such as "land reconveyance," which aids in the development of land for poorer classes, is subsequently weakened. In the 2001 panchayat elections, reports revealed that an auction of seats took place (Vyasulu 2001).

Most of the intermediate local bodies are elected under development partner pressure. Government departments are given targets to set up self-help groups and other people's organizations for better people's participation. Allegations have been made about the government by the Bellandur *gram panchayat* and surrounding villages, which were selected for the proposed information and technology corridor project in the City. In September 2004, Janata Dal (Secular) Secretary-General C. Narayanswamy demanded a high-level inquiry into land grabbing by private land developers and influential persons (*Deccan Herald* 2004).

It has been reported that despite preliminary notification for land acquisition by the BDA and the Karnataka Industrial Area Development Board, influential persons, middlemen, and private land developers have cheated the farmers by paying them less than the market value for their lands and then selling the acquired lands at prevailing market rates to information technology companies like Intel. The India Urban Indicators Programme developed by the Society for Development Studies was well received at the United Nations Habitat II Conference held at Istanbul in June 1996, and won the "Best Practice" award for excellence from among 110 participating countries. Bangalore was among the 11 Indian cities included in the program and Karnataka accounted for five of them. Thus in Bangalore also, a loose regulatory environment for land use is oriented toward mixed land use, as a result of which developers hold sway over its development and retail sale.

The Bangalore model serves governance parameters better than the Gurgaon Model and this is for one single reason. They have better civil society activism and two important measures of downward accountability: first, the gram sabhas as deliberative bodies and, second, the system of *jamabandhi* (social audit). When gram sabhas started deteriorating, efforts such as citizens' charters, Report Cards on Public Utilities, and right to information became important. Similarly, citizens' groups in Bangalore such as Public Affairs Survey and Swabhimaan collected a set of crucial data from candidates contesting elections and then disseminated the data to help voters make a better choice. Their survey of the industrial environment in Karnataka State has also spurred reforms in the Karnataka industries (Simplification of Procedures and Documentation Act/Rule 2001).

LOCAL GOVERNANCE AND EPISTEMIC BONDS

The last part of this paper brings out a model of governance based upon quantum physics that explains why local governance weakens when exogenous trends start dominating the processes of globalization and transnational investments. This model also explains that the weakening of local governance is the main impetus behind the rise of electoral fallacies in modern democracies. Quantum mechanics offers a method to understand the structures of society and about the ecological bonds that may be referred to as epistemic bonds [EB], which bring people together and sustain them in a common mode of beliefs, values, and culture, or more appropriately, in an ecosystem. Thus, EB is a "strong attractive force" composed of a set of relationships between the resources and the resource-dependent community. These bonds also provide stability and security of habitation and of the availability of needed resources from the ecosystem. All this is assured due to internal governance systems nurtured and sustained over a long period of history within the framework of ecological relationships, which an exogenous mode of development fails to visualize. The two figures given below explain the pressures of production strategies that do not adapt themselves to the community's carrying capacities within the local constraints of resources. The result is the reduced and shrinking community spaces leading toward retrogressive development or an unsustainable development. As this trend continues, the cost of governance increases and visible negative effects of growth such as inequities, lawlessness, violence, spread of diseases, and loss of environmental resources block the achievement of good governance within any society.

5

Leadership and Change Management: A Comparative Analysis

The subject of leadership, especially leadership in government, is not fully understood, despite the fact that it is often mentioned as a critical element that accounts for government's success or failure. Consultants abound; popular how-to-do-it management books, available around the world, especially in airport bookstores for the time-pressured senior manager, often provide checklists and simplistic advice about becoming an effective leader. Serious reflection about leadership and its relationship to performance is less common. Almost all commentators on the subject of leadership mention that effective leaders have a *vision* and share that vision with members of the organization. A vision is not something precise. Rather, it provides the person who assumes a top-level position with the opportunity to share his or her ideas about what the organization should become, what it should do, how it should perform, and, perhaps most important, what the role and responsibilities of members of the organization should be. A vision is abstract; it is broader than goals and it is more expansive than a mission statement.

Leaders are effective when they inspire others. This is an important theme of E. H. Valsan's article, "Leadership in Public Administration for Alleviating Poverty and Development: A Conceptual Approach." As he points out, many models of administration have ignored what he calls "inspiration" as a core element of effective leadership; he uses the example of Mother Teresa and her work with the poor in Calcutta to illustrate his point. Valsan steps away from the formal attributes of leaders—especially their organizational roles—to develop the psychological underpinnings of effective leadership. By extension, one can employ his concepts to investigate how leaders try to create positive change.

Leadership is no longer only about "great men." Rather, contemporary portraits show that leadership applies equally to women—and not only great women like Mother Teresa. On the contrary, gender is a central part of development and leadership can make some gender-based programs successful. This theme is present in Sheila Rai's article, "Gender-Responsive Governance in India: the Experience of Rajasthan." Her conclusion, however, is sobering, since she points out that a large gap yawns between the rhetoric of gender and the realities of effective gender initiatives, at least as illustrated by her case study of Rajasthan.

A similar theme is found in Ahmad Martadha Mohamed's "Administrative Discretion and Representative Bureaucracy: Linking Descriptive Representation to Substantive Representation." Drawing largely on the Western academic literature of representative bureaucracy, Mohamed shows that in his sample of Malaysian public administrators, women and minorities will act to pursue policy issues relevant to these groups when they internalize these characteristics. The implication of both articles is that policies aimed at advancing the interests of women and minorities require leaders who both share these interests and pursue them via effective leadership. Formal representation through affirmative action programs, by themselves, will not automatically lead to substantive change.

As the well-known management theorist John P. Kotter points out in his book, *Leading Change* (Boston, MA: Harvard Business School Press, 1996), leadership and management are not identical, and this can be seen, especially, by observing that well-managed organizations are not necessarily high-performance organizations. The reason lies in the differences between management and leadership. Management and leadership are often used interchangeably, but there are important differences between them. High-performance organizations have both strong management systems and effective leadership. We all know what the essential management functions are. They include

- planning and budgeting,
- organization and staffing, and
- controlling and problem-solving.

These are the traditional and essential functions found in all large organizations. These functions provide the foundation of higher education university degrees in business and public administration as well as short-term training programs. We constantly try to improve human resources methods and financial practices in organizations. High-performance organizations certainly need effective management processes to produce positive results— *but they are not sufficient to guarantee long-term success*. Tatsuo Oyama's article, "Educating and Training Japanese Government Officials: Current Trends and Policy Study Aspects," surveys the education and in-service training of Japanese civil servants. His conclusions are telling and they point out the knowledge gaps of current civil servants. But, in reading between the lines, one can find a substantial shortcoming in the lack of attention to leadership qualities, clearly missing from the formal and informal curriculum. Here is a short list of those qualities:

- *Establish Direction*: This refers to the importance of vision—providing members of the organization with a sense of what the organization is, and what it might be. Vision creates the setting for the members of the organization to see how their performance fits into the "big picture."
- *Align people by creating an environment of cooperation in the organization.* It is often said that much of what is done in organizations is done in groups. Leadership includes the facilitation of teamwork by creating the appropriate atmosphere.
- *Motivate and Inspire Members of the Organization.* All of the public officials I referred to above viewed it as their task to nurture employees so that they will perform up to their potential.

While effective managers produce stability in organizations and are therefore important for the survival and maintenance of organizations, leaders who have the qualities listed above are capable of producing positive changes. These changes may be new services, improved services, and, more broadly, even new missions.

High-performance organizations need both effective managers and effective leaders. Kotter's book helps us think about the relationship between both management and leadership in an organization embarking on substantial change. If both leadership and management are nonexistent, efforts to change will go nowhere. When leadership is strong but not backed up by effective management structures, efforts to undergo significant change may show some initial progress, but will soon be stymied by the lack of core management functions that must support the change. When management is strong but leadership is lacking, short-term positive results are likely to occur, but significant organizational change will not take place. When management and leadership are both strong, the organization is likely to be successful in undergoing large-scale change. The last combination is not only desirable but also achievable. It is the task of public administration educators to make this point to the next generation of public servants.

LEADERSHIP IN PUBLIC ADMINISTRATION

The importance of public administration for poverty alleviation and development was recognized in the NAPSIPAG region more than 50 years ago, when colleges and institutes of public administration were started and later, when the Eastern Regional Organization for Public Administration organized annual conferences and seminars where major issues of poverty and development were discussed. Several academic experts from the West, especially from the United States, came to the region with technical assistance programs and made recommendations for the reorganization of governmental machinery. Paul Appleby's report on public administration in India was accepted by the then Government of India with acclaim in 1953 and it led to the inauguration of the Indian Institute of Public Administration by Prime Minister Nehru, who continued to be its President till his death in 1964.

Postgraduate studies in public administration that started in university departments and colleges in India, South Korea, the Philippines, and Thailand were largely influenced by the "theories" of public administration taught in American universities. This was because it was in the United States that the subject was developed as an academic discipline, though often in departments of political science. Conceptually, much was borrowed from terminologies developed in the armed forces and applied to business management situations in the West. Asian scholars who wrote textbooks on public administration were largely influenced by these concepts and terminologies in describing their own systems of administration.

A mainly descriptive structural approach was followed, with very little consideration for behavioral aspects of relevance to their own societies. Subjects like leadership were neglected in their curricula until recently. Perhaps this was due to the prevailing notion that it was a subject to be dealt with in political science; the closest discussion of the subject came under the rubric of "POSDCORB," described as the "Functions of the Executive" by Gulick and Urwick. As is well known, the acronym stood for Planning, Organizing, Staffing, Directing, Coordinating, Reporting and Budgeting. These functions implied scope for leadership, yet critics found the model mechanical and without concern for the ground realities of situations under which bureaucracies operated.

The exposure to administrative situations in Asian countries helped American scholars like Fred Riggs, Ferrel Heady and William Siffin realize the need to understand the history and background of administrative systems in Thailand, the Philippines and other countries, before ideas and institutions developed in the United States were applied. Fred Riggs in particular emphasized through his lectures on the ecology of public administration the need to describe administrative ecology before considering prescriptions for reform. His Prismatic Model further attempted to provide hypothetical characteristics of administrative environment in developing societies. Influenced by such innovations in the thinking and study of public administration, many Asian scholars like Hahn-Been Lee and Jose Abueva came out with analytical propositions based on field research in their respective countries. Research done by this author in India and the Philippines (Valsan 1970) helped in developing a conceptual framework applicable to development administration beyond the POSDCORB criteria, which are universally relevant.

Later experience and observations in Bangladesh, Egypt, and Sri Lanka all the more convinced the author that development administrators, while discharging the functions of POSDCORB, needed to be aware of the importance of the "Five 'I's"— Information, Inspiration, Innovation, Introjection, and Integration. Development administrators found an awareness of these dynamic elements valuable in helping them perform well in the leadership roles often required for development administration. For the sake of clarity and for emphasizing their contemporary relevance, an elaboration of each concept is attempted below:

INFORMATION

Unlike the 1960s, when this conceptual formulation was identified, the importance of information for leadership in public administration is easier to understand today. The information revolution that the world has witnessed during the last few decades has made data and ideas from anywhere in the world available to the leadership. It has also helped make field research and feedback information essential for decision making by administrators. It has helped attempts to replicate successful projects in countries far away with locally relevant modifications. A famous example is the Grameen Bank concept originated in Bangladesh under the dynamic leadership of Muhammad Yunus, which has spread all over the developing world, helping rural women through microcredit projects.

Information technology (IT) initiatives in E-government have spread out to several countries with varying degrees of success, but definitely influencing the thinking and functioning of leaders and administrators. The availability of information windows at the village level has expedited the process of applying for benefits and services available to common citizens, and for their speedy delivery. Under the POSDCORB formulation, information as a function was included under reporting, which was more in an upward direction in a hierarchical organization. Reporting back to the people or subordinates was unknown in such a dispensation. Today, information as a dynamic element in development administration can be accessed and passed on from any direction and utilized for accomplishing the goals of the organization. Awareness of its importance and familiarity, if not mastery of its computer utilization, has become an essential qualification for dynamic leadership.

For developing democracies of the Asia–Pacific region, political parties and representatives find IT useful to collect and analyze information and to project popular demands more meaningfully in parliaments and public forums, thus influencing policy formulation. For instance, in Kerala, India, the Marxist Communist Party, which had in the early days opposed the introduction of computers on grounds of its leading to massive unemployment, is reported to have equipped its own offices with modern computers. Rajiv Gandhi was a modernizer in this respect, inviting technically competent Indians from abroad to introduce a revolution in the field of telecommunications using IT. In short, awareness of the importance of information with all its technological implications is a must for development leadership. It is equally important for coordinating all activities concerned with the plight of the poor, thus avoiding the duplication of efforts and funding that often occurs because of development partner contributions or scarce budgetary allocations of governments.

INSPIRATION

Mechanical models of administration and theoretical analyses of leadership have neglected the importance of inspiration, whereas it can be one of the mobilizing forces for development administration and poverty alleviation activities. Inspiration here is being looked at both as an individual experience and as a collective requirement for successful administration, contributing to development as well as in tackling the problems of acute poverty. This writer was impressed by its role in community development programs of the 1950s and 1960s in Bangladesh, India, and the Philippines. Leaders like S. K. Dey, who was the first community development minister in India; Akhtar Hameed Khan, who resigned from the prestigious Indian Civil Service and followed Gandhian idealism in launching a community development program in Comilla in East Pakistan (now Bangladesh); and Ramon Magsaysay, who established the Presidential Assistant for Community Development in the Philippines, were all inspired by the desire to serve their respective communities or nations by tackling the problems of the rural masses. They in turn were able to inspire hundreds of their countrymen to join these movements, imbibing the spirit of public service.

One example is that of Muhammad Yunus, who started the Grameen banks. As a student at the Comilla Academy, he was inspired by the leadership of Akhtar Hameed Khan. Similarly, Jimmy Yen, who launched the Philippine Rural Reconstruction Movement (PRRM) in order to uplift the living conditions of the rural population, was able to inspire people like Dr. Juan Flavier, who later took over the mantle of PRRM. Hence, the relevance of the "chain of inspiration" concept for development, which is to be seen as a parallel with the "chain of command" concept in the mechanical model of management. That inspiration is equally important in the alleviation of poverty is clearly demonstrated in the life and contributions of Mother Teresa. Apart from her claim of divine inspiration, which is not part of our analysis, it was a fact that the poverty and misery of the sick and the dying inspired her to take care of those mortals. In turn, she was able to inspire a large number of young Sisters of Charity, who continue to serve the poor in several countries, even since her passing from the scene. The fact that they survive based on donations by private individuals belonging to all religions and institutions who are inspired by the message of the Mother and the service of her followers is equally important for the purpose of this analysis.

Looking at more productive projects for reducing poverty using the potentials of the healthy among the poor, one finds the livelihood programs of PRRM and the Kudumbasree projects of Kerala, meant for augmenting the income of women in need of support, succeeding wherever political, social, or bureaucratic leadership is inspiring. Here, it is important to emphasize that bureaucratic leadership is possible wherever there is ideal political leadership. Good examples of commitment set by political leaders or ministers can inspire civil servants and civil society volunteers to contribute to the success of development programs. Conversely, corrupt, greedy, and incompetent political bosses can kill the enthusiasm of even the most honest and competent subordinates. In short, it is only the inspired who can inspire.

The above discussion naturally leads to the question of the *sources of inspiration*. In the original work mentioned earlier, this writer attempted to compare the concept of charisma with that of inspiration and, among other points of comparison, mentioned that whereas charisma is supposed to have only one supernatural source, inspiration can have a multiplicity of sources. For instance, even when one's boss is corrupt and uninspiring, the goals of the organization and the needs of the poor or the clientele, as well as the dedication of one's own subordinates, can sometimes sustain one's inspiration to serve. Charisma as a concept can be even antidevelopment, or go against the interest of poverty alleviation programs. For instance, those who attribute charisma to Mother Teresa sometimes withdraw from the movement, saying that the Mother was charismatic, which they are not, and they cannot be expected to serve the way she did. The same is applicable to the discussion of Gandhi, who was also considered charismatic and thus even worshipped, but seldom followed by his so-called followers. On the contrary, if they can draw inspiration from the causes for which Mother Teresa or Mahatma Gandhi worked, more success will be achieved in attaining the goals they shared with their leaders. A rational understanding of the concept of inspiration and attempts to instill it in organizations and administrative systems can lead to attaining organizational goals for human development. A caveat must be added, however, that our analysis excludes the role of what may be called negative inspiration for destructive activities commonly reported in the media in the new millennium.

INNOVATION

Another dynamic element in this conceptual model is innovation. Bureaucracy in general and public administration in particular are well known for routine and blind following of established practices. Awareness of the need for innovative thinking on the part of administrators was considered essential in order to achieve the development goals that could not wait for slow and incremental methods at the expense of suffering masses. Especially in the case of programs for alleviating poverty, bureaucratic excuses and corrupt practices have to be met with innovative initiatives. IT, as mentioned earlier, has opened avenues for more innovative approaches to decision making and service delivery. Also, as indicated earlier, information about other successful programs can be utilized for introducing innovative activities in a new setting. India's green revolution introduced many innovations in agriculture, leading to higher productivity, but the distribution system did not match the success of the scientists and the farmers, with the result that poverty and malnutrition continue to haunt rural areas in some states. Political leadership in such situations also did not come up with innovative solutions for bureaucracies to implement.

In tackling abject poverty and facing natural calamities like floods, drought, cyclones, and earthquakes, bureaucracies and social and political workers are challenged to introduce quick and effective innovations and makeshift arrangements. An awareness of the importance of innovation in such critical situations is important in the training of civil servants for administrative leadership.

Innovative approaches in communicating with the masses are important for implementing sensitive activities like family planning. The successful utilization of local political leadership for canvassing and mobilizing the masses for attending male sterilization camps in Kerala, India, in the 1970s introduced many innovative incentives to the participants and their families (Valsan 1977). Literacy campaigns also try out incentives and innovative methods of teaching in order to attract women and elderly illiterates.

INTROJECTION

During the last 3 decades, public administration and management sciences have seen major innovations and terminologies like Total Quality Management, New Public Management, and Human Resources Development. The concept of introjection suggested by Fred W. Riggs is important in the context of trying to introduce innovations successfully implemented in the West to Asian, Pacific, African, and Latin American countries. Borrowing from psychology, which calls for the selective internalization of values, Riggs implies here accepting reforms or innovations that can work in a society, and rejecting those that are not suitable or may even cause disturbance to the polity.

The concept can be applied even while trying to imitate in one part of a country a policy or practice that has proved successful in another part. A typical example was the attempt to introduce male sterilization in North India, copying successful innovative methods adopted in Kerala mentioned earlier. Kerala being a highly literate state, it was possible to mobilize the masses for the family planning program. In Uttar Pradesh, with poor literacy rates, on the other hand, the bureaucrats and politicians who wanted similar results even used force, thereby causing political damage to the ruling Congress Party in the election that followed and making family planning an untouchable subject even for the federal Government, thereby causing the increase of the national population beyond a billion.

Had they been aware of the importance of introjection, such a situation could have been avoided. The failure of many programs for poverty alleviation is also traceable to the inability of bureaucrats and social workers to take into account the sociocultural background of the population and the special conditions of poverty prevailing in each society. In short, awareness of the concept of introjection is important for leaders trying to introduce reforms simply because of their success elsewhere.

INTEGRATION

Closely related to the concept of introjection is integration, which is most important for the stability of any society. As modernization is supposed to be accompanied by differentiation of functions, developing countries in their urge for development through modernization imitate developed countries in introducing institutions and structures that are expected to function in the same way as in the West. However, the proliferation of institutions and agencies without sufficient coordination leads to chaotic situations, causing administrative breakdown or political instability. In this connection, it is worth remembering the Riggsian addition to his revision of the prismatic model, in which he emphasized the role of integration for diffracted societies. Prismatic conditions prevail where no integration of differentiated functions occurs.

Awareness of the importance of introjection helps in understanding the need for integrating the departments and institutions created. Reforms that are likely to tear the society apart due to lack of information should be kept in abeyance until objections to their implementation are explained and public acceptance obtained. In short, by taking into account ecological factors affecting development in a society, leaders can introduce reforms without disturbing the integration and the integrity of the society concerned.

The dynamic model of development administration suggested by the above analysis does not ignore the role of POSDCORB executive functions, but urges the awareness of the importance of the "Five I's"—Information, Inspiration, Innovation, Introjection, and Integration—for performing a leadership role in the society. Extensive discussions on the model were held during graduate seminars with participants from different countries, many of whom supported its validity as a supplement to POSDCORB. However, in the context of poverty and problems faced by the weaker sections of society, leaders involved in alleviating misery, pain, and humiliation of those sections of the population, to be effective, need to call on some special attributes that they may have or that can be consciously cultivated. These, I suggest, are Empathy, Enthusiasm, Efficiency, Entrepreneurship, and Ethics.

EMPATHY

Here again, Mother Teresa's example is unique. Inspiration for undertaking the task of picking up the old, sick, and needy from the streets of Calcutta and treating, feeding, and housing them could have been effective only because of her capacity to empathize with their lot. It is one thing to feel sympathy and to donate some amount, food, or clothes as many of us do, but another experience to put oneself in their situation and to cater to their felt needs. Empathy is equally important for those involved in crisis management situations tackling natural calamities. Other instances of exemplary capacity for empathy can be cited, but other attributes of equal importance need our attention.

ENTHUSIASM

Any movement involving mobilization of people needs leaders who are not only inspired by its goals, but are enthusiastic about achieving them. Their commitment, the way they articulate goals, methods, and details, and their electrifying influence over their followers reflect that enthusiasm. It is an attribute that is important for fund-raising for noble causes. Juan Flavier of PRRM, who later became a cabinet secretary in the Philippines and is now a Senator, is an example that comes to one's mind. Watching him in the early years of PRRM, making inspirational talks full of ideas, wit, and humour to enthuse the volunteers going to the barrios, was a pleasure.

EFFICIENCY

Lest it be felt that all our talk of inspiration, empathy, and enthusiasm in leadership is devoid of concern for practical aspects of running organizations, it is important to emphasize the attribute of efficiency, without which no leadership in public service or administration is possible. Akhtar Hameed Khan, who was trained in the erstwhile Indian Civil Service, was conscious of this at Comilla. He attached considerable importance to bookkeeping and training volunteers in financial management. Especially for organizations depending upon donations or government subsidies, accountability depends upon the efficiency of the leadership. Many organizations begun with good intentions for public service did not survive beyond the lifetime of their founders, because no mechanism was built in for continuation of an efficient system of management. Punctuality, dependability, and fairness in the treatment of clientele, colleagues, and subordinates constitute this important attribute essential for public service. Unfortunately, very often institutions for charitable purposes run by governments lack efficient leadership.

ENTREPRENEURSHIP

Normally considered a business management concept, entrepreneurship as an attribute for leadership in public administration and poverty alleviation activities is increasingly becoming important due to the challenges faced by modern organizations. Closely related to the concept of innovation suggested earlier, success in achieving organizational goals, especially in commercial organizations run by governments, largely depends upon this attribute. An example from India would be the Managing Director of Kochi International Airport Authority, V. J. Kurian, who is a member of the Indian Administrative Service. Though building the airport was a political decision, the financing of it through public contributions and donations, which were later converted into shares in the commercially constituted airport company, were all achieved to a large measure due to the entrepreneurship of this government officer. The story of the successful operation and continuing development of this airport is itself worth a case study in leadership. Mother Teresa, in addition to all her inspiring qualities, was also considered during her lifetime as an entrepreneur who was able to start branches of her Missionaries of Charity in several countries. The Grameen Bank concept in Bangladesh is another example of encouraging the spirit of entrepreneurship among rural women by providing microcredit for starting small commercial activities.

ETHICS

When all the qualities and attributes of leadership for public administration are discussed, one cannot ignore the importance of ethics. A universal outcry against corruption in government organizations has occurred during the last decade. This implies unethical practices and deals between individuals serving in public and private enterprises at the expense of the taxpayers of the countries concerned. Even charitable activities and relief operations are not immune to allegations of corruption. Private greed getting accommodated in public organizations is despised, but such practices seem to continue to multiply. This is a challenge to the leadership of all countries and from it arises the need to identify honest men and women in administration and to assign them to leadership positions, giving necessary training in other attributes required in performing leadership tasks. Negative reporting in the media and casual description of all bureaucrats and politicians as corrupt does not solve the problem. A positive approach to cultivating ethical attributes among civil servants and politicians and giving prominent recognition to men and women of integrity can go a long way in generating leadership in public organizations.

A natural question that may be raised while discussing the attributes of leadership mentioned above is that of the cultivability of these qualities among political and bureaucratic personnel. A general answer will be that it is possible, not only through training programs designed for human development, but through exemplary leadership of eminent individuals who should be assigned the task of mentoring their colleagues and subordinates. Watching the efficiency, enthusiasm, entrepreneurship, capacity for empathy, and ethical attributes of a leader can inspire those around him or her to perform better and to prepare themselves to wear the mantle. Delegation of responsibilities is important under such a dispensation, so that the leaders can make sure about the capabilities of their colleagues and subordinates who are one day going to be in charge. Concentration of all authority in one person's hands can be detrimental to the creation of leadership capabilities in organizations.

ECONOMIC AND FINANCIAL MANAGEMENT: A WORKSHOP

Economic and financial management presents the most complex issues to the nation states of the 21st century. The economic issues concern national income, growth, productivity, and equitable distribution of wealth. The financial issues deal with revenues, expenditure, management of budgetary deficits, and management of public enterprises. The central economic and financial management issue besetting the nation states is poverty eradication. Gunnar Myrdal in *Asian Drama* has said that poverty anywhere is considered a threat to prosperity everywhere. A large chunk of the world population suffers from acute poverty, which deprives them of two square meals every day, primary education, child protection, maternal health, and old-age security. A majority of the world population is considered poor from the point of view of consumption intake of a given minimum of cereals. The question of food security has been engaging the minds of policy makers for very long. Many see rural poverty as the crux of issue. It is true that a considerable part of the global population lives in villages, but urbanization has added a new dimension to the problem of poverty, as noted by Gugler in a paper entitled "Overurbanization Reconsidered" (1988). In many countries, the percentage of the urban population living below the poverty line is higher than that of the population in rural areas. Poverty and environmental degradation have been found to be closely associated, as discussed by de Steiguer (1995) in "Three Theories from Economics about the Environment." Poverty and increases in population have also been found to go hand in hand, as revealed by Meadows (1997) in "The Key to Population Is Poverty."

Poverty is a hydra-headed problem. New dimensions of the problem are emerging at a rapid pace. In terms of gender, poverty among women has overtaken poverty among men. A study by the African Development Bank (2004) entitled "Gender Poverty and Environmental Indicators on African Countries" reveals the frightening magnitude of gender poverty, which results in tremendous suffering. Occupational poverty is repeatedly referred to. The agricultural laborer is considered to be poorer than the industrial labourer. Poverty is also associated with lack of education, employment, and social standing. A. K. Sen (1994), in his paper entitled "Population: Delusion and Reality," explains at length the coexistence of poverty with undernourishment, child labour, and lack of education and basic health care facilities.

Poverty is reckoned as the biggest menace of the 21st century. A number of tools have been employed to counter this menace. The United Nations has declared 2005 as the year of microfinance, and microfinance programs are intended to reach the poorest of the poor. The United Nations earlier endorsed the Millennium Development Goals, the most prominent of which is the halving of the numbers of the extreme poor. The sociologists have been advocating promotion of multiethnic and multicultural societies. The new economic world order is being discussed to bridge the disparity between the North and South.

However, we have to agree that no "silver bullet" is available to solve the problem of poverty. Any solution has to be people-centred. The magnitude of the problem of poverty varies from country to country. The evolution of country-specific poverty definitions, institutions, and monitoring systems is needed to promote capacity building among the poor and empower them to find lasting solutions to the problem of poverty. The lack of effective delivery mechanisms has impeded the success of poverty eradication programs. Nongovernment organizations, grassroots institutions, and national and international organizations are being involved to design and implement suitable programs to make program delivery more effective. Some countries have strengthened the rule of law and enacted and vigorously implemented laws to protect the poor. The poverty-affected countries are also trying to learn from each other's experience, which has helped them in introducing best practices. Promotion of self-employment and the culture of entrepreneurship has been adjudged by many countries a powerful tool to eradicate poverty. The approach of the People's Republic of China of "blocking and pushing" is being followed by many other countries to prevent any further rise in the population affected by poverty.

The problem of poverty has to be tackled as an utmost priority and as "now or never." Undoubtedly, it is the biggest challenge for public administration advocating good governance.

6

Poverty Alleviation through Effective Public Service Delivery

INTRODUCTION

The panelists of this group explored the poverty alleviation avenues available through e-government, bureaucratic reforms, the welfare state, public programs, and other means of effective public service delivery. While the panelists cover a wide range of topics, the focus here is the four papers included in the symposium.

E-GOVERNMENT

In their paper, R. F. I. Smith and Julian Teicher observe three ways that e-government can help governance and public service:

- e-government can help improve governance and service delivery by refocusing consideration of the purposes and tools of government;
- e-government initiatives pose challenging questions of management, especially about coordination in government and the design of services for citizens; and
- progress toward implementing e-government raises critical questions about preferred styles of governance and about how governments relate to citizens.

The authors conclude that interactions between citizens, the institutions of government, and information and communications technology raise more agendas than governments can handle. Nevertheless, e-government helps improve governance and services by asking questions. Another point is that e-governance can accelerate economic development and the empowerment of individual citizens, as well as bringing about good governance and development to overcome the problem of poverty alleviation. E-initiatives will promote new agendas of relationship management and institution construction, playing an increasingly critical role in reconnecting citizens and governments.

BUREAUCRATIC REFORM

In his paper "Improving Public Service Delivery Through Bureaucracy Reform," Dr. Awang Anwaruddin examines the current status of the bureaucracy in Indonesia and proposes some recommendations for improvement.

The author identifies three kinds of problems with Indonesia's bureaucracy. First, Transparency International reports indicate that Indonesia is among the most corrupt countries in the world in recent years and the *World Competitiveness Yearbook 2003* demonstrates that the performance of bureaucracy in Indonesia is ranked the world's worst along with those of Viet Nam and India.

Second, there are problems with the overlapping structure of bureaucracy, vague divisions between government functions and citizen obligations, and unclear political process of policy formation. In both central and local government, the bureaucracy is now getting bigger and more swollen. Therefore, the bureaucracy becomes inflexible and slow in responding to emerging problems.

Third, there are problems with human resources quality. About 60% of public employees are educated at high-school level, while only 15.6% graduates are university graduates. The remuneration is not based on merit that considers the work performance. Thus, there is no correlation between salary and productivity.

In countries like Indonesia, the main problem is low public service performance and excessive service cost. Therefore a positive prescription is a comprehensive approach of bureaucratic reform, including the bureaucratic institution, management, human resources, and service culture. Other efforts may include i) establishing an interagency committee, ii) assistance from academic institutions/NGOs, iii) collaboration between government and academic institutions, iv) program evaluation, v) absorption of funding from ADB and other foundations, and f) encouraging comprehensive participation.

Anwarudin's detailed approach to reform efforts is offered through preliminary, implementation, and evaluation stages.

WELFARE STATE

In his paper, Dr. Djonet Santoso examines the role of the Social Safety Net (SSN) program in Indonesia in poverty reduction. It is a general understanding that government should work to boost economic growth, reduce poverty, and develop the human resources through expanding public health spending and schooling. In this regard, the Indonesian Government created the SSN program in 1998. Though the effectiveness of the program varies across regions, the study reveals that on many occasions the program has missed the target groups. The SSN program has four subprograms: food security, employment creation, education, and health care. To further improve the effectiveness of the SSN program, the author recommends that the Government implement several strategies: consult with nongovernment organizations; take new approaches; improve the transparency of information dissemination to the public; bring about effective and efficient public consultation; monitor the progress of programs or projects; encourage citizen participation; and look for accurate demographic data.

PUBLIC PROGRAMS

In their paper "Rural Poverty Alleviation In India: An Assessment of Public Programs," B. S. Ghuman and Gurpinder Chima use secondary data and identify the impact of public programs on rural poverty alleviation as well as highlighting the collective role of both policy and nonpolicy variables in rural poverty alleviation.

The authors use regression analysis to find out that four variables—per capita (rural poor) expenditure on wage employment generation and selfemployment programs for the rural poor, per capita monthly supply of rice and wheat by the Public Distribution System (PDS) for below-poverty-line rural people, per capita funds advanced by regional rural banks for the rural poor, and rural nonfarm employment—help in reducing the percentage of India's rural poor.

Thus, from the public policy perspective, the authors recommend allocation of more public funds for wage employment and self-employment programs, and for the PDS. Moreover, the number of rural regional banks should also be increased, which would be effective in reducing the number of rural poor.

Our panelists cover a number of issues that manifest the value orientation of conventional public administration, such as efficiency, effectiveness, social equity, democratic participation, and public accountability. While traditional values are emphasized, the more contemporary ideas of New Public Administration are also highlighted, such as entrepreneurship, market orientation, and result and outcome orientation.

Poverty is a historical phenomenon; only if economic development reaches an advanced level can poverty ultimately be eliminated. Nevertheless, even in rich countries like the USA, fighting poverty is still a significant issue. Therefore, public administration shoulders the responsibility of redistributing social wealth through a number of means, such as tax policy, diverse welfare programs, and other regulatory policies. Public administration has a large role to play in facilitating economic growth as well as ensuring social equity. Although our panelists and other participants have greatly contributed to our understanding of the state of the arts of poverty alleviation in so many countries and areas of Asia-Pacific region, they do not exhaust the issue.

New problems and questions will surely emerge from time to time. In this regard, we look forward to the next NAPSIPAG conference for the new means and new ideas about governance from and for Asia-Pacific areas.

IMPROVING GOVERNANCE AND SERVICES

Since the late 1990s, the prospect of using information and communication technologies (ICTs) to improve effectiveness, fairness, and accountability in government has attracted widespread enthusiasm. However, early hopes that e-initiatives would bypass intractable questions of government organization and transform citizen experience of the delivery of public services have given way to more modest claims.

At the same time, thinking about how to use ICTs most effectively in government has generated widening questions about what governments should try to do and how they should do it. As Fountain (2001) has argued, einitiatives reconfigure bureaucracy and disturb settled understandings about politics and the nature of the state.

ICTs open up diverse patterns of personal and group interaction. But managing ICT infrastructure and applications to provide better government demands coordination. Within government, e-government initiatives pose sharp questions about the roles and capabilities of the executive. They challenge the executive to organize itself for integrated policy making and management, respond to what citizens actually need, and manage multilayered and reciprocal interactions between government organizations and technology.

These challenges are linked, but linking them in a "whole-government" agenda creates large tests of executive capability.

A recent study by the Organisation for Economic Cooperation and Development (OECD) sets out key dimensions of the challenge in these terms: "Key questions include: How to collaborate more effectively across agencies to address complex, shared problems; how to enhance customer focus; and how to build relationships with private sector partners" (OECD 2003: Such questions lead directly to a familiar dilemma "How to capture the benefits of coordinated action and shared approaches while maintaining individual agency responsibility and accountability for operations and results" (OECD 2003: 15).

Many governments have gone to great lengths to craft pluralist or decentralized strategies for improvement. In such models, connections between diverse initiatives depend on consultation and negotiation. Many large and complex businesses have followed similar paths.

However, the opportunity costs of e-initiatives are high. Such initiatives need to provide value. For governments, e-initiatives need to provide policy, management, and service outcomes that citizens value. The concept of public value provides a useful framework for making such assessments (Moore 1995; Kelly and Muers 2002; Stoker 2003; UN 2003; Smith 2004). For businesses, e-initiatives need to grow the business, build shareholder value, or maximize dividends. This has led to steadily more assertive rethinking of the role of coordinating and framework-setting bodies for the use of ICT in both business and government.

Themes of decentralization, devolution, and differentiation associated with New Public Management, neoliberal, or Washington Consensus agendas, which had a pervasive influence in the 1990s, are critically reconsidered. The OECD e-government project team (OECD 2003: 99) sets out a long list of benefits of central coordination. For the private sector, Nicholas Carr argues controversially that similar considerations apply: Hierarchies... may outperform markets when it comes to integrating complex information systems, leading to a re-emergence of the vertically integrated company (Carr 2004: 12).

In a major study of information technology (IT) governance, Peter Weill and Jeanne Ross (2004) go further; they concentrate on the private sector but include significant public sector cases. They set out a concept of IT governance in which decision rights about IT are carefully allocated to ensure that business strategies drive IT investments. They propose that as dependence on IT spreads throughout organizations, IT governance increases in importance. In words that mirror the phrasing of the OECD team, Weill and Ross argue that the task of good governance is to handle effectively a longtime management paradox—encouraging and leveraging the ingenuity of all the enterprise's people while ensuring compliance with the overall vision and principles (Weill and Ross 2004: 236).

Governments introducing e-initiatives thus face contradictory pressures. Making e-government initiatives work demands significant resources. E-initiatives are hungry for political, organizational, human, and financial capital. Investments and potential gains are large. But to date, actual gains, however measured, are modest. Further, the price of even modest gains is to open up controversial agendas of governance. Central coordination is back. And it is joined by demands for more responsive and participative government. The propositions outlined above provide a framework for exploring these issues. Examples will be drawn from international surveys of e-government (OECD 2003; UN 2003; Yong 2003) and from the state of Victoria and the federal government in Australia. This paper argues that

- e-government can help improve governance and service delivery by refocusing consideration of the purposes and tools of government;
- e-government initiatives pose challenging questions of management, especially about coordination in government and the design of services for citizens; and
- progress toward implementing e-government raises critical questions about preferred styles of governance and about how governments relate to citizens.

REFOCUSING THE PURPOSES AND TOOLS OF GOVERNMENT

E-government initiatives focus attention on the long-term impacts of the interaction of technology and organizations. E-government is not just about using ICTs throughout the institutions and operations of government. It is also about how organizations in government perceive and apply technology. The reciprocal relations between technology and organizations drive longterm change (Fountain 2001, Bellamy 2002). Ambitions for e-initiatives in government are large. A recent UN survey argued that E-government is about opportunity. Opportunity for the public sector to reform to achieve greater efficiency and efficacy. Opportunity to reduce costs and increase services to the society. Opportunity to include all in public service delivery. And opportunity to empower the citizens for participatory democracy. But the greatest promise of e-government is the historic opportunity for the developing countries to "leap frog" the traditionally longer development stages and catch up in providing a higher standard of living for their populations (UN 2003: 182).

Similarly, in Australia the state government of Victoria stresses the need for positive social impacts. Recently, it reframed its e-government strategy around people-centred government. Its aim is [t]hat Victorians [be] assisted to meet their everyday needs through timely, convenient and relevant support from government, made possible by harnessing the capabilities of information networks and communications technologies as they evolve (Government of Victoria 2002:1). Further, E-government should be about people, not technology... Putting People at the Centre... is our vision for creating a new era of richer interaction between the government and citizens (Government of Victoria 2002: 2). E-government is thus about the potential for a transformation of government and governance. Many early discussions of e-government outlined stages in the development of e-government in which the final stage was "transformation," "integration," "seamless service delivery," or some similarly ambitious state. However, the path to transformation is tricky.

Early, discrete, and bottom-up e-government initiatives tended to meet barriers. Such barriers included costs of ICT infrastructure, lack of interoperability, and problems of coordination. It proved easier to initiate specific projects than to bring together integrated packages. It also proved easier to use the Internet to provide information than to facilitate transactions.

Thinking about the path to transformation raises large questions. Three deserve particular attention. First, is how is change in the application of technology is to be managed?. Whether the focus is on determining requirements for IT infrastructure, finding funds to invest and accounting for those invested, outsourcing responsibility for technology supply, redesigning office procedures, or redefining requirements for skills and knowledge possessed by public employees, governments are expected to assume substantial responsibilities for the management of change.

In a study that combines technical and organizational perspectives, Lionel Pearce uses the evolution of selected stages models to set out the extent of the change agenda. He argues that the specialists in information systems management who originated stages models found themselves drawn progressively more deeply into issues of organization and management. He advocates an organization development model in which each step forward is checked against progress in four dimensions: financial, business process improvement, organizational learning, and customer satisfaction (Pearce 2004:147).

The second question is how to determine the focus of desired transformations. Much discussion focuses on citizens as customers. Government is treated as a retail business and initiatives focus on individual transactions, for example, paying taxes, receiving benefits, renewing licenses, or finding information. E-government in Singapore is notable for the number of transactions now available electronically. Victoria Online provides users with access to Victorian agencies through a single entry point. It also provides access to federal and local levels of government. At the federal level australia.gov.au provides access to a series of portals with entry points to federal government services and to state governments.

However, citizens expect more from governments than to be treated as customers (Mintzberg 1994). Pressures emerge for holistic initiatives that benefit citizens as a group. Such initiatives may include institution building, policy development, or the management of information on which both the internal operations of government and the delivery of services depend. The statements quoted above from the UN and the government of Victoria make this explicit. However, progress on such initiatives is at a very early stage. The third question is how to measure progress and learn lessons. Initiatives need to provide value to citizens and to be integrated. The country recognized consistently as an outstanding leader in e-government, Canada, makes a point of using citizen surveys, focus groups, benchmarking tools, and advisory groups (Government of Canada 2003). Canada also explicitly links the achievement of efficiency gains with improving and integrating services.

The federal Government in Australia follows a similar course. In a recent study, it found that e-initiatives returned favorable cost-benefit ratios and that, if anything, agencies underestimated "the financial benefits to people of government online initiatives." It also found a demand from citizens for more participation: Focus group participants indicated a strong desire for more information, greater interaction with government agencies and active participation in development of future community-focused e-government initiatives (AGIMO 2003).

For the two largest countries in Asia, the People's Republic of China and India, a whole government perspective is also emerging as critical. James S. L. Yong and Janice L. K. Leong provide an example of the management difficulties facing e-initiatives in the Beijing Government: We still lack a clear uniform standard in constructing e-Government, since different departments have different standards. Also, it's very difficult to redefine the work responsibilities of those departments (Yong and Leong 2003: 86).

Unless such problems are addressed, Yong and Leong foresee that "islands of automation" will emerge in different government agencies, and the overall e-government interface will remain disjointed (2003: 93). Yong and Sachdeva identify similar issues in India, stating that ...the road to an integrated e-Government system in India is still a long one. The projects are emerging disparately without much replication and interoperability... There is a great need for a comprehensive national e-Governance Plan (Yong and Sachdeva 2003: 142–143).

If such issues assume high priority in countries that are making conspicuous efforts, they assume even more significance in countries that are still starting out. In Indonesia, for example, Ayuning Budiati (2004) found that e-government initiatives needed stronger leadership from the President and central agencies. Progress was further inhibited by the strong tendency for agencies and levels of government to work alone.

E-government thus refocuses the purposes and tools of government by contributing to agendas that place a high priority on coordination, integration, and providing citizens with value.

RETHINKING COORDINATION AND DESIGN OF SERVICES

Ensuring that ICT infrastructure supports e-government strategies requires explicit strategies for the governance of ICT. Once information and transactions are available online, attention refocuses on integrated services. In turn, this leads to proposals for service redesign. Both governance of ICT and service integration have consequent impacts on the distribution of agency responsibilities and relations with users.

Governance of IT: The approach to IT governance proposed by Weill and Ross is designed to manage change. They argue that the need for IT governance increases as change accelerates (2004: 184). In brief, their case is that good IT governance pays off: IT is expensive, IT is pervasive, new ITs bombard enterprises with new business opportunities, IT governance is critical to organizational learning about IT value, IT value depends on more than good technology, senior management has limited attention spans, and leading enterprises govern IT differently (2004: 14-18). Through an extensive survey of IT management practices in leading corporations and several public sector agencies, including the Metropolitan Police Service in London and UNICEF, they aim to identify effective governance strategies. For governments, their argument about organizational learning is especially important. Weill and Ross state that [e]nterprises have struggled to understand the value of their IT-related initiatives because value cannot always be readily demonstrated through a traditional discounted cash flow analysis. Value results not only from incremental process improvements but also from the ability to respond to competitive pressures... Effective governance creates mechanisms through which enterprises can debate potential value and formalize their learning (2004: 16-17).

The examples cited above reflect the difficulties many governments have in managing contending e-initiatives. Governments need to learn how to manage them better and convince citizens that they are getting value for money. Further, governments need to learn how to learn about managing egovernment. Weill and Ross's analysis is based on an IT governance arrangements matrix related to different governance archetypes for different kinds of decisions. They identify five interrelated IT decisions:

- IT principles—clarifying the business role of IT;
- IT architecture—defining integration and standardization requirements;

- IT infrastructure—determining shared and enabling services;
- business application needs—specifying the business needs for purchased or internally developed IT applications; and
- IT investment and prioritization—choosing which initiatives to fund and how much to spend. (2004: 10-11).

They identify six archetypes for the kinds of people involved in making IT decisions:

- business monarchy—top managers;
- IT monarchy—IT specialists;
- feudal—each business unit makes independent decisions;
- federal—combination of the corporate centre and the business units with or without IT people involved;
- IT duopoly—IT group and one other group (e.g., top management or business unit leaders); and
- anarchy—isolated individual or small group decision making (2004: 12).

They use the matrix to plot the distribution of arrangements used by the organizations in their study, relate arrangements for the overall making and monitoring of strategic business decisions, and identify effective patterns of governance.

Weill and Ross find that any decision archetypes can be associated with effective business strategies (2004: 158–175). However, patterns fall into three main groups. Companies that focus on operational excellence use highly centralized IT governance to facilitate high-volume, low-cost transaction processing. Companies that focus on customer intimacy face more complex needs and try to combine decentralized organizational structures with strong business and IT monarchies to "define and enforce shared technology, business processes, and data definitions" (2004: 168). Companies that focus on product leadership need to encourage creativity while sharing results and building synergies. They can use duopolies and IT monarchies. They can even use feudal arrangements for identifying IT application needs. Generally, Weill and Ross argue that IT governance in corporations is moving from "more autonomous to more synergistic organizational designs. As firms evolve toward more synergistic designs, they adopt more complex IT governance" (2004: 175).

The distinguishing features of most government organizations are greater organizational complexity and difficulties in performance measurement. Weill and Ross recommend

- using joint business and IT decision making for setting IT principles,
- considering IT infrastructure principles to be strategic business decisions,
- not using a feudal model for business application needs, and
- using joint decision making for IT investments. (2004: 203–205).

They suggest that high-performing public sector bodies regularly use the following mechanisms

- executive committees focusing on all key assets including IT,
- IT council comprising business and IT executives,
- IT leadership committee comprising IT executives,
- architecture committee,
- tracking of IT projects and resources consumed, and
- business/IT relationship managers (2004: 205–206).

The most conspicuous result of improved IT governance is improved management of information. For example, they attribute the transformation of business processes in the United Nation Economic and Social Council to construction of an effective intranet.

Weill and Ross conclude that, compared with corporations, government and not-for-profit organizations need to govern IT in subtly different ways: Successful IT governance in not for profits relies even more on partnerships and joint decisions between business leaders as well as heavier use of formal mechanisms such as committees. More and more not for profits will include representatives from outside the organization on their IT governance mechanisms to reflect their broader definition of value (2004: 214).

The strength of Weill and Ross's analysis is that it is based on case studies of large government or not-for-profit organizations and reinforced by considerable familiarity with government operations. However, it does not examine arrangements for whole governments. The following brief examination of governance arrangements in the federal Government in Australia and the state government of Victoria makes a start at filling the gap. This examination reinforces Weill's and Ross's conclusions about business complexity and improved governance by evolution. However, as Canadian observers have noted, a government is an "enterprise of enterprises." For this reason, federal models are highly attractive. The problem is that, as Australian experience shows, "whole-of-government" models are very difficult to sustain. Making business-IT duopolies work at agency level does not necessarily create support for a cohesive, whole-of-government federal system. Federal models provide thin restraints on feudal temptations, and the culture of agencies and departments operating in isolation is well entrenched.

Federal Government in Australia: In the federal Government, the history of IT governance and of e-government initiatives is of successive attempts to improve coordination, which decay, and a profusion of single-agency or single-transaction initiatives, which succeed but do not always connect. Whole-of-government approaches to IT governance began in the early 1990s with a review commissioned by the Minister of Finance.

The Finance portfolio had, and still has, a leading role in management reform across the federal public sector. While the review recommended improved coordination between agencies, it also recommended contestability and outsourcing for IT solutions. A new Government in 1996 attempted to drive outsourcing from the Department of Finance. Although it was forced to abandon this strategy, because of it a substantial legacy of mistrust of central direction of IT remains.

In 1997, the Government set up the National Office of the Information Economy (NOIE) as a separate office within the portfolio of Communications, Information and the Arts. The office had a dual role: it encouraged internal coordination of e-initiatives; it also had responsibility for developing the regulatory and physical infrastructure for e-commerce. NOIE absorbed responsibilities from other departments, including the Office of the Government Online, but it did not have overall responsibility for e-government. Meanwhile, in 2002, the government set up an Information Management Strategy Committee (IMSC), supported by a Chief Information Officer Committee. The IMSC included heads of significant service delivery agencies and the Department of the Prime Minister and Cabinet. The head of Communications, Information Technology and the Arts chaired the committee. The Department of Finance was not represented. The committee encouraged a "big picture" approach to ICT issues, but agencies continued to be responsible for their own arrangements. As Teicher and Dow have commented, these arrangements reflected ...the fragmented nature of public management and the difficulty of achieving a whole-of-government perspective in the wake of two decades of managerialist reforms which have been partially successful in developing an organization specific culture (Teicher and Dow 2003: 243).

However, the Management Advisory Committee, a meeting of departmental and significant agency heads, began to take a larger interest in the use of ICTs. The e-government benefits study, referred to above, also developed a substantial whole-of-government agenda:

- consistent methods for demand assessment and a demand assessment approach that will respond to the whole-of-government perspective;
- consistent mechanisms for tracking all government service delivery options so adoption of e-government can be placed in perspective;
- consistent methods for assessing value and determining which projects have an acceptable benefit/cost ratio and should proceed;

- a whole-of-government e-service architecture that focuses on the user and the interface to the user that will honor the intention of citizencentric and cross-agency expectation;
- a mechanism for cross-agency cooperation that allows agencies to take the lead as well as deliver services on each other's behalf; and
- a funding mechanism that responds to the social value being created and supports e-government initiatives that reflect cross-agency cooperation and citizen-centric development (AGIMO 2003).

In 2004, the Management Advisory Committee followed up with a forthright report on coordination entitled *Connecting Australia: Whole of Government Responses to Australia's Priority Challenges* (MAC 2004). Also in 2004, the Government split NOIE, absorbed it into the Department of Communications, Information Technology and the Arts and created the Australian Government Information Office (AGIMO). AGIMO inherited NOIE's internal coordination tasks. Further, as part of a post-election reshuffle, the Government created in the Finance portfolio a new Department of Human Services, charged with improving service delivery, and transferred AGIMO to Finance. The impact of these changes is yet to be seen. After several years and by a zigzag path, the federal Government has put together arrangements that may be able to fulfil Weill and Ross's governance tasks. It has moved from a stance of differentiation and outsourcing to one of collective leadership by department and agency heads. Setting up the Department of Human Services suggests that it may also be willing to tackle the task of integrating services by redesigning their organizational architecture, and in the process reconfiguring the bundles of government services. Putting AGIMO and Human Services together in the Finance portfolio provides a platform for serious reform. Under NOIE the federal model tended to become confederal. Under the new arrangements it has gained a potential centre.

Victoria: In Victoria, the history of e-government is of initial enthusiastic political leadership, substantial redirection following a change of government, and recent steps to institutionalize political and bureaucratic leadership in the interests of further ambitious initiatives.

In the early 1990s, a neoliberal government created Multimedia Victoria as a new agency to encourage e-commerce and e-government. In 1999, a new government, as noted above, introduced themes of "people-centred government." It recognized also the need for a holistic approach, including

- effective governance—the mandate or authority to act in a given situation, a framework for reporting and accountability, a recognized budget process and reward system;
- business systems—the operating business and decision-making processes that support cross-government activities; and
- physical infrastructure—the ICT and other systems needed to combine agency services for presentation to the community in an integrated way (Government of Victoria 2002: 14-16).

It developed Victoria Online as a joint venture between Multimedia Victoria and the Department of Premier and Cabinet, in conjunction with a range of external stakeholders. The project relied on extensive social research. Victoria's approach is a counterpoint to its initial centralized, politically led initiatives, with a strategy to link citizens, technology, and community development.

However, this strategy was easier to articulate than to implement. More recently, Victoria has opted for a radical reorganization of decision making. Central to the new arrangements is a new position of system-wide Chief Information Officer (CIO) "to improve efficiency, promote innovative and integrated service and cut waste" (Moran 2003). A new position of Chief Technical Officer (CTO) was also created.

The initiative was supported by a report by the Boston Consulting Group (Government of Victoria 2003). The consultants made extensive studies of private sector CIO models and of government ICT management roles that the consultants thought to be overly decentralized.

The office of the CIO is located in the Department of Premier and Cabinet, which, with the Department of Treasury and Finance, provides advice across the full range of government responsibilities.

The office of the CTO is located in the Department of Infrastructure. As with NOIE at the federal level, Multimedia Victoria has been divided. The CIO supports an ICT Strategy Project Board at head-of-department level and an ICT Strategy Sub Committee of the Expenditure Review Committee at Cabinet level. Similar central consolidation of roles, consistent with Weill and Ross's recommendations discussed above, is envisaged for each department and agency.

The Boston Consulting Group consultants made extensive studies of private sector CIO models and of government ICT management roles which the consultants thought to be overly decentralized.

The approach is designed to build a continuing conversation among stakeholders about governance principles and a thorough examination of all existing plans and investments. It includes significant foundation projects, such as a single data centre servicing all agencies, a government-wide document management system, and a shared application hosting environment (Office of the Chief Information Officer 2004; Woodhead 2004).

The foundation CIO received praise for his diplomatic approach to securing the support of secretaries of departments: "he accepted they held unambiguous accountability for the outcomes of their departments. He adopted mechanisms to make allies rather than trying to wrest power from them" (King 2005).

In the words of the foundation CIO, He argued that the approach provides strong reasons for people to work together (Woodhead 2004): What we've established are mechanisms for ensuring that agencies have discretion in regard to the evolution of decisions that their operations depend on, but in exercising that delegation we reversed the onus of proof. We essentially said that secretaries are to have regard to plan developments and to demonstrate why non-compliance would be beneficial (Woodhead 2004).

In terms of Weill's and Ross's archetypes, the approach places strong emphasis on joint decision making based on shared understandings of complex patterns of interdependence. It aspires to a federal model in which business and IT infrastructure needs are bound tightly together.

In the short run, the results of the Victoria initiatives are ambiguous. Two other states have followed Victoria's appointment of a CIO with overall responsibility for ICT. However, in Victoria itself, the foundation CIO resigned unexpectedly after less than a year. While the government promptly appointed a respected replacement, speculation has continued about the viability of the role. Such speculation is fuelled by the high turnover of CIOs in both business and government in Australia (King 2004, 2005). However, how to make CIO positions a part of stable top management teams remains vigorously contested.

In different ways, the federal government in Australia and the government of Victoria have raised the priority of IT governance in plans for e-government. They have accepted that it is essential to align IT infrastructure with business needs. Like Weill and Ross, they have tried to solve the puzzle of how to encourage creativity by allowing discretion while ensuring effectiveness by providing leadership.

RECONNECTING CITIZENS AND GOVERNMENTS

The cumulative impact of e-government initiatives holds out the prospect of creating substantial public value. Recent initiatives in Australia recognize the need to provide citizens not only with improved services but also with improved opportunities for participation.

Strengthening links between the current internal focus on IT governance and the benefits made available to citizens will become urgent. E-initiatives will promote new agendas of relationship management and institution building. Five examples make this clear.

First, initiatives in single electronic transactions, including procurement and licensing, improve transparency, accountability, and timeliness in decision making. Some citizens will be satisfied with quick, fair decisions. Others will want to develop wider agendas of transparency and accountability.

Second, looking at government services as retail operations has led to initiatives in service integration. Such integration has proved harder than it looked because service redesign leads to agency redesign. In turn, agency redesign changes relationships with users.

Third, sharing information within the public sector raises questions about accuracy, security, and privacy. Within government, sharing information poses challenges of technology and management. Information once gathered can be shared and analyzed. Aggregating information can itself create new information. In turn, this may lead to new policy and management options.

However, within the community, such activity raises questions of accuracy, security, and privacy. High value is placed on ensuring that information shared is accurate, that it is not shared between organizations serving conflicting interests, and that personal information is not shared without safeguards. How to determine citizen preferences about what can be shared and what must be kept private is emerging as a task of strategic importance.

Fourth, experiments with e-consultation and e-democracy join e-government agendas with wider agendas about new forms of national governance. As Canada has shown, citizen surveys can help shape effective einitiatives.

Weill and Ross and recent Australian initiatives acknowledge the need for stakeholder involvement. So far, experiments with e-democracy are modest. However, together with other e-initiatives, especially about the management of information, they have the potential to raise new agendas. These include demands to renegotiate relations between executives, legislatures, and the citizens on whom both executives and legislatures depend.

Fifth, e-initiatives have the potential to transcend national boundaries. So far the strongest impacts on organizational boundaries have concerned agencies in government. Initiatives to integrate services have already led to questions about the realignment of responsibilities within federal systems. In Australia, relations between federal and state levels of government have swung between competition and collaboration.

Current relationships are strongly competitive. Building integrated e-government initiatives will depend on negotiating a new agenda for collaboration. This suggests that similar attempts to collaborate between national governments are likely to open up substantial new agendas.

Many discussions of e-government have kept it quite separate from agendas in e-governance. This discussion suggests that these agendas are already merging.

7

Teaching Public Policy and Administration

Ever since Plato's *Republic,* the question of how to groom future public leaders for their future roles has been laden with philosophical, even moral, significance. Answers touch on core beliefs: What makes good public policy? What skills and dispositions would, if possessed by public managers, both inform and lend authority to their decision making? The authors in this section engage in three interconnected debates that in a generic form were probably as relevant to the *Republic* as they remain today. Briefly, they concern the *content, methods,* and ultimately the *consequences* of policy education.

THE CRUX

To begin with the obvious, the fields of public policy and administration have a bountiful and diverse inheritance. Dan Durning's chapter traces the rise of public policy programs since the 1960s and the more recent advent of public management programs modelled to some extent after schools of business administration. Leaving aside the question of what separates such programs from public administration—an added layer of complexity—multiple disciplinary identities and influences have led to perennial debates over what belongs to the "core" of a policy or administration curriculum. What knowledge of economics, political science, and management is vital for public administrators or policy analysts to possess, and with what skills of integration? Durning makes an interesting observation that mainstream policy analysis in quest of technical sophistication has moved away from the problem-solving orientation that inspired scholars to launch public policy as a separate discipline.

An anecdote may help to illustrate the diversity of views within public policy circles alone. Our colleagues at the newly established Lee Kuan Yew School of Public Policy recently conducted a review of the core curricula of major policy schools worldwide. It revealed a wide range of configurations of such programs.

Most included some form of economics, statistics, and political analysis in the core, but the relative emphasis varied from one to several courses in each of those fields. Other programs incorporated management or leadership courses as well.

Clearly a range of visions of what an appropriate policy program should look like are available among the leading purveyors of such education. Not least because faculty members in these departments are as likely to identify themselves with component disciplines (such as economics or political science) as with the less well delineated "policy sciences," it is likely these debates will be with us for some time.

The same review turned up a mandatory course entitled "Democratic Governance" at a prominent policy school. The course title itself might sit uneasily in the core curriculum of some countries otherwise keen to promote policy education, even though the content is probably not vastly different from less colorfully entitled courses in "political and organizational analysis" at other institutions.

This raises a second area of tension regarding the content of policy education. To what extent, and how, is it necessary to localize the content of policy education to fit non-Western contexts? Or to put it more radically, are entirely new models of, and modalities of teaching, policy and administration necessary for such settings?

The question takes on a particular edge in the attempt to transplant core curricula—and the content underneath course titles—from countries with long-established "democratic" traditions to authoritarian or one-party governance settings. And it takes the form of a visceral frustration for many educators of policy and administration programs in non-US settings in particular; because so many of the basic texts—let alone the textbooks—of public policy and administration are built around that country's rather unique set of institutions.

Several of the authors in this section address such issues. Ngok Kinglun outlines the development of teaching of public administration and policy in the People's Republic of China (PRC). Developing a relevant curriculum has been especially important due to the PRC's shift from a planned to a market economy requiring new institutions and mindsets in the public sector.

Baulderstone and O'Toole highlight the interesting case of international students studying public administration in Australia, for whom the existing curriculum and mode of delivery may not be entirely appropriate and require modification. It is far from easy to introduce modifications to key courses in these fields that maintain coherence while catering to a diverse student body.

Robert Laking gives a detailed account of how this challenge was addressed in training Vietnamese participants in public management in New Zealand.

EFFECTIVE TEACHING

The question of what teaching methods would best serve adult learners has long been debated in universities and in the specialist literature on pedagogy. One form this challenge takes for teachers of policy and administration is how to prepare students for the complexities of a public sector environment, in which ethical dilemmas, conflicting notions of the "public interest," and multiple accountability pressures are all common.

The generic answer in many professional schools has been to promote *problem-based learning* in various forms. It arises from a long-standing critique—much in vogue in university centres devoted to teaching methods, and given a new interpretation in Steven Aufrecht and Xie Ming's chapter— of hierarchical, lecture-based methods. These methods take various forms. Faculties of medicine perhaps have the most plausible application: rigorous, closely supervised clinical education to accompany theoretical learning. Yet the subjects of policy analysis and administration are rather unlike the controlled environment of hospital examination rooms. Business schools have developed a more applicable model, emphasizing group work, internships, and applied case analysis. An important point to note is that none of these methods is free of controversy or practical challenge.

Take the use of case studies. They are widely employed in both business and public administration classrooms, and are widely thought to provide the opportunity to integrate political, economic, and organizational analysis for "real-life" problem-solving and to stimulate the development of managerial "wisdom." Yet typical public policy cases have also been criticized as portraying the policy world in terms of "high-level, lone protagonists beset by hostile political forces," and of de-emphasizing the institutional and historical contexts of policy action (Chetkovich and Kirp 2001: 283).

If the critique rings true for American policy contexts, it may have even greater traction when case studies "cooked" in Western contexts are served to current or future public managers from developing or non-Western country settings.

Several chapters look beyond case analysis for problem-based learning methods. Carole Comerton-Forde and her colleagues from the University of Sydney explore group work in public policy programs, while Richard Hayllar offers a detailed description of the use of extended role-plays "to develop policy and decision-making skills in cases where interpretations of what is in the 'best public interest' are strongly contested," as he puts it in his evocative title. While no chapter focuses on e-learning methods, there is little doubt that this new technology will be increasingly important in the years to come, and an important way to provide distance education and in-service training to public sector personnel in a wide catchment area.

SIGNIFICANCE

This is a third type of question that can be asked of policy education. Put differently, what impact does training in public policy and administration have on the practice of governance or the quality of governmental decision making? The question may sit uncomfortably for educators; indeed, only one of the chapters in this section—that by Mangahas on the potential impact on Millennium Development Goal attainment—addresses this type of issue.

The reluctance stems largely from the general difficulty of quantifying the impact of higher education in any field—except on the subsequent wages of graduates, a measure which is decidedly unhelpful for the public sector. The question may also be uncomfortable for university administrators. After all, policy and administration schools—particularly those catering to students from developing countries—probably have among the highest percentages of students whose tuition is paid by third parties among all the professional schools. Are these generous funders, whether donors or governments, getting their money's worth?

In this regard one might recall Chambers' (1983) evocative (if simplistic) description of the cultural and attitudinal gulf separating "positive practitioners"—for whom every problem is solvable with the right mix of resources and skills—and "negative academics"—annoyingly insisting on the profound structural constraints on effective policy intervention. Professional schools of public administration and policy everywhere straddle, even embody, this divide. But it is a tension that can border on "schizophrenia" when the context is policy education in less developed settings.

We know that the productivity and "room for maneuver" for individual public managers depends heavily on how facilitative their work environments are: on the incentives, resources, information, and public authority that these managers can mobilize. If all such incentives and resources are weak to the breaking point in many developing country settings (as many "negative academics" might contend), what will a better grasp of benefitcost analysis bring our well-trained public servant? To put the question more strongly, how tenuous is the link—for it must be tenuous—between the short exposure of mid-career managers to expensive, short-duration executive education programs and the quality of policy outputs emerging from the systems in which they must operate?

There may be good answers to this question. Indeed, some aspects of developing country environments may *enhance* managerial discretion and, by extension, the importance of its sensitive application (Grindle and Thomas 1991). But to ask the question underlines the difficulties of moving the pedagogical discussion from one based (to use public management-speak) on the "process and outputs" to the "outcomes and impacts" of policy education.

Ultimately, educators of the "guardians" of once and future *Republics* can always fall back onto Oscar Wilde's famous dictum: "If you think education is expensive, try ignorance." But perhaps we can do better than this. Examining the impact of policy education in producing not just more capable, but more *effective* public managers is an important future arena for discussion—one the chapters point toward without directly addressing.

8

Enhancing the Role of Public Administration Education

INTRODUCTION

The Millennium Development Goals (MDGs) establish targets for reducing poverty, improving health care and education, promoting economic growth, empowering women, and creating an enabling environment for sustainable development (UNDP 2003). The magnitude of the challenge for achieving the MDGs is formidable. Unless drastic and concerted actions are undertaken at all levels—from global to local—it is unlikely that the desired results and outcomes will be significantly realized (DFID 2003). The attainment of the MDGs requires collective action and commitment of international, national, and sub-national institutions involving governments, civil society, and the private sector.

Addressing the enduring problems of poverty and environment degradation is predicated on the successful implementation of governance reforms to rectify the policy and institutional frameworks that discriminate against the historically disadvantaged and marginalized sectors.

The MDGs are expected to be resisted, since new concepts and paradigms must be introduced to the policy arena, together with new administrative systems that challenge strongly held views and practices. Any effort to promote citizen-centred policies and pro-poor change will understandably be opposed by well-organized and influential groups that benefit from the status quo.

Critical to the achievement of the MDGs is the promotion of institutional and organizational development, which requires the learning of new skills, strategies, approaches, and tools. Building capacity for identifying and responding to citizens' needs, particularly those of the poor, is an imperative for most developing countries. Functional skills in cooperating with others, managing stakeholders, and establishing networks and partnerships should be improved. Measuring and reporting performance to enhance efficacy and promote accountability of public officials are also necessary.

To meet the MDGs, public administration education must play a key role. Despite the global interest in and broad support for work toward realizing the MDGs, they are yet to be formally introduced in the teaching and learning processes of many schools of public administration in the Philippines. This paper seeks to suggest what such schools can and should do to support actions toward fulfillment of the MDGs. It also aims to examine how the academic curricula for teaching public administration may be strengthened to develop competencies for institutional and organizational development looking toward the MDGs.

This paper begins with a brief discussion of what will it take to achieve the MDGs. This is followed by a description of the agenda for promoting good governance and its link to reaching the MDGs. The paper then explains a framework for promoting institutional and organizational development. A discussion of perspectives in effective curriculum design follows. Next, the paper provides some general observations on academic curricula in public administration. The paper concludes with recommendations to strengthen programs of instruction and educative roles to help achieve the MDGs.

PROVIDING AN ENABLING ENVIRONMENT

Targeting poverty reduction, women's empowerment, and environmental sustainability require substantial changes in political, economic, and social systems (Brinkerhoff 2004). The enduring problems that the MDGs seek to address are the consequence of decades of policies and practices at international and national levels. As such, significant improvements in living conditions in developing countries will be realized through specific reform measures at the national and sub-national levels, matched with focused interventions from the international community.

International and national instruments are the key to reaching the MDGs. International instruments involve effective debt reduction, trade-related policies, reform of the Bretton Woods Institutions and the World Trade Organization, and increased quantity and better quality of international aid (GFID 2002). National instruments include improving the delivery of basic services, particularly to the poor; a more equitable and transparent taxation system; and a guarantee of peace and order (GFID 2002). Public policies are too often insufficiently focused around issues related to poverty, health care, education, gender, and environment. Likewise, administrative capacities are inadequately prepared and resources are scarce for promoting change and pursuing pro-poor development.

Although the attainment of the MDGs is not the sole responsibility of governments, governments actually play a critical role in making services work for the people and raising the quality of life. Governments perform thousands of functions, but in essence, they perform four major types of activities that affect almost every aspect of living: i) they formulate and monitor policies; ii) they raise revenues to implement policies; iii) they implement policies, some through provision of goods and services; and iv) they provide an enabling environment for private sector growth and social development (ADB 2003). The reduced or nonexistent capacity for good governance has nonetheless weighed down government performance. Good governance or sound development management is therefore a sine qua non for achieving the MDGs.

Governance is broadly defined as the sound exercise of political, economic, and administrative authority to manage a country's resources for development. It involves the institutionalization of a system through which citizens, institutions, organizations, and groups in the society articulate their interests, exercise their rights, and mediate their differences in pursuit of the collective good (ADB 1995).

It embraces not only the affairs of government, but also the proactive role of the private sector and civil society in national development. Governance is, thus, not the sole province of government. Instead, its functions are delegated to, or assumed by, other institutions and organizations in the business sector and civil society (UNDP 1997). Its concern with the sound exercise of authority underscores its ethical moorings. Thus, its basic elements are accountability, participation, predictability, and transparency, which are also the key principles of sound development management (ADB 2003). The basic elements of governance, its key dimensions, and specific areas of action. Promoting good governance poses opportunities as well as challenges as it brings together the public sector, civil society, the private sector, and communities in the tasks of evolving policies, programs, organizational and operational mechanisms, and institutional arrangements that can effectively respond to the needs of the people, ensure the judicious and transparent use of public funds, encourage growth of the private sector, promote effective delivery of public services, and uphold the rule of law.

Mainstreaming good governance not only requires capacitating individuals and institutions, but also providing the appropriate policy environment to institutionalize reforms (ADB 2005). At the individual level, capacity building for good governance focuses on the process of equipping civil servants and stakeholders with the understanding; skills; and access to information, knowledge, and training that enable them to work together and perform effectively.

At the organizational level, governance reforms involve the elaboration and establishment of enabling management systems, structures, processes, and procedures, not only within organizations but also in the management of relationships between and among the different organizations and sectors. At the institutional level, capacity building includes making legal and regulatory changes to enable organizations, institutions, and agencies at all levels and in all sectors to enhance their capacity.

Sound development management identifies the roles of the state as:

- creating a conducive economic environment,
- protecting the vulnerable,

- improving government efficiency and responsiveness,
- empowering people and democratizing the political system,
- decentralizing the administrative system,
- reducing gaps between rich and poor,
- encouraging cultural diversity and social integration, and
- protecting the environment.

ORGANIZATIONAL DEVELOPMENT

Institutions are often creations and instruments of the powerful elite, and usually discriminate against the poor (DFID 2003a). Without institutional reform, policies and programs to support the MDGs can be stymied. Poor development performance is rooted in institutional factors. Institutional causes of poverty can be:

- *Economic:* inadequate funding for basic services, inefficient allocation and use of resources, debt burden, weak planning and budgeting links, lack of competitiveness, weak revenue generation capability, and poor access to credit;
- *Legal*: poor regulatory framework, corrupt administration of justice and law enforcement, policy conflicts/gaps, and a closed system of policy making.
- *Political*: political instability, a strong patronage system, a highly politicized civil service, and corrupt leaders.
- *Social*: low labour productivity, unemployment, a poor work ethic, a high incidence of crime, insurgency (DFID 2003a).

The 2002 World Bank Development Report emphasizes the importance of institution building for poverty alleviation (World Bank 2002). The United Kingdom's Department for International Development (DFID) similarly points out the pressing need for governments to enhance their capabilities if they are to work better for poor people to achieve the MDGs (DFID 2003a). As such, building capabilities for good governance and MDGs is very much a matter of institutional development. It is in this context where teaching and research in public administration can make a difference.

Promoting good governance and achieving the MDGs are likely to succeed if they pursue improvements in wider institutional capacities as well as in technical competencies. More efficient and responsive services for the poor require technical competencies (i.e., knowledge, skills, and attitude) for doing so; but these must be matched with institutional changes to allow the technical improvements to work. For example, Filipino civil servants need technical competence to identify and improve specific aspects of service delivery through application of bench marking and continuous improvement techniques. At the same time, their superiors and work structures should allow them to perform better and make the necessary improvements. According to DFID, technical interventions (e.g., training or ICT applications) that leave unsatisfactory institutions intact achieve nothing (DFID 2003b).

Institutional/organizational development must be directed at achieving a specific outcome. In the context of realizing the MDGs, the change intervention should clearly identify what is to be done and why. Once the purpose has been defined, a timeframe is set for achieving the milestones and results. The context or starting point is then situated. Participants and allies to the change process are identified and managed. Accountability measures are likewise established.

The institutional development process consists of five stages. The first phase involves analysis and diagnosis that examine the overall institutional framework. It seeks to answer questions like "What is to be achieved and why?" and "What are the main institutional strengths/ weaknesses?" The second phase refers to the analysis and diagnosis of the concerned organization in its wider institutional context. This stage aims to identify the main organizational strengths/weaknesses. The third phase is designing the intervention, which identifies the best way to promote change. Next is implementation or managing the change intervention. Finally, the monitoring and evaluation phase is concerned with establishing mechanisms for measuring performance.

PERSPECTIVES ON CURRICULUM DESIGN AND DEVELOPMENT

Blueprint for Teaching and Learning Processes: The academic curriculum is an essential component of any educational institution. The curriculum is the blueprint for instruction and student assessment. It sets out the learning objectives and the means for achieving them. The curriculum therefore sets out not only the content of each course but also the interconnectedness and sequence of courses to systematically provide the learners with a rational process for acquiring and building upon their know-how and skills over a specified period of time. Being at the core of educational functions, resources must support the successful achievement of curriculum goals and objectives.

A carefully planned and well-structured curriculum provides a strong foundation for quality delivery of education, thus realizing the desired learning outcomes. Serious curriculum design involves a long and iterative process. Curriculum development stresses the importance of identifying educational opportunities that are most critical to an organization or community. The learner groups and their learning needs are properly identified. Learning objectives are subsequently determined and ordered in relation to required competencies.

The appropriate number and mix of courses or modules are likewise specified. The content outline is developed for each course. Instructional strategies and media are selected. Lesson plans are also developed for each course including the timing and duration. Logistics of the total curriculum delivery system are planned and finalized. The design may be scaled down or expanded based on the resources that will be made available. The content and objectives of the curriculum design are validated and field tested prior to adoption and full-scale implementation. Other mechanisms must be put in place to monitor and evaluate whether or not the curriculum is meeting its intended purpose. Moreover, the system of responsibilities and accountabilities for managing and implementing the curriculum must be established.

Poor curriculum designs achieve minimal educational benefits. Too often they are manifested by the lack of goal orientation and convergence in the program of instruction, unnecessary overlaps of courses, disjointed subjects, wasteful use of scarce resources, low completion rates, substandard teaching, and ineffective assessment of learning. At the end of the day, the curriculum should be able to effectively, efficiently, and economically provide the desired learning outcomes.

Curriculum development is a complex process. It requires iteration, dedication, perseverance, and, more important, the technical expertise to get it going. Pitfalls can be avoided by observing the principles and logical process of curriculum design, applying bench marking and continuous improvement techniques, and enhancing learner participation in curriculum development.

There is an increasing trend for curriculum designs to shift from the traditional subject-based, input-oriented, and teacher-centred learning to systems-integrated, competency-based, community-oriented, and student-centred programs. The continuing challenge for educational institutions is how to make their academic curricula respond to changing needs and demands, thus bringing about favorable results and outcomes.

The curriculum must be directed at providing students with the necessary competencies to make them productive members of society. The curriculum must not only respond to individual learning needs of students, but also to societal and/ or organizational demands. Such needs and demands serve as the bases for developing a responsive and viable curriculum. The curriculum defines the scope and content of what students should learn and what must be taught. Teaching and learning methods are assembled around achieving curriculum goals and objectives. Formative and summary assessment techniques are likewise formulated and administered to measure/ improve the curriculum and instruction.

Curriculum design encompasses the horizontal and vertical organization. The horizontal organization is concerned with the side-byside arrangement of curriculum components. The vertical organization, on the other hand, is concerned with the longitudinal arrangement of curriculum elements—the placement of additional skills development. Under the horizontal organization are scope and sequence. Scope is the breadth and depth of the content of a curriculum—from simple to complex principles, required common content, and elective or special content. Sequence is the order by which the curriculum content is presented. Under vertical organization are continuity and integration. Continuity refers to the vertical reiteration of major curriculum elements. Integration refers to the horizontal relationships of curriculum activities. Inasmuch as the academic curriculum is a very important element in ensuring quality delivery of educational services, it must be emphasized that learning outcomes are shaped by i) university/school factors, ii) system/ supporting inputs, iii) student characteristics, and iv) contextual factors (Cortes 1993). Overall, the effectiveness of a university or school is conventionally measured in terms of learning achievement, completion rate, and competitiveness of graduates in the labour market.

University/School factors consist of i) university/school vision/mission, ii) university climate/culture, iii) curriculum and instruction, iv) leadership and quality of staff, and v) teaching/learning processes. Although the vision/ mission statement predictably sets high expectations, it needs to clearly state the expected outcomes. The educational institution must have a strong commitment to excellence and the organization geared toward delivering better services and results.

The university/school must have a capable teaching force. It also requires competent leadership to manage school resources and, more important, provide effective instructional supervision. A system of responsibilities and accountabilities must also be established and operationalized. Rewards and incentives are likewise necessary. Teaching/ Learning processes alongside assessment/testing techniques must be aligned with the curriculum. Both teachers and students must strive for academic excellence. Students have to assume learning responsibilities.

The university/school must have supporting inputs from the educational system as well as from the community and parents/families of students. The concerned educational institution must have the legal mandate and resources to carry out its functions. Of course, the quality of students admitted into the degree programs is contributory to the success of the university/school. Institutional, political, economic, language, and cultural factors are also important in appreciating the capacity of the university/school to produce good graduates.

What Makes a Good Curriculum?: A quality curriculum must be very clear about what is to be covered, how it is delivered, and how to measure/assess learning. Learner objectives, activities, and assessments must be closely linked to one another. An effective curriculum requires the following (MDESE 2004):

- a rationale that relates the goals and objectives of each subject area and course to the educational mission and philosophy;
- a general description of the content of subject areas at the undergraduate and graduate levels;
- statement of general goals for students in each subject area;
- specific, measurable learner objectives for each subject;
- alignment of the measurable learner objectives for each subject to the knowledge, skills, and attitudes that students need to meet the curriculum goals and standards;
- instructional strategies (activities) and specific assessments (including performance-based assessments for a majority of the learner objectives);
- evidence that individual learner objectives have been articulated by subject and by course sequence; and
- review and approval for each curriculum guide.

Another perspective of an effective curriculum identifies five critical components: i) meaning, ii) coherence, iii) articulation, iv) high standards, and v) alignment. The first element, *meaning*, refers to setting measurable objectives that focus on fundamental knowledge and processes. It includes a clear, defensible rationale and contains explicit course descriptions. In addition, meaning should articulate scope and sequence. Furthermore, meaning should provide assessments and instructional activities to measure established objectives.

Coherence pertains to the provision of adequate opportunities at each level in the curriculum or certain points in the learning process to build on prior knowledge and learning experiences.

Articulation in the effective curriculum model focuses on the promotion of learning at different year levels that is appropriately sequenced and related. It also connects topics within year levels/courses by unifying themes/ concepts.

High standards establish a core set of challenging benchmarks or yardsticks of performance for all students. High standards promote in-depth learning and they help address student learning styles through a variety of instructional strategies. High standards in a curriculum also utilize a variety of assessments to evaluate levels of student understanding (and achievement).

Alignment is equally important in a curriculum. The curriculum must exhibit strong connections between written, taught, and evaluated learning. The curriculum must likewise provide direction to the course content, process of delivering instruction, and methods for measuring progress of learning. Other characteristics of an effective curriculum, instructional strategies and activities, and assessment program, which reemphasizes alignment and integration of the curriculum content, pedagogical tasks and activities, and assessment. Formation of the curriculum content begins with defining and sequencing aims, goals, and objectives of instruction. Knowledge and skills to be taught are prioritized in the curriculum in terms of being mandatory (must know), essential (need to know), and worthy (nice to know).

Themes and topics are included and prioritized in the curriculum as a result of a systematic, well-informed, and highly consultative process. The vertical and horizontal linkages and interconnectedness of courses/ subjects are likewise decided. It is also preferable that the philosophy or tone of a curriculum be guided by specific and acceptable learning models. Instructional delivery is another important aspect that can make or break a good curriculum. Apart from the curriculum, instruction is shaped by teacher quality, pedagogical approaches, and instructional materials.

The teacher (or medium) needs not only to have mastery of the subject matter, but must also apply appropriate processes and methods. The organizational structure and mechanisms to govern curriculum implementation and improvement must likewise be put in place. Assessment relates not only to measuring if and how learning has taken place, but is also concerned with evaluating whether the goals and objectives of the delivered curricula have been obtained. Assessment methods are formulated to accurately provide information to measure learning and to improve instruction and curriculum.

Curriculum Design Prototypes: Prototypes of curriculum design are represented by three types: i) subject centered, ii) learner-centred, and iii) problem-centred. The relative strengths and limitations of three prototypes. The *subject-centred curriculum design* is the oldest and most widely used. The scope and content of the curriculum are determined by the conventional range of subjects worthy of inclusion. The sequence of topics is largely a function of the logic of the subject matter.

The *learner-centred curriculum design* emphasizes individual development. This kind of curriculum design is more sensitive to learning needs, which makes it more effective than the traditional subject-centred design. The design is developed based on the needs, interests, and purposes of students. It is not "pre-planned" or "off-the-shelf." It evolves as teacher and students work together on content and tasks. The scope and content depend on what the learners need to learn. The sequence of topics is aligned with the absorptive capacity and even preferences of the learners. The *problem-centred curriculum design* is similar to the learner-centred design, as they are both rooted in individual-centred epistemological assumptions. It is focused on building and strengthening competencies to enable the learner to function more effectively and productively in the community or society. The design aims to perform strongly in providing problem-analysis and problem-solving skills. Problem-centred design is nonetheless "pre-planned" in the sense that it is oriented to addressing pressing or common problems, which shape the scope, content, and sequence of instruction.

Approaches to Curriculum Review and Development: Academic review of high degree programs in United Kingdom is conducted using a phased approach. First, necessary preparations for the review are undertaken. Scope and preference surveys are undertaken to gather information on the following: i) the range of subjects offered, ii) desired programs to be included under each subject heading, iii) the estimated number of full-time equivalent students for each program, and iv) the institution's preferred timing for the review and any preferences for subjects to be reviewed. With the time schedule mapped out, initial profiles are prepared to commence a dialogue with the concerned educational institution on the overall approach to and intensity of the review. Self evaluation documents and program specifications are prepared at this stage.

Second, the points of reference for the review are laid down. A framework of higher education qualifications is used to provide reference points to determine whether the intended outcomes for programs and actual student achievement are appropriate to the level of the qualification awarded. Subject benchmarks are likewise established, which represent the general expectations about standards for the award of qualifications at a given level in a particular subject area.

Third, the review is conducted. One approach involves a peer review, where judgments are made by those who understand the subject under scrutiny and who are familiar with the teaching and learning processes. The other approach is to review against the broad aims of the concerned educational institution.

Fourth, judgments are made on academic standards and quality of learning opportunities based on the results of the review. Reports are written, disseminated, and discussed to come up with decisions on what to do with the curriculum under review. The University of British Columbia in Canada suggests a step-by-step circular procedure to design an effective curriculum: i) convene faculty members, ii) develop the concept, iii) draft the content, iv) consider the learners, v) prioritize the substance, vi) evaluate learning, and vii) organize for learning (UBC 2004).

Convene Faculty Members: When proposing a new curriculum/course or revising an existing curriculum/course, the idea must be explored with colleagues. Questions that might be helpful in identifying who could join the dialogue include

- Who is willing to talk about teaching?
- Who will be involved with the course?
- Who should be part of the discussion?

Develop the Concept: Faculty members usually have a good grasp of the courses they teach and why they are taught. What is clear to them, nonetheless, may seem vague when made public to the students and to colleagues. When preparing a course, a series of courses, or university-wide curricular objectives, it is useful first to establish a clear understanding of the course. A very helpful way to do this is to ask and answer relevant questions about the important aspects of the "what" and "why" of any course. Some guide questions may include

- What is the critical idea, skill, or attitude that students must learn from the course?
- How will this course improve the present program?
- What are the specific problem(s) this course is meant to address?
- Why should this course be included in the departmental and program offerings?

Draft the Content: Having deliberated on the concept and how it will fit, the question now becomes, exactly what i) knowledge, ii) skills, and iii) attitudes or beliefs the concerned educational institution wants its students to learn. Options may include wanting students to understand concepts or master ideas, to be able to critique established ideas and formulate something better, or to demonstrate the ability to follow a procedure. Attitudes or beliefs may focus on personal growth and the appreciation of certain ideas. Possible content may consist of all suggestions of individual faculty members, disciplinary strictures, degree program requirements, and university objectives. The end result is a pool of rich ideas from which the course will be structured.

Consider the Students: Courses/Subjects are taught to students who enroll/ take them with both homogeneous and heterogeneous levels of knowledge, skills, and attitudes. Since the aim of the curriculum is to build on what they already know, thus helping them reach new levels of competence, it is important to know what they know, which is helpful in determining course level and the necessity of prerequisites. Some useful questions to ask are

- Who should take the course/subject?
- What should they know, be able to do, and believe before they take the course/subject?
- Who else may take the course/subject?
- What will they most likely know, be able to do, and believe before they take the course/subject?

Prioritize Topics: After the possible substance has been gathered and the potential student identified, topics for inclusion in any course/subject must be prioritized. Establishing a ranking system not only helps in identifying the course/subject content, but also provides areas of enrichment for students or possibilities of further course development. Useful questions include

- What must a student know, be able to do, or believe as a result of this course?
- What might be nice to know, but not as essential?
- What is redundant?
- What is less relevant? Or irrelevant?

Evaluate Learning: The evaluation of the course, if properly designed, provides the operational definition of the course. As such, the "what", "when" and "why" of course evaluations are essential in any type of assessment. Evaluations are the most powerful feedback to teaching and learning instruments and it is necessary to begin immediately to determine how to know what students are learning.

Evaluations should be focused and specific. If the goal is to make students learn to think, then thinking is evaluated. Similarly, if the goal is for students to learn a skill, evaluation should require demonstration of the skill. Learning goals related to changes in attitudes and beliefs are obviously more difficult to evaluate. Such evaluations are usually derived through feedback from their peers, colleagues, and coworkers. Before structuring how a course is to be taught, it is best to decide if it is appropriate for students to compose a term paper, do a synopsis of a journal article, critique a chapter of a book or the entire book, make an oral report, answer a quiz or examination, prepare a role-play, analyze a case, solve a problem, or answer ambiguous multiple choice questions. Other useful questions:

- How frequently should evaluation be conducted?
- What should be the weighting of various evaluations?
- How will fairness be monitored?

Organize for Learning: Once the content of learning has been formulated, it is imperative to think about how to make this knowledge and these skills, attitudes, and beliefs accessible to students. Teaching methods should be selected on the basis of how students can learn most effectively and efficiently what the concerned educational institution wants them to learn. Some questions to ask include

- How can the material be sequenced most effectively?
- What will the students need to do to enable them to learn? (Will they need to talk, listen, argue, do experiments, write, compute, discuss, criticize, analyze, apply, synthesize, evaluate, or what?)
- Which teaching methods will work best for what we want students to learn? (lecture, discussion, lab seminar, self-study, cooperative learning group, problem session, etc.)
- What additional material will facilitate student learning? (Would a course manual, a case study, a field trip, a lab exercise, a problem set, a question sheet, or a simulation be helpful?)
- What needs to be included in the course outline?

STRENGTHENING PUBLIC ADMINISTRATION EDUCATION

In light of the agenda set by the MDGs, how can schools of public administration make themselves more relevant? What must public administration students know? What should be taught? In sum, what is the appropriate program of instruction in support of the MDGs?. Learning competencies in the study and practice of public administration need to emphasize the following:

- Communicating the MDGs to leaders, policy makers, service providers, and citizens;
- Generating and sustaining policy and institutional commitment;
- Building partnerships and networks;
- Translating the MDGs into specific actions that can be taken at the national, sub-national, community, and family levels;
- Identifying the process and implementation arrangements for achieving the MDGs;
- Bench marking, monitoring, evaluating, and reporting progress on the MDGs;
- Generating and allocating resources for the MDGs; and
- Promoting and managing institutional and organizational development.

Some fundamental issues need to be addressed to improve existing curriculum designs in public administration. First, the MDGs need to be integrated into academic curricula of public administration. A survey conducted by this author involving 102 participants in the recent national conference of the Association of Schools of Public Administration in the Philippines reveals low levels of awareness of the MDGs among the participants before attending the said conference and a desire on their part to learn tools and techniques for achieving the MDGs.

Second, curriculum development needs to be more systematic, research based, and oriented toward addressing student learning needs. As a matter of practice and norm, the teacher has complete flexibility and discretion in what themes or topics to include in his/her course. The teaching methods, course references or readings list, and course requirements are likewise decided by the teacher. Previous course syllabi or the experience of having studied the same subject before serves as a guide in designing and delivering the course. There are no explicit guidelines or standards to follow in teaching the subjects. Institutional mechanisms for instructional supervision or peer review—which are key in ensuring quality and high academic standards—are scarce, if not nonexistent. In the absence of written guidelines, newcomers may find it difficult to teach.

Academic curricula commonly lack efficient organization of subjects. In addition to the vague vertical and horizontal integration of subjects, the curriculum is unclear as to relative emphasis that needs to given to an "agreed" set of topics (e.g., what topics should be discussed and how much time should be given to discussing each). The lack of clarity and specificity of learning objectives and outcomes can create problems in delivering instruction and assessing teaching/learning. Third, most academic curricula in public administration tend to be subject-centred. The logical structure and sequence of courses and topics of academic curricula are greatly influenced by textbooks or references. Too often, curriculum designs have been oversimplified and reduced to a mere list of courses with the corresponding academic credits that must be accrued over a prescribed period of time. Even worse, such a list has been copied or drawn from other schools perceived to be leaders in the field. Written and explicit curriculum guidelines are rather uncommon.

When the curriculum is subject-centred, there is a tendency for lessons to be fragmented, to the extent that students find it difficult to appreciate the interconnectedness of the different subjects studied. The courses also generally tend to be detached from concerns and events of the real world. A study shows that graduates and students clamor for more practical examples (Mangahas 2004).

Degree programs are usually shaped by what the school wants to teach instead of what the student needs to learn or what the larger community demands. Many programs of instruction favour passive concepts of learning, which rely heavily on lectures and oral reports. Fourth, curriculum objectives should be made more specific and measurable. Similarly, the learning objectives and outcomes should be clearly articulated. The contents and instructional strategies will therefore be organized around the desired learning objectives and outcomes. The statement of objectives and outcomes also serves as the reference points to measure learning. The desired curriculum must be properly disseminated with adequate guidelines and standards to implement it.

In a recent curriculum study, content analysis of course syllabi indicates varying interpretations of public administration courses among the faculty members (Mangahas 2004). Course requirements for the same subjects vary according to the teacher. The study also points out wide variations in the number and emphasis of course topics or sessions for a course being taught by different teachers. Teaching and learning inputs similarly vary.

Issues have therefore been raised regarding the validity and fairness of questions during the examinations. Summary and formative forms of evaluating learning, such as examinations, should be congruent with what has been taught to the students. The quality of current degree programs in public administration can be further strengthened by putting in place reasonable, consistent, and objective standards for providing teaching/ learning inputs. Improving the curriculum is absolutely a step in the right direction by aiming to provide quality education in public administration and governance.

Given the challenges facing public administration education in this country, the Association of Schools of Public Administration in the Philippines should be able to provide leadership in standards setting, curriculum development, and measurement of learning outcomes.

9

Executive and Public Administration

CONSTITUTION AND ARTICULATION OF GOVERNANCE GOALS

The Constitution of India has clearly articulated the social and economic goals and has specified agents for achieving the promised social revolution. Matters concerning formation and working of the executive agencies (both political and civil) are spelt out. Citizens have been assured that the Executive together with other organs of the State (Legislature & Judiciary) would uphold their rights and remove the inequities from which the anti-democratic forces derive their sustenance. Good Governance, it was hoped, would transform the social, political and economic life of the people, within the framework of democracy.

In the beginning the constitutional arrangements relating to governance worked more or less to general satisfaction and provided the people with a fairly safe and secure life. However, as time passed their inadequacies have become evident and Government has lost its elan as it has failed to live up to the expectations of the Constitution to give real substance to the policies designed to promote social well being. Even the most modest expectations have remained unfulfilled.

The present situation is characterised by a pervasive disenchantment with the way things have worked out. It is futile to debate whether it is the institutions provided by the Constitution that have failed or whether the men who work these Institutions have failed. While we cannot abolish the men and the women who command the strategic heights of governance, we can improve and update the present Institutions, which have developed visible fault lines.

Inability to ensure the socio-economic goals cannot be attributable to scarcity of resources but to the failure of Governance. It is the insufficient attention paid to such a transformation that has deepened the fissures between the people and the administration. The failure to regenerate society lay in the basic conceptual weakness that encouraged the untested assumption that people are best served when the ruling classes originate, execute and administer policies, plans and programmes for their welfare from above. This misconceived paternalism has reinforced the tyranny of the *status quo* and has gravely weakened forces of change. The 'Law and Order' pre-occupation of the bureaucratic mind has led to the entrenchment of the system that the Constitution had promised to transform.

Another fundamental flaw vitiating governance emanated from the lack of conviction that the consent of the people is the basis of democratic government. The over-arching theme, a legacy from the colonial days, that people remain a passive category subjects rather than citizens remained firmly rooted on official mind. People were aroused only at intervals of five years or there about to choose their rulers and to go back again to a life of political passivity. Political mobilisation of masses mostly remained neglected. This produced all manner of infirmities and has given rise to alienation of the people from the political system.

Rights of the people are inalienable. The words "We, the people" signify not only the moral and historical insight of founding fathers but they serve to reaffirm they are the source of all constitutional authority and that the test of Good Governance was measure of people's well being. However, the functionaries of the State have failed to realize that they are servants of the people and not their masters. Test of a vibrant democracy is the degree of success in calling its Executive to be accountable to the people.

The new administrative class, working under the mesmeric spell of colonial attitudes, was reluctant to consider the people as citizens. They continued to treat them as subjects or '*ryots*' both owing allegiance to a superior master. This denial robbed them of power and made it possible for the Executive to diminish the significance of the people. It is the possession of power that gives people control over their destiny and authority over those whom they have chosen to serve them.

Another fundamental flaw in governance outlined above is inherent in the centralized nature of the Indian State which lays down the parameters of the administration. There is an indissoluble link between the two. This was evident when the norms of colonial administration, with their long ancestry, came early to stamp their features on the post-independence dispensation. Colonial administration had created a top-down system of command and obedience in which State and local units of government were treated as subordinate to the Central Government. There is no reason why the Central Government should have large and unwieldy ministries handling subjects like education, health, agriculture, rural development, social welfare, industry, power, etc. when these areas can more conveniently and appropriately be handled at the State, regional or district levels. The Centre can at best be a clearing house of ideas and knowledge but for it to be actually involved in shaping policy and in allocation of resources is an over-lapping of jurisdiction. Reallocation of subjects from the three Lists given in the Seventh Schedule could be looked into in this context. Downsizing of the Government should also follow. Big Governments are not always conducive to efficiency and promptness. People should know where the buck stops. But it should always be kept in view that when the Centre does not hold, societies become polarised.

Democracy implies intellectual acceptance of the position that self government is better than even good governance. Unless self government is ensured by clear devolution of power from the centre to the periphery, people are prevented from participation in Governance. They can not eliminate arbitrariness in executive actions which generally tilts the balance in favour of the privileged. Moreover the 'top-down' state of affairs does not legitimise 'self-government' which is of primordial value. 'Top-down' administration stifles public initiative. To make people effective they must consciously enjoy and assert their constitutional entitlements and not be mere supplicants for or objects of administrative largesse. That is the rationale of the 73rd and 74th amendments to the Constitution. A strong sense of public duty comes from empowerment. People's attitude changes from one of obedience to authority to active participation in governance. It is only when the gap between the executive and the people is narrowed down through decentralisation that democratisation can occur. The whole configuration of governance changes if democratic order is conceived not as a 'once in five year ritual' of changing the guard but as a continuous renewal of democratic life from a knowledgeable and participative citizen body. A citizen as a political and social unit could alone take responsibility for transformation of the state of the society. The essence of the matter is that there should be effective participative democracy at all levels; once people become the fountainhead of power, their role in governance becomes meaningful and effective. It encourages an active sense of public duty, replacing emphasis from authority and obedience to active participation. The Commission holds that while improving the nature and institutional response of administration to the challenges of democracy is imperative, the system can deliver the goods only through devolution, decentralisation and democratisation thereby narrowing the gap between the base of the polity and the super structure.

DEVOLUTION, DECENTRALISATION AND DEMOCRATISATION

The new architecture of governance has to be built on the basis of devolution of authority, responsibility and resources to appropriate levels. If corresponding dispersion of resources and personnel is not accompanied with devolution of authority it perpetuates mentality of dependency. Resources do not mean only financial resources. Human resources are as important. Experience shows that monitored and supervised by the local authorities, who are also their employers, the professionals at the district and local levels have performed better. If a primary school teacher looks to a distant education director for his promotion or any other improvement in his conditions of service, he is not going to be accountable and responsive to the needs of the local community he is supposed to serve. This simple example brings to the fore the question of the present structure of social and economic services and how it needs to be remodelled or refashioned to bring it in line with the requirements of the age of decentralization. There is no reason why the District Councils cannot recruit, train, manage cadres of school teachers, supervisors, administrators for primary and secondary education leaving the areas of high speciality to professionals like curriculum developers. Coordination functions can be handled by regional or state level bodies. Similar logic can be applied in regard to other services which are needed at the district levels and it can be extended upwards to the State level.

What is urgently required at this juncture is a straightforward recognition at the highest policy level that a district is a basic unit of planning for development – social, cultural, economic and human. Functions, finances, and functionaries relating to such programmes would have to be placed under the direct supervision and command of elected bodies at the district levels of operation to give content and substance to the different programmes of development and public welfare. This would to a substantial degree, correct the existing distortions and make officials directly answerable to the people to ensure proper implementation of development programmes under the direct scrutiny of people.

Land is the most valuable natural resource whose planning and development offer major prospects for increases in output and incomes for the people, especially for those who are near or below the poverty line. For efficient land planning and optimum use, it is essential that there be clarity and certainty about title to land. In India land records are in a very poor shape and there is maximum litigation in the rural areas about ownership. It has been estimated by reputed agencies that India loses 1.3 per cent economic growth as a result of disputed land titles, which inhibits supply of capital and credit for agriculture. It is therefore exceedingly important that a fundamental change is brought about in the way land records are maintained. At present land records are presumptive in character. In August 1989, the Supreme Court stated that "revenue records are not documents of title". Millions of productive man-hours are lost in time consuming litigation. The Commission recommends that we move to a system where the State guarantees the title to land after carrying out extensive land surveys and computerizing the land records. It will take some time but the results would be beneficial for investment in land. This will be a major step forward in revitalizing land administration in the country as it would enable Right to access, Right to use, Right to enforce decisions regarding land. Similar rationalization of records relating to individuals rights in properties other than privately held lands (which are held in common) would improve operational efficiency which left unattended foment unrest. The Commission is of the view that a coherent public policy addressed to the modern methods of management would contribute to better use of assets and raise dynamic forces of individual creativity. Run away expansion in bureaucratic apparatus of the State would also get curtailed by new management system.

THE CIVIL SOCIETY

Dispersal of power through local autonomy maximizes opportunities for popular participation and helps change the nature of the relationship between the State and civil society. Instead of being merely passive recipients of welfare, citizens become active agents. A democratic society cannot function properly if everything in it is left only to the State or even to statutory bodies. Statutory action itself will be infructuous if it is not underpinned by voluntary action. The exercise of political power through civil society opens the way for concomitant democracy. Civil society consists of open and secular institutions that mediate between the citizen and the State. In the absence of civil society, the State machinery and civil servants become the dominant repository of power. The modern idea of civil government requires emergence of civil society which would make people self-reliant rather than remain dependent on State institutions and subject to their all pervasive control.

One of the marked weakness of the present regime has been its failure to effectively play its role in the socializing process. It has failed to use the machinery of the state to create a society of equals founded on the principles of social justice, secularism and eradication of casteism. In this regard, the situation of the Dalits and backward castes points to glaring failure of the state. In spite of several programmes launched by it, the state has failed to energetically lift up the Dalits and members of other lower castes and also failed to liberate a large sections of society from gender discrimination. As the executive has overwhelmingly identified itself with the stratified sections of the privileged few, it remained insensitive to the calamities that befell the weaker sections of the society and reluctantly took steps to repel the most injurious actions perpetrated against them. Large sections of these people remained docile, submissive, passive and tame. Piecemeal changes improved the conditions slightly, but the very spirit of the people by which the Constitution was to be sustained continued to rap.

It is the civil society that has to take the lead in helping create a society based on principles of social justice, secularism and non-casteist approaches to social action. It should be one of the serious endeavours of civil society to strengthen the mosaic of India's pluralism and not let it be broken up lest endless tensions and increasing violence come in the way of peoples' progress. In India the relationship between the civil society and the State may have moved some distance from distrust and antagonism to a more tolerant status but the continuing ambivalence comes in the way of a full blown cooperation for chosen ends.

The procedures and the processes adopted for executing policies supposedly designed to help the poorer sections to regain control over their social and economic circumstances have accentuated the distance between the haves and the have-nots. The barriers come not only from old vested interests but also from new sources of privilege. The instrumentalities of the State appear substantially inadequate to cope with the challenge of change. In fact some of the institutional devices intended to be remedial measures against inequities had regressive consequences reinforcing socio-economic barriers. In several cases, programmes adopted by the administration to handle issues of inequity failed to deliver. Bureaucracy cannot deliver unless countervailing power of the interest group most directly involved is harnessed. The Commission recommends that energetic efforts be made to establish a pattern of cooperative relationship between the State and associations, NGOs and other voluntary bodies to launch a concerted effort to regenerate the springs of progressive social change. State and civil society are not to be treated antithetical but complementary.

ALL INDIA SERVICES AND ADMINISTRATIVE REFORMS

The structural problem of two of the All India Services, namely, the Indian Administrative Service and the Indian Police Service, is that they were founded on the imperial idea of territorial control. It was at the district level that the Raj became an operational reality. This colonial idea was not abandoned when the country became independent for reasons which emerge clearly from the Constituent Assembly debates. Thus the present structure of the All India Services would appear to be incompatible with the development of full fledged democratic representative government at the district level. In plain language it means that 'law and order' has also to be brought within the ambit of the elected district panchayat which is constitutionally entrusted with responsibility for developmental activity. It is only thus that public service at the district level would acquire significance and be the real stepping stone for political leadership at higher levels.

The absence of clear cut relationship between the people and the state functionaries is responsible for much which has gone wrong. All this happened because, inadvertently or otherwise, we allowed the colonial legacy of administration to continue to hold sway in the post-independence era as well. For instance, the change of nomenclature from ICS to IAS did not even constitute a cosmetic change. The so-called 'steel frame' of the British Empire became the role model for the fledgling IAS fraternity. The '*guru mantra*' of the old guard, viz, the I.C.S., was the maintenance of the *status quo* and the new guard, viz. the IAS, was only too willing to oblige and follow suit. It is a naive hope to expect status quoist to initiate or welcome changes for a variety of reasons. First, they have a vested interest in perpetuating their dominant advantageous position along with the privileges flowing from it. Second, being bureaucrats rather than intellectual leaders, they lack the vision and imagination to devise new and innovative policies, preferring to tread the beaten track, follow precedents and to continue familiar programmes.

The end of the imperial continuum in the administrative set up may require a different conception of the generalist services. The brightest university graduates who wish to enter the Indian Administrative Service could then be trained in a variety of subjects having to do with the economic and financial administration of the States and the Union and policy making in higher branches of administration such as security, science and technology, international trade, international monetary system, alternative approaches to energy and environmental issues, social and economic issues connected with affirmative action, etc. to constitute a truly elite corps of administrators. They would be mobile within defined fields but would not perform the present generalist jig of moving from animal husbandry to defence or to women welfare which makes a total mockery of any concept of administrative policy making in the present age of knowledge explosion.

MODERNIZING THE CIVIL SERVICES

Arbitrary and questionable methods of appointments, promotions and transfers of officers by political superiors also led to corrosion of the moral basis of its independence. It has strengthened the temptation in services to collusive practices with politicians to avoid the inconvenience of transfers and to gain advantages by ingratiating themselves to political masters. They would do the politicians' biddings rather than adhere to rules. Lest the situation becomes more vicious, it is necessary that a better arrangement be conceived under the Constitution. The question of appointments, transfers and placements is not to be left to the discretion of the politicians or administrative bosses but be entrusted to independent and autonomous boards. The Commission, therefore, recommends that the questions of personnel policy including placements, promotions, transfers and fast-track advancements on the basis of forward-looking career management policies and techniques should be managed by autonomous Personnel Boards for assisting the high level political authorities in making key decisions. Such civil service boards should be constituted under statutory provisions. They should be expected to function like the UPSC. Reputed management experts from institutes of management, well known for their excellence, should be inducted into these boards to provide a broad based pool of expertise. The principle is not to take politics out of personnel policy but to make knowledge and information institutionally available to the political decision-makers on the basis of appropriate parliamentary legislation under article 309. The sanctity of parliamentary legislation under article 309 is needed to counteract the publicly known trends of the play of unhealthy and destabilizing influences in the management of public services in general and higher civil services in particular.

Above a certain level—say the Joint Secretary level-all posts should be open for recruitment from a wide variety of sources including the open market. We should specialize some of the generalists and generalize some of the specialists through proper career management which has to be freed from day to day political manipulation and influence peddling.

Social audit of official working would be another way of developing accountability and answerability. Officials, before starting their career, in addition to the taking of an oath of loyalty to the Constitution, should swear to abide by the basic principles of good governance. This would give renewed sense of commitment by the executives to the basic tenets of the Constitution. It is important to recognize that change in existing policies and procedures will not come from the initiatives of those who stand to benefit from the existing arrangements. It needs the combined efforts of political avant-garde, activists in diverse fields, academic, and civil society institutions to generate pressures for change. Otherwise institutional decay will proceed apace with distressing consequences.

Systematic debasement as a consequence of high handed conduct by certain sections of the executive has seriously dented the moral authority of the government. The functioning of the civil and police services have been far from satisfactory. Hence a negative perception of the Police that it ill serves the people has become deeply rooted in the psyche. The letter of the law may have been observed, but the spirit has been emasculated. Corruption and illegality have vitiated the course of justice. All this has contributed to a massive decline in the prestige of the public office. Evidence of moral and professional failure of administrative apparatus is too overwhelming to ignore. Yet the services have remained largely immune from imposition of penalties due to the complicated procedures that have grown out of the constitutional guarantee against arbitrary and vindictive action (article 311).

The constitutional safeguards have in practice acted to shield the guilty against swift and certain punishment for abuse of public office for private gain. A major corollary has been erosion of accountability. It has accordingly become necessary to re-visit the issue of constitutional safeguards under article 311 to ensure that the honest and efficient officials are given the requisite protection but the dishonest are not allowed to prosper in office. A comprehensive examination of the entire corpus of administrative jurisprudence has to be undertaken to rationalize and simplify the procedure of administrative and legal action and to bring the theory and practice of security of tenure in line with the experience of the last more than 50 years. The need is not to discourage the good people; the need is to discourage the bad people which objective can be served only by sufficient and speedy procedures to bring the guilty to the book.

The present methods of evaluation of performance need drastic reform. At present neither the quantity nor the quality of output of individuals and collective units is properly measured. The result is that the good, the bad and the indifferent are all lumped together. Mostly chronology determines who goes ahead and who does not. The civil service regulations need to be changed radically in the light of contemporary administrative theory to introduce modern evaluation methodology.

The administrative structure and systems have to be consciously redesigned to give appropriate recognition to the professional and technical services so that they may play their due role in modernizing our economy and society. The specialist should not be required to play second fiddle to the generalist at the top. Conceptually we need to develop a collegiate style of administrative management where the leader is an energizer and a facilitated, and not an oracle delivering verdicts from a high pedestal. It is essential to bring forward a parliamentary Bill under article 312(1) and to have it extensively debated in professional circles as well as by the general public.

The professional bodies like the Institution of Engineers, the Chartered Accountants, Medical Council, Bar Council of India, etc. which could have played a vital role in buttressing the role of civil society in governance have been content to act as lobbyists fighting for benefits to their constituency but not much else beyond narrow self-interest. Thus we have arrived at a situation in the judicial administration where courts are deemed to exist for judges and lawyers and not for the public seeking justice.

CENTRAL ADMINISTRATIVE TRIBUNAL

The Central Administrative Tribunal and various State Administrative Tribunals were established under the Administrative Tribunals Act, 1985 which was enacted in pursuance of article 323A of the Constitution. Since their decisions are subject to the supervisory jurisdiction of the High Courts, a suggestion was made that the institutions of these tribunals had not served the purpose for which they were established. The Commission examined the matter with reference to the actual results and felt that there is a case for their continuance.

UNION PUBLIC SERVICE COMMISSION

The Commission has carefully examined the suggestions made by a delegation of UPSC Members led by their Chairperson in regard to the proviso to article 320, the jurisdiction of the UPSC and its reports, the rank of the UPSC Members, the composition of UPSC and its powers regarding recruitment of its own personnel.

It feels that some suggestions like laying of the UPSC reports on the table of each House of Parliament can be implemented through executive orders. Others depend on development of healthy conventions regulating the relations between the UPSC and the executive branch. The Commission does not see any need for change in the existing provisions concerning the UPSC (or other Public Service Commissions).

The Right to Information

Major assumption behind a new style of governance is the citizen's access to information. Much of the common man's distress and helplessness could be traced to his lack of access to information and lack of knowledge of decision-making processes. He remains ignorant and unaware of the processes which vitally affect his interest. Government procedures and regulations shrouded in a veil of secrecy do not allow the clients to know how their cases are being handled. They shy away from questioning officers handling their cases because of the latter's snobbish attitude and bow-wow style. Right to information should be guaranteed and needs to be given real substance. In this regard, government must assume a major responsibility and mobilize skills to ensure flow of information to citizens. The traditional insistence on secrecy should be discarded. In fact, we should have an oath of transparency in place of an oath of secrecy. Administration should become transparent and participatory. Right to information can usher in many benefits, such as speedy disposal of cases, minimizing manipulative and dilatory tactics of the babudom, and, last but most importantly, putting a considerable check on graft and corruption.

Freedom of Information Bill, 2000

The object of the Freedom of Information Bill, 2000 now pending before Parliament is to promote transparency in government activity. The public has a right to know what decisions are being taken and why. Dissemination of information about policies and actions in the public realm leads to a more accountable government. This deserves full support. The Commission recommends that the Union Government should take steps to move the Parliament for early enactment of the Freedom of Information Legislation. It will be a major step forward in strengthening the values of a free and democratic society.

THE CHALLENGE OF GLOBALISATION

The advent of globalisation presents a new series of challenges to the administration. Activated by technological improvements, a new international relationship of our interests across issues and boundaries has come into being. Trade and financial developments have tightened to mesh the economic linkages across boundaries and regardless of preferences. The new state of affairs just cannot be wished away but must be engaged with. We should build up expertise to ensure that the interests of our country and the people are not overwhelmed by the forces of globalisation. We must evolve our foreign and domestic policies to control our future. We cannot mortgage our interests nor can our security be left to the mercy of others. Government cannot abdicate its responsibility to affect international events and conditions to our advantage. Without the capacity to handle this new situation, we would be striking empty postures and would fail to seize the opportunity to develop in the context of globalisation. The executive of the State should learn to anticipate global developments and endow our policy with more knowledge-packed inputs to handle them to our advantage. At the same time, the aim has to be to tap the wellsprings of patriotism and give our people a sense of patriotic duty to harness the energy for economic and social development to spearhead programmes and develop national pride and self-confidence. Mass political education and raising of political consciousness become inescapable. This is the task to be performed by political parties. To remain actively involved in new development programmes the people would also need the support of well organized, well prepared, knowledge-oriented personnel and well thought out policies. Think-tanks and organized intellectual groups would have to be promoted through state funding, etc. without abridging their autonomy.

The survival and competitiveness in the emerging global economic order requires resources that are knowledge based and outcomes which are knowledge driven. It is, therefore, recommended that the Union Government having regard to the importance of the higher scientific and technological research should have an apex body called the National Science and Technology Commission as an umbrella organization for policy making, planning, promoting and funding of higher scientific and technological research. This is necessary that such a body should have the Prime Minister as its Head. However, National Commission on Science and Technology will retain the distinct identity from the Departments/Organization of Atomic Energy,

Space, Defence Research and Development, Scientific and Industrial Research, Bio-Technology, Ocean Development, etc. Their present internal structures, some of whom have the management structure of Commissions with delegated powers, will not be disturbed but the Commission will deal with overall common issues bringing about greater coordination and integration in planning, promoting, policy making, funding and securing unified vision of the future and the future technologies. The Commission should also take into account the funding priorities in the private sector and provide over all policy guidance. The principal functions will include evaluation of science and technology policy for the country, evaluation of the models of appropriate managerial structures in scientific/ research organizations and responsibility for rationalizing allocation of funds. The Commission, therefore, recommends that a funding pattern for investment of about 2% of the GNP exclusively for scientific and technological research and development needs to be examined.

COMMON MARKET

A major achievement since the attainment of freedom has been the creation of a common Indian market that approaches in size to some of the biggest markets in the world. This is the foundation of our political unity. Anything that weakens or threatens to weaken or destroy India's political unity has to be prevented. Therefore, no unit of the Union can be empowered to weaken the foundation of the common market. However the Commission has recommended certain measures in para 8.8.2 to remove the barriers to smooth flow of goods and services which would reflect a seamless flow of inter-state trade and commerce.

DUALITY IN FOREIGN AND DOMESTIC POLICIES

The structural problems of foreign policy would be to constantly aim at making the best possible use of the international order and use it to our advantage. In the country's governance, the duality of foreign and domestic policy should end. The two should not be antithetical. A serious effort is required to combine the two to recast relations and launch a creative initiative to achieve strategic partnerships the world over on the principles of inter-dependence without domestic interests being relegated to the background. This calls for a thorough change in the form, working and structuring of Foreign Affairs mechanisms including the External Affairs Ministry. Foreign policy implementation is now more than mere diplomacy. It calls for cutting through the mind-set of a generation.

THE INSTITUTION OF THE PRIME MINISTER

The question of prerogative of the Prime Minister in the Parliamentary System to advise the dissolution of the House was raised. It was urged that one of the methods of restoring stability and cohesion of functioning in Parliamentary system of Government was to strengthen the Institution of the Prime Minister and one of the ways of doing so is to empower the Prime Minister to advise dissolution of the House whenever he thinks that House has exhausted its mandate and a fresh appeal to the electorate is called for. The proposition as raised contemplates such a power in the Prime Minister even after he has lost confidence of the House. This proposition has the familiar ring of the Parliamentary convention in Britain. One learned Member was strongly of the view that recognition of such a power in the Prime Minister would impart much needed stability to the political system in the country and would enable the Leader of the House to address determinedly towards issues of development, national security etc.

On a consideration of the matter, the Commission is of the view that the present constitutional position needs no modification.

Probity in Governance

Integrity, in the widest sense of the term, in the holders of public offices is what distinguishes a good public administration from a bad one. There may be other indicators but in the absence of integrity other competencies are not capable of yielding the desired results. Integrity is much more than financial honesty in official dealings. Unless public office is regarded as a trust that a public servant holds for public good, even the most enlightened policies for promoting the welfare of the society will not work. How to restore this ethical and moral dimension to public life in India is one of the most crucial issues of governance at present.

We cannot hope to succeed in this endeavour if we rely solely on legislation. For instance, the spirit of cooperative, team work, helping the deprived and the weak to obtain the protection and the benefit of the law require a vigorous social and political movement to really become part of our work culture and social behaviour. However, we should at the same time block some of the escape routes that the dishonest find to their advantage in the existing laws.

One of the measures adopted in several western countries to fight corruption and mal-administration is enactment of Public Interest Disclosure Acts which are popularly called the Whistle-blower Acts. Similar law may be enacted in India also. The Act must ensure that the informants are protected against retribution and any form of discrimination for reporting what they perceived to be wrongdoing, i.e., for *bona fide* disclosures which may ultimately turn out to be not entirely or substantially true.

Misfeasance in Public Office

The current situation is that public servants cannot be held personally responsible for their arbitrary, malicious, and outrageously unfair actions that cause injury to the public and loss to the State. A person can be detained illegally and subjected to unauthorised violence in custody, resulting in death, without any individual being called to account and having to pay damages for his patently illegal and arbitrary action. Other such examples can be cited. There is no law at present that defines the principles on the basis of which misfeasance can be rendered punishable. Time has come to consider framing a law that would place responsibility on public servants for damages/compensation for patently *mala fide* actions. The basis for action under the law may be an audit report or a report by a commission, committee or body competent to examine the relevant facts. The Commission recommends that the Government examine the proposal for enacting a comprehensive law to provide that where public servants cause loss to the State by their *mala fide* actions or omissions, they would be made liable to make good the loss caused and, in addition, would be liable for damages.

Liability in Tort

The Commission had issued a consultation paper on 'Liability of State in Tort' for eliciting public opinion. After considering the responses and fully discussing the matter, the Commission decided that no recommendation in regard to the suggestions made in the consultation paper was necessary.

Benami Transactions (Prohibition) Act, 1988

This law was enacted to penalise public servants and others who acquire property in a clandestine manner out of ill gotten money. The property thus acquired stands in the name of others but the real beneficiary is the person who has used illegitimate funds to acquire it. The law provides that *benami* properties can be acquired by the government without any compensation. But this provision which is under Section 5 can be implemented only if rules are made under Section 8 for prescribing the authority, the manner and procedure for acquiring *benami* properties by the State. Such rules have not been made so far. The Commission recommends that the Union Government frame rules, without further loss of time, under Section 8 of the Benami Transactions (Prohibition) Act, 1988 for acquiring *benami* property and that a law be enacted to provide for forfeiture of benami property of corrupt public servants as well as non-public servants.

Confiscation of Illegally Acquired Assets

The Supreme Court has urged in *Delhi Development Authority v. Skipper Construction Co. (P) Ltd. 2.*, a well known case of abuse of authority and corruption, that "...a law providing for forfeiture of properties acquired by holders of public offices (including the offices/posts in the public sector corporations) by indulging in corrupt and illegal acts and deals, is a crying necessity in the present stage of our society." The Commission recommends that Government examine enacting a law for confiscation of illegally acquired assets on the lines suggested by the Supreme Court.

There is perhaps no need to set up an additional independent Authority to determine this issue of confiscation. There is already, under the Smugglers and Foreign Exchange Manipulators (Forfeiture of Property) Act, (SAFEMA) 1976, a Tribunal to deal with similar situation arising out of other statutes. The same Tribunal may be conferred additional jurisdiction to determine cases of confiscation arising out of the Benami Transactions (Prohibition) Act, 1988 and the Prevention of Corruption Act, 1988, (as may be amended) and other legislations which empower confiscation of illegally acquired assets. The Tribunal will exercise distinct and separate jurisdictions under separate statutes.

The Commission also recommends that the Prevention of Corruption Act, 1988 be amended to provide for confiscation of the property of a public servant who is found to be in possession of property disproportionate to his/her known sources of income and is convicted for the said offence. In this case, the law should shift the burden of proof to the public servant who was convicted. In other words, the presumption should be that the disproportionate assets found in possession of the convicted public servant were acquired by him by corrupt or illegal means. A proof of preponderance of probability shall be sufficient for confiscation of the property. The Commission recommends that the law should lay down that the standard of proof in determining whether a person has been benefited from an offence and for determining the amount in which a confiscation order is to be made, is that which is applicable to civil cases, i.e. a mere preponderance of probability only. A useful analogy may be seen in Section 2(8) of the Drug Trafficking Act 1994 in United Kingdom.

Lok Pal Bill

The Lok Pal Bill has a long and chequered history. An agency like the Lok Pal would help forces working for a cleaner government. The most recent Bill introduced in Parliament is the Lok Pal Bill 2001, introduced in the Lok Sabha on 14 August, 2001. It follows the pattern of the 1998 Bill especially insofar as it includes the Prime Minister within its purview. The Commission has carefully examined the point relating to the inclusion of the Prime Minister within the jurisdiction of Lok Pal. In the parliamentary system, the Prime Minister occupies a unique position. He is the kingpin of the entire governmental structure.

It is his personality, his image and his leadership that drives the government and, indeed, other major institutions of the State. Major threats of destabilisation and subversion of democratic governments cannot be ignored. In this context, the Prime Minister as the symbol of the stability and continuity of the regime, should not be exposed to the risks of well orchestrated and well planned attempts to malign his image and reputation on which the entire functioning of government depends. The entire structure can be undermined by malicious character assassination. The Commission recommends that the Constitution should provide for appointment of Lok Pal. It also recommends that the Prime Minister should be kept out of the purview of the Lok Pal.

With the above amendment, the Lok Pal Bill needs to be expeditiously considered and passed by Parliament. If possible, it may be further strengthened by providing that its findings should be final and form the basis for action by government. The Commission thinks that a start should immediately be made on the basis of the Bill. Let experience be gained of working a high level body to enforce standards of rectitude and propriety in the conduct of public affairs.

CENTRAL COMMISSION OF VIGILANCE

The Commission recommends that the Central Vigilance Commission Bill, already introduced in Parliament, be passed as speedily as possible.

STATUS OF LOKAYUKTAS

The Conference of the Lokayuktas and Upa-Lokayuktas at their Sixth All India Conference had passed a resolution requesting this Commission to take up for consideration the issue of conferment of a constitutional status on the institution of Lokayuktas and Upa-Lokayuktas.

After considering the matter, the Commission recommends that the Constitution should contain a provision obliging the

States to establish the institution of Lokayuktas in their respective jurisdictions in accordance with the legislation of the appropriate legislatures.

INQUIRY COMMISSIONS

The Commissions of Inquiry Act, 1952 enables both the State and Central Governments to appoint Commissions of Inquiry to inquire into and report on definite matters of public importance within a specified time. The Commission has noted that even though these Commissions have to submit their report in a specified time, yet they take unduly long time in submission of their report. Such delays cause disillusionment and loss of faith of the people in such Commissions of Inquiry.

It is, therefore, recommended that when once a Commission of inquiry is constituted under the Commissions of Inquiry Act, 1952 or otherwise, the Government should consult the Chairperson of the Commission in respect of time required for completion / finalisation of the report Once such a time is specified, the Commission should adhere to it. It is also recommended that Action Taken Report should be announced by the Government within a period of three months from the date of submission of the report.

IDEAS ON GOVERNANCE

Inadequacies and Failures: In the beginning the constitutional arrangements relating to governance worked more or less to general satisfaction and provided the law abiding citizens with a fairly safe, and secure life. However, as time passed their inadequacies have become evident and Government has lost its elan as it has failed to live up to the expectations of the Constitution to give real substance to the policies designed to promote social well being even the most modest expectations have remained unfulfilled.

Failure to ensure the socio-economic goals is now no longer attributable to scarcity of resources but to the failure of Governance. It is the insufficient attention paid to such a transformation that has deepened the fissures between the people and the administration. The failure to regenerate society lay in the basic conceptual weakness that encouraged the untested assumption that people are best served when the ruling classes originate, execute and administer policies, plans and programmes for their welfare from above. This misconceived paternalism has reinforced the tyranny of the Status Quo and has gravely weakened forces of change. The Indian problem, Nehru had recognised, was not to foster stability in the system but to transform it. The 'Law and Order' pre-occupation of the bureaucratic mind led to the entrenchment of the system that the Constitution had promised to transform. This mind-set thwarted the initiates for legislative to socio-economic well being of all sections of people. Repeated surgery, in the shape of constitutional amendments, had to be resorted to instill even minimal transformative features. Examples include land reforms and steps to deal with the entrenched injustices of the caste system and halting measures for evoking rights to property as transcendental.

The words 'we the people......' were not empty rhetoric; they were earnestly inscribed to recognise and respect India's political sovereign – the people. The highest rank of a person in a democratic country is to be its citizen. But the new administration class, working under the mesmeric spell of colonial attitudes, was reluctant to consider the people at large as citizens. They continued to treat them as subjects or 'ryots' both owing allegiance to a superior master. This denial robbed them of power and made it possible for the executive to snuff out the significance of the people. It is the possession of power that gives people control over their destiny and authority over those whom they have chosen to serve them. Ambedkar had cautioned: "By independence we have lost the excuse of blaming the British for any thing going wrong. If hereafter things go wrong, we will have nobody to blame except ourselves".

Self Government is better than even good Governance. Unless self-government is ensured by clear devolution of power from the centre to the periphery, people are prevented from participation in Governance. They can not eliminate arbitrariness in executive actions which generally tilts the balance in favour of the privileged. Moreover the 'top-down' state of affairs does not legitimise 'self-government' which is of primordial value. 'Top-down' administration stifles public initiative. To make people effective they must consciously enjoy and assert their constitutional entitlements and not be mere supplicants for or objects of administrative largesse. That is the rationale of the 73rd and 74th amendments to the Constitution. A strong sense of public duty comes from empowerment. People's attitude changes from one of obedience to authority to active participation in governance. It is only when the gap between the executive and the people is narrowed down through decentralisation that democratisation can occur. The whole configuration of governance changes if democratic order is conceived not as a 'once in five year ritual' of changing the guard but as a continuous renewal of democratic life from a knowledgeable and participative citizen body. A citizen as a political and social unit could alone take responsibility for transformation of the state of the society. Adequate constitutional amendments in this regard could alone make it possible for strengthening people's say in governance involving beneficiaries in implementation, introducing flexibility through greater autonomy to States and local bodies, enabling greater involvement of voluntary agencies, introducing better delivery systems through self-help groups and so on. The essence of the matter is that there should be effective participative democracy at all levels; once people become the fountainhead of power, their role in governance becomes meaningful and effective. It encourages an active sense of public duty, replacing emphasis from authority and obedience to active participation. The system can deliver the goods through devolution, decentralization and democratization, thereby narrowing the gap between the base of the polity and its super-structure.

Institutions and structures do impinge on the working of the fundamental law of the land. There is, however, a substantive problem of the philosophy that underlies such institutions and structures. And that has to do with the role of the State. Immediately after the Second World War, when the decolonised world began its quest for development, the intellectual context favoured a strong, in fact a leading, role for the State in the development process. It was partly a legacy of the Great Depression, but it was also a reflection of the major changes brought about by the October Revolution in 1917. An alternative route to the process of industrialisation, which held the key to the removal of poverty, in which the role of the market in the allocation of resources was believed to be marginal, was the lynchpin of the strategy for development enshrined in our Constitution.

Some of the shortcomings in the governance outlined above are inherent in the centralized nature of the Indian State which lays down the parameters of the administration. There is an indissoluble link between the two. This was evident when the norms of colonial administration, with their long ancestry, came early to stamp their features on the post-independence dispensation. Colonial administration had created a top-down system of command and obedience in which State and local units of government were treated as subordinate to the Central Government.

Reallocation of Subjects in the 7th Schedule: Reallocation of subjects from the three Lists given in the Seventh Schedule is a prerequisite in this context, to make governance come closer to the people. The Central List of subjects should contract drastically, confining the Centre to subjects of national importance such as defence, National Security, foreign policy, Interstate-rivers, communication, macro-economic, planning, environment, etc. The list of subjects meant for the States and for other layers of government will have to be augmented with the Centre refraining from involvement in matters best addressed at the lower levels.

Rationalisation of Size of Governments & Devolution of their Functions: There is no reason why the central government should have large and unwieldy ministries handling subjects like education, health, agriculture, rural development, social welfare, industry, power, etc. when these areas can more conveniently and appropriately be handled at the state, regional or district levels. The centre can at best be a clearing house of ideas and knowledge but for it to be actually involved in shaping policy and in allocation of resources is an overlapping of jurisdiction. Down sizing of the Government should also follow Big Governments are not always conducive to efficiency and promptness. People should know where the buck stops.

Similarly, if the state governments do not delegate authority and resources to units below the state, similar acts of aggregation and aggression occur depriving local bodies of initiative, capacity for innovation and experimentation. The richness and diversity of experience across tens of thousands of communities in locations across the country is sought to be standardised and homogenised by such straitjacketing as is involved in the present arrangements. We need to break away in a decisive manner from this dogma of centralisation which had its counterpart in centralised planning. There must be power in the local governments to 'remould through experimentation, our economic practices and institutions to meet the changing social and economic needs. A single courageous unit of local government may serve as a laboratory and try a novel, social and economic experiments without risk to the rest of the country.

However we need a few cautionary sign posts. A major achievement since the attainment of independence has been the creation of a common Indian market that approaches in size some of the biggest markets in the world. This is the foundation of political unity. Anything that weakens or threatens to weaken or destroys India's political unity has to be prevented. Therefore no unit of the Union can be empowered to weaken the foundations of the common market. It is because of this predominant consideration that currency belongs pre-eminently to the realm of the Union government. So does the defence of the realm, the hallmark of national sovereignty. Further it should always be kept in view that when the Centre does not hold societies become polarised. Similarly, the fact that some items belong to the union list does not mean that the Union can act in any manner it things fit as long as it is assured of legislative support. The concept of continuous renewal of consent means that, within limits central policies are publicly debated and agreed to. The citizens should have access to information, data, arguments that go into the making of executive or legislative decisions. Only then can citizens feel that they have contributed to the functioning of the polity.

This has to be considered with devolution of authority, responsibility and resources to appropriate levels. Decentralisation cannot work without the devolution of resources. If the major sources of revenue remain with the centre then the notion of the state autonomy would lack substance. Therefore, along with re-configuration of the three lists of the constitution there has also to be a re-configuration of the sources of revenue. The states should be able to raise resources for the tasks they have to undertake. This would bring into broad relief issues of regional imbalance. However they cannot be swept under the carpet by making the comfortable assumption that the centre can act as a big brother to help the weaklings. The last four decades have amply demonstrated that regional imbalances have grown in spite of these subventions provided by the centre to help the weaker states.

The principle that responsibility must be accompanied by corresponding resources can be dispensed with only at the cost of perpetuating the beggars mentality. The gap between the rich and the poor states within the country has to be bridged by policies that stimulate growth in the poor states, rather than by handouts which end up in the hands of the undeserving. The existing policy regime has only stimulated competition between the states on the size of the plan. The bigger the size the more successful is the political leadership of the state supposed to be. Performances and outcomes do not matter. Thus U.P. and Bihar can continue to wallow in illiteracy while state leaders go about trumpeting the size of the plan they have secured from the Planning Commission. The states must have the matching resource to do what they ought to but they must also take the responsibility, fiscal, political and administrative, for what has to be done.

The present policy regime is an elaborate subterfuge for seeking scapegoats. The Constitution has encouraged this charade. The sooner it ends the better it will be. This is the only way to harmonise the imperatives of all round development with those of reducing, and ultimately eliminating, caste-based iniquities. The list of subjects allocated in the 3 lists indicated under Schedule 7 will have to be drastically reallocated to make the States operate on a more federal bases than at present. This is inseparable from an equal insight in financial framework in which generation of fiscal resources acquires greater and balanced autonomy. Consistent with this principle, it would be desirable to provide in the constitution that the additional terms of reference under Article 280(3)(d) in the interests of sound finance should be finalised in consultation with the States, preferably through an endorsement of the National Development Council. Also the time would appear to have come to give to the recommendations of the Finance Commissions the status of a legally binding award. This would enforce accountable and responsible behaviour throughout the spectrum of the institutions of governance.

Human Resource Management and Involvement of Community: When one talks about resources it does not only mean financial resources, it implies human resources as well. You cannot ask a district councillor to take charge of primary or secondary education at the district level without giving the elected district council control over administrators and teachers who run the school system. If a primary school teacher looks to a distant education director or the education minister or state level elected representative from the area for his promotion or any other improvement in his conditions of service, he is not going to be accountable and responsive to the needs of the local community. This simple example raises the question of the present structure of social and economic services and how it needs to be remodelled or refashioned to bring it in line with the requirements of the age of decentralisation. We have to think in terms of services being owned by the communities which use these services. There is no reason why the district councils cannot recruit, train, manage cadres of school teachers, supervisors, administrators for primary and secondary education, leaving the area of high speciality professionals like curriculum developers to be handled by regional or state level bodies. This would bring local communities in intimate relationship with the education personnel and create appropriate environment for bringing forth responsibility and accountable behaviour from services to the local communities that pay them. It will also ensure that the communities themselves fulfil their obligations towards such personnel and towards the larger objectives of creating and sustaining a healthy and vibrant education system. Similar logic can be employed in regard to other services which are needed at the district levels and it can be extended upwards to the state level.

What is urgently required at this juncture is a straightforward recognition in the fundamental law, cutting through the verbiage of devolution, that a district is the basic unit of planning for development-social, cultural, economic and human. Along with this it is necessary to provide that creation of new districts has to conform to the criteria of viability. Otherwise the political process already under pressure of the forces of fragmentation would be unable to at least moderate the present trends.

More Powers to Local Elected Bodies: Functions, finances and functionaries would have to be placed under the direct supervision and command of elected bodies at relevant levels of operations. This would, to a substantial degree, correct the existing distortions and make officials answerable and accountable to the people. This has implications in respect of devolution of political and financial powers from the Centre, too. Devolving as much power as possible to local and regional levels of government increases the ability of the system to foster citizenship and to enhance the citizen's decision-making abilities. Officers at local levels have greater initiative in implementation under the watchful eyes of the people directly effected.

Dispersal of power through local autonomy maximises opportunities for popular participation and helps change the nature of the relationship between the State and the civil society. Instead of being merely the passive recipients of rights, citizens become active agents. A democratic society cannot function properly if everything in it is left only to the state or even to statutory bodies. Statutory action will be infractuous if it is not underpinned by voluntary action. The driving force for regeneration comes not from the state or its institutions but from social movement. People acquire more characteristics of a ruler than ruled where they set up associations and NGOs to assert their rights and preferences in the domain of public policies. This exercise of political power through civil society originated as different from statutory (bodies) opens the way for concomitant democracy. Civil society consists of open and secular institutions that mediate between the citizen and the state. Thereby state and civil society do not work as antithetical or substitutable but as complementary to each other. Private associations and pressure groups act as a powerful brake on state Institutions and also monitor the conduct of public servants. In the absence of civil societies the state machinery and civil servants becomes the dominant nexus of power. The modern idea of self-government requires emergence of civil society which would make people self-reliant rather than remain dependent on state institutions and subject to their control.

One of the marked weakness of the present regime has been its failure to effectively play its role in the socializing process. It has failed to use the machinery of the state to create a society of equals founded on the principles of social justice, secularism and eradication of casteism. In this regard, the situation of the Dalits and backward castes points to glaring failure of the state.

In spite of several programmes launched by it, the state has failed to energetically lift up the Dalits and members of other lower castes. As the executive has overwhelmingly identified itself with the stratified sections of the privileged few, it remained insensitive to the calamities that befell the weaker sections of the society and reluctantly took steps to repel the most injurious actions perpetrated against them. Large sections of these people remained docile, submissive, passive and tame. Piecemeal changes improved the conditions slightly, but the very spirit of the people by which the Constitution was to be sustained continued to rap.

Poverty which had its roots in the old system of land holding and wealth accumulation also remained by and large unvanquished by the programmes launched to eradicate it. The executive machinery failed the basic aims of the Constitution to eradicate mass poverty and illiteracy and to improve the standard of health and general well-being. These received scant support from the regime in spite of big promises made to fulfil the scheme of things enshrined in the Constitution. The administrative classes emerging as an elitist class failed to identify themselves with the meek and helpless, nor did they strengthen social movements wedded to social transformation. Relevant provisions of the Constitution in this respect remained mostly neglected by the executive agencies.

The arrangements of administration (bed-rock of governance) under the Constitution now appeared inadequate to meet the situation. The effectiveness of premier services to play its role in augmenting the socialising process remained limited and foreclosed possibilities of finding just solutions.

Civil Services: One of the problems that remains to be addressed in the context concerns the All India Services. The structural problem is that these two services (Administrative & Police) were founded on the imperial idea of territorial control. It was at the district level that the Raj really became an operational reality. The territorial integrity of the imperial domain rested on the territorial control over hundreds of districts from over the length and breadth of the country.

Therefore services were recruited for the purpose of maintaining political control over the vast territories of the empire – and their counterparts could be found everywhere in the colonised world governed by Britain – but were expected to do sundry other jobs such as tax collection once again the major part being from land, regulating trade and industry and supervising urban centres, but the numbers involved in staff jobs in the central and provincial secretariats were minuscule compared to the presence of the services at the district level.

This colonial idea was not abandoned when the country became free for reasons which become clear from the constituent assembly debates. Be it as it may, the present situation is that the structure of the All India Services would appear to be incompatible with the development or full fledged democratic representative government at the district level. In plain words it means that law and order has also to be brought within the ambit of the elected district council which should also be in-charge of developmental activity.

It may well mean the disappearance of the post of the district collector, an institution traditionally venerated by the advocates of the All India Services. We would need cadres trained to detect, prevent and investigate crimes and to maintain the peace and public order but the need for a generalist officer to maintain public order may be questioned. In fact if the force to combat crime and maintain public order should in a substantive sense be subjected to the control of the elected representatives at the district level. It is only thus that public service at the district level would acquire significance and be the real stepping stone for leadership at higher levels.

These are several ways in which the IAS can be improved and rationalised and made to play an important role in transforming governance and attention should be given to them. Above a certain level – above the present Joint Secretary to GOI level – the posts should be manned by persons drawn from different services and sources and even from industry, corporate houses, NGO's and the Posts of Secretaries should not be the near monopoly of IAS officers. We should specialise some of the generalists and generalise some of the specialists through proper career management. Such persons alone should hold the top posts. Career management has to improve greatly and be freed from day to day political manipulation. The system which has come into vogue of a minister choosing his Secretary to Government from among the officers of his own State has to be given up at once. In the early years upto 1970s it was recognised that a Secretary was Secretary to Government and not Secretary to the Minister and case was taken in postings most of the time to ensure that the two did not belong to the same State. Exception was made only on the basis of the individual work of officer for a particular job and not because 'x' minister wanted 'y' officer from some State or community.

For career management and preparation of lists of persons suitable for senior appointments on an objective basis, international experience is available. The political leadership should be willing to give up its hold.

The absence of clear cut relationship between the people and the state functionaries is responsible for much which has gone wrong. All this happened because, inadvertently or otherwise, we allowed the colonial legacy of administration to continue to hold sway in the post-independence era as well. For instance, the change of nomenclature from ICS to IAS did not even constitute a cosmetic change. The so-called 'steel frame' of the British Empire became the role model for the fledgling IAS fraternity. The 'guru mantra' of the old guard, viz, the I.C.S., was the maintenance of the status quo and the new guard, viz. the IAS, was only too willing to oblige and follow suit. It is a naive hope to expect status quoisto to initiate or welcome changes for a variety of reasons. First, they have a vested interest in perpetuating their dominant advantageous position along with the privileges flowing from it. Second, being for the most part bureaucrats rather than intellectual leaders, they lack the vision and imagination to devise new and innovative policies, preferring to tread the beaten track and to continue familiar programmes.

Many other failings of the executive machinery leading to violation of fundamental rights have also become obvious. The obscene and atrocious acts systematically employed by certain sections of the executive devalued and debased the moral authority of the Government. The civil and police services failed to serve the people well. Corruption and illegal ways vitiated the course of justice and fairplay. Hardships, negligence and injustices accumulated, which had adverse political consequences.

Perks, fringe benefits, special arrangements and privileges provided exclusively to executive officers and political masters set them apart from the people. What is still more galling is that most of these freebies had no legitimate sanction but were self-appropriated by the high and mighty ruling elites as some sort of a divine right. A massive decline in the prestige of public office occurred in the public eye. Corruption, like cancer, proliferated in the whole body politics. Delivery agencies were rendered ineffective and partial. Credibility of government organizations suffered very badly with the runaway expansion in the bureaucratic apparatus of the State does not serve society but it served itself. Disillusionment with democratic governance became pervasive.

Making the Civil Servants Amenable to Discipline: The need for well-orchestrated administrative effort on the part of the Union and State level administration in achieving constitutional goals and national targets is well recognized. While it cannot be denied that administration have assisted the government of the day in making and implementing the policies. Cases are increasing where they have failed morally and professionally and yet remained immune from imposition of penalties due to complicated procedures provided for taking action against them as per Article 311 of the Constitution (against the erring officers). This has had a bad effect on the overall discipline. The safeguards provided to civil servants could only be justified if they were to exercise exceptional probity in their activities and conduct and were to put public service before self, not otherwise. Though the state functionaries do need safeguards against harassment, malice and witch-hunting by superiors and political masters or even from some self-styled activists, in practice it is carried too far, becoming counter productive.

The excessive safeguards have emboldened the civil servants to flout or circumvent rules with impunity and engendered a feeling of irresponsibility. It has also become a principal threat to the doctrine of accountability to the people. Thus it has become extremely difficult to punish the guilty and put the working of the executive on proper rails. (CBI and like agencies have not proved equal to the task either.) Hence the need to modify the existing provisions and procedure and make the civil servants more amenable to discipline without any injustice being done to them. The doctrine of permanency will have to undergo a radical change. Measures weeding out personnel lacking probity or competence and induction of outside talent on contractual basis should also be encouraged.

There is no doubt that the way the administrative law has operated in the country and the way it has been interpreted by the higher courts has tended to confer an immunity against action to meet out swift punishment to the delinquent officers. But that only points to the need for a thorough reform of the administrative law as well as an overhaul of a judicial system. One cannot take away guarantees of fair and impartial treatment of services and still hope to get competent and devoted performance from public servants. The need is not to discourage good people; the need is to discourage bad people which objective can be served only by efficient and speedy procedures to bring the guilty to the book.

Methods of Evaluation: Stability of tenure and guarantee against arbitrary punishment are essential if you want to get the best out of public servants. AT the same time the present methods of evaluation of performance need drastic reform. At present neither the quantity nor the quality of output of individuals and collective units in myriad organizations of government is properly measured with the result that the good, the bad and the indifferent are all lumped together and mostly chronology determines who goes ahead and who does not. These would also require extensive changes in the civil service regulations. This has to be a continuous process of bringing knowledge of organization into play in relation to our institutional set up.

Lok Pal: Cases have multiplied, giving rise to questions regarding the impartiality of the civil service. Critics blame them for putting self-interest above public interest and bending too willingly to do extra-legal dictates superiors and political masters instead of performing duties impartially and conscientiously as per law. Sections of people ill-served clamour for relief and for restoration of the rule of law and justice in transactions. Amidst a spate of corruption scandals and financial scams, it is imperative that the long-awaited Lok Pal Bill becomes a law. The other institutional arrangements like 'whistle blowing', etc. should also be put in place to curb corrupt practices.

A pliable civil service influenced and manipulated by the political executive has severely strained the authority of governance and the executive personnel have lost confidence in their own value of service to the people. They are consumed by a desire to achieve and hold high offices for their own personal gains. People have remained secondary and are treated more as subjects than citizens. It alienated administration from people and contributed to the prevailing malaise of misgovernance and significant demoralization all over. The system seems unable to solve problems that people face. Unsolved problems at times start driving some sections of society to violence, while the powers that be little realize that sporadic violence can lead to major upheavals in society.

Civil Services Board: Arbitrary and questionable methods of appointments, promotions and transfers of officers by political superiors also led to corrosion of the moral basis of its independence. It has strengthened the temptation in services to collusive practices with politicians to avoid the inconvenience of transfers and to gain advantages by ingratiating themselves to political masters, which was at the expense of being fair and independent. They would do the politicians' biddings rather than adhere to rules. Lest the situation becomes more vicious, it is necessary that a better arrangement be conceived under the Constitution. The question of appointments, transfers and placements is not to be left to the discretion of the politicians or administrative bosses but be entrusted to independent and autonomous boards constituted (under the Constitution) on the lines of UPSC. Clear and predictable guidelines and revised rules of service may also be worked out.

The vertical hierarchy as against the horizontal one makes officers less accountable to the people for whom they have been employed to serve and more accountable to their official or political superiors situated away from the people lodged in places far away. This is inherent in the present arrangement where functions, functionaries, and finances are not placed in one place in the hands of those who run and preside over the local affairs, including local government. This requires to be changed.

Transparency in Administration and Right to Information: A major promise of a different style of governance is the citizen's excess to information. The right to information cannot be hedged by so many restrictions as to render it meaningless. The idea is not as it is often supposed by the supporters of the proposal that people at the district level or village level would know what has been allocated for their respective territories and how it is being spent. The concept is much broader and much richer. How much should a country spend on its defence preparedness? What kind of weapons it ought to have and why?

If democracy has to have any meaning in the modern context, questions like this kind cannot be reserved exclusively for the experts to discuss and decide. Political education of the citizens has to embrace these and other similar questions that have bearing on the kind of society that we wish to build. It is only if the right to information is legislated and develops from precedent to precedent that rights and responsibilities will begin to go together. Currently we only worry about our rights but do not spare any thought for our responsibilities because we do not either care to know or have no means of knowing what is involved in making one policy choice rather than another. We therefore also do not know what kind of obligations go with different options that we can choose from. It is comparatively easy to mislead people about the consequences of a policy option. If a full knowledge about the implications is vouch-safed only to the chosen few, and the common folk, the unshaven lot, are ignored on the ground of their ignorance and irresponsibility, then the act of detonating a bomb can be represented as a major enhancement of the country's status without altering the existential reality of the weakness within.

Much of the common man's distress and helplessness could be traced to his lack of access to information and lack of knowledge of decision-making processes. He remains ignorant and unaware of the processes which vitally affect his interest. Government procedures and regulations shrouded in a veil of secrecy do not allow the clients to know how their cases are being handled. They shy away from questioning officers handling their cases because of the latter's snobbish attitude and bow-wow style. Establishment of right to information should be promulgated and needs to be given real substance. In this regard, government must assume a major responsibility and mobilize skills to ensure flow of such information to citizens. The traditional insistence on secrecy should be discarded. In fact, we should have in place of an oath of secrecy, an oath of transparency. Administration should become transparent and participatory. Right to information can usher in many benefits, such as speedy disposal of cases, minimizing manipulative and dilatory tactics of the babudom, and, last but most importantly, putting a considerable check on graft and corruption.

Accountability: Social audit of official working would be another way of developing accountability and answerability to the people. Without such an arrangement, neither performance nor delivery systems could be monitored or improved. The social audit by free and independent agencies could also lay the ground to harness resources of men and material to improve human conditions. This would also be a pre-condition to secure the over-riding objective of people's participation in government and a means to evaluate the utility of the services on the touchstone of its performance.

It may also be worth considering that officials, before starting their career, take an oath of loyalty to the Constitution and swear to abide by the basic principles of good governance. This would give renewed sense of commitment by the executives to the basic tenets of the Constitution and would prove important both substantially and symbolically. This might also clear their minds marvellously.

During the course of these fifty years that our Constitution has been in operation, many new avenues of work and responsibility have come up which were not there earlier. Government was responsible for maintenance of general law and order apart from implementing certain governmental programmes of economic development. Government cannot any longer confine itself to these only. The role of government and civil servants has to undergo a striking change. If the new services and new avenues are to be harnessed and put in the service of the people, governance has to recast its responsibility to tap the wells of new avenues based on new technologies and new knowledge by employing expertise and agencies specially engaged to handle them. Indeed many new professional services have since been harnessed. In fact, in relative terms, the importance of general service administration has receded into background and the need for technical professional services are in the forefront of developmental activities. The new services have indeed found the way up. But it is nevertheless imperative that their role, status and importance, vis-a-vis the IAS should be clearly spelt out, reformulated and given a meaningful and dignified status. Other non-IAS, Secretariat Services which have many legitimate grievances should also be upgraded to play their role more effectively. General administration would remain important but its role has to be clearly redefined. Controversies between the new and the old services, and within the services if allowed to develop, would become a formula for disaster.

Specialists and Generalists: Technocrats and experts have been employed in the past, but they had to play second fiddle to the generalists. But specialization has reached such levels of sophistication that a specialist is no longer going to be satisfied with a subservient position in the dispensation where changes in the field science and technology are taking place at a bewildering speed.

All this calls for suitable legislative action, provision for which should clearly be laid down in the form of an Act for which a provision exists in article 311 and which has not yet been done (except that an Act related to IAS was promulgated).

Over the years several Committees were appointed to review the state of administration. Their reports have spelt out measures to correct malpractices. Some of their recommendations, though sharp and sound, have failed to redeem the situation. While all efforts should be made to take full advantage of these reports and implement their recommendations, the malaise is far too deep to be set right by mere technical or administrative reforms. Much more is needed to be done. It is imperative to devolve power from the Centre to the periphery and modify and add some provisions to the existing constitutional arrangements to gear up the working of the executive machinery by making it more accountable to local government.

The decline in quality of governance has been augmented by the excessive governmentalisation of all public activities. Autonomous public institutions like para-statals, banks, financial institutions, universities and even cooperatives were micro-managed resulting in failure to achieve their declared objectives. Because of micro-management they could not held responsible or accountable. Every organisation had an alibi for failure. It should be recognised that a mature democracy is a polyarchy of several institutions and not merely Government at various levels. Government's role is to get the laws enacted, provide for the framework of a category of public institutions and provisions to regulate them and protect the public from fraud. As stated above, an even more important role is to implement the laws fairly and effectively, but not to interfere and micro-manage.

The decline in governance is no less due to the failure of professional groups (which are privileged sections of the society) to uphold standards. It is the duty of a member of each profession to uphold the dharma of that profession. It is the duty of each professional organization to prescribe and uphold standards and take action against the deviant. That is the whole object of setting up self-regulating organizations like, Institution of Engineers, Chartered Accountants, Medical Council, Council of Technical Education, Bar Council, etc. But these organisations have been functioning more as lobbies for each profession. Professions are instruments of public service.

They and the perceived benefits of their members have become ends in themselves. For example, it has now come to the position in judicial administration that courts are for lawyers and not for the public. Every suggested reform of the judicial system is obstructed by strikes and agitations of lawyers. No low-cost alternative redressal system is allowed to come up. Even simplified systems incorporated in statutes regarding family courts, consumer protection, etc. are subverted and made complicated. Examples can be cited from every other profession.

The contribution of the judicial arm, with the assistance of lawyers as mentioned above, in the decline of governance has to be recorded. It is not a small contribution. The delays in courts, the frequent adjournments, the lengthy trials and hearings, the insistence on special privileges and perks during service and after retirement, the subordinate corruption etc. are well known. Of course, one has to record that the higher courts have in recognising public interest litigation become the last refuge of the harassed citizen and have done a magnificent job in drawing attention of the executive to its failures. At the same time, in the High Courts, the writ jurisdiction has been used indiscriminately in the opposite direction resulting in protection of tax evaders, delinquent and inefficient civil servants, forest and works contractors and so on. In many cases, the public position has been faulted on technical grounds and the dishonest let off against public interest. The judicial system has to reconcile this paradox.

New Challenges: The advent of globalisation presents a new series of challenges to the administration. Activated by technological improvements, a new inter-national relationship of our interests across issues and boundaries has come into being. Trade and financial developments have tightened to mesh of economic linkages across boundaries and regardless of preferences. The new state of affairs just cannot be wished away but must be engaged with. We should build up expertise to ensure that the interests of our country and the people are not overwhelmed by the forces of globalization and that our interests are properly served. We must evolve our foreign and domestic policies to control our future and serve our interests better. We cannot mortgage our interests nor can our security be left to the mercy of others. Government cannot abdicate its responsibility to affect international events and conditions to our advantage. Without the capacity to handle this new situation, we would be striking empty postures and would fail to seize the opportunity to develop in the context of globalization.

The executive of the State should learn to anticipate global developments and endow our policy with more knowledge-packed inputs to handle them to our advantage. At the same the aim has to be to tap the wellsprings of patriotism and give our people a sense of patriotic duty to harness the energy for economic and social development to spearhead programmes and develop pride and self-confidence. Mass political education and raising of political consciousness become inescapable. This is the task to be performed by political parties. To remain actively involved in new development programmes the people would also need the support of well organized, well prepared, knowledge-oriented personnel and well thought out policies. Think-tanks and organized intellectual groups would have to be promoted through state funding, etc.

Governance and Foreign Policy: The structural problems of foreign policies would be to constantly aim at making the best possible use of the international order and use it to our advantage. Use of force to impose the will of one country over another has become less potent. A totally different style of foreign policy has to be designed to attain the basic principles laid down in the Constitution. In the country's governance, the duality of foreign and domestic policy in country's governance should end. The two should not be antithetical. A serious effort is implied to combine the two to recast relation and launch a creative initiative to achieve strategic partnerships the world over. Recasting of relations with other countries on the principles of inter-dependence so that domestic interests are furthered through it. Our domestic interests cannot be put off. We must know how to implement our constitutional convictions in this regard. This calls for a thorough change in the form, working and structuring of Foreign Affairs mechanisms including the Ministry. Foreign policy implementation is now more than mere diplomacy.

There is lost of fuzziness in widespread talk about erosion of moral values, loss of character so and so forth. This kind of debate leads nowhere. There are no constitutional remedies against downright theft, cheating, chicanery, moral and political hypocrisy and deliberate falsehood. We cannot produce good people out of nothing and out of nowhere. The basic thing is to adopt right policies in all spheres – education most of all, but also economic and security. The government that fails to protect the life and property of citizens and their human rights and dignity can hardly face the challenges of prejudices, habits and failings of peoples morality. These are not matters of high metaphysics. There is a great deal of accumulated wisdom available on the subject. That it has not been used is true. It stands to reason that its non-use must benefit some people. Very often, people who benefit may be found in the garb of rulers. The fundamental political question before the country is how can such people be unmasked and overthrown? Only organised political parties can answer this question. If they do not societies may crumble. History offers many consolations but rarely if ever solace for the politically naive.

Good governance proveset on the ability to strike a balance between morality and pragmatism. The educational institutes, think tanks and media should play an important role in this regard. Good governance also calls for good leadership. It is imperative that such a leadership should be sensitive to the needs of the people and should have knowledge of the alternatives which would meet their needs and possess the capacity to mobilize public opinion in their favour. Such a leadership would also guide political and civil executives to ensure good governance.

Prime Minister, the Undisputed Leader: One of the methods for restoring stability and cohesion of functioning to governance in a parliamentary government is to empower the Prime Minister to emerge as an undisputed strong leader in office. One of the ways of doing this (apart from other Parliamentary reforms) is to empower the Prime Minister to dissolve the House when he thinks that the house has exhausted its mandate and an appeal to the country is called for. This will reinforce leadership in maintaining standards of integrity and public morality in the performance of the ministers and members of parliament and reduce the influence of special interests. This is really a matter of stating a political doctrine of high constitutional import and getting it ratified by the Supreme Court.

Comptroller and Auditor General: As and when the office of the ombudsman, or in local parlance the Lokpal, comes into being, there is legitimate hope that the scope for veniality and gross wilful negligence by political and administrative bosses will be appreciably reduced. However, the Lokpal cannot act effectively as a 'lone ranger', his hands will have to be strengthened from all possible sources. One such unfailing source is the periodical mandatory reports of the Comptroller and Auditor General of India (CAG). Hitherto, CAG reports have not often been treated with the seriousness and sincerity they demand. At times they are treated in a somewhat cavalier fashion. Preparation of CAG reports understandably time-consuming and by the time they appear, the officials indicted for financial malpractices or some other grave lapses have retired or gone to pastures new and in the process the domain of accountability and answerability gets a severe jolt. The constitutional office of CAG, therefore, need some more teeth to expeditiously and effectively back individual malefactors and delinquent agencies even if virtually speaking some of them are half lying in their graves. (Read separate chapter on CAG)

Power not only corrupts but also inebriates. This attribute of power leads the state or its agencies, at times, to use unwarranted or excessive force or to indulge in some other reprehensible activity. Today public opinion of media are alert enough to compel the state to institute a commission of enquiry in the event of some such act of commission by an official agency. However, an enquiry commission lumbers upon with its tortuous sittings and hearings and by the time its findings come out, the passion of the agitated public have almost cooled down if not altogether vanished. Moreover, for lack of full judicial status to an enquiry commission equivalent to that of a judicial court politicians, officials and other concerned persons do not take the summons and proceedings of the commission with appropriate seriousness and deference. And to top it on the findings of the commission are reluctantly acted upon, if not all, especially when the indicted party happens to be politicians or officials in power. An impartial enquiry commission, whenever deem necessary, acts as a healthy check on the arbitrariness and high-handedness of the state and its agencies, provided, of course it completes its findings without avoidable delay and the state is mandatory obligated to act on its findings within a reasonable time-frame. Hopefully, the Constitution can take cognizance of this aspect so that enquiry commissions can become effective tools for initiating corrective or even punitive measures wherever government or administration exceeds its brief.

10

Rural Poverty Alleviation in India: An Assessment of Public Programs

DATA AND METHODOLOGY

This study is based on secondary data. The data have been compiled from various sources such as publications of the Planning Commission of India (1993, 2001, 2002), Census of India, Central Statistical Organisation of India, Reserve Bank of India (1999), and Government of India (2000, 2003, and 2004).

After a careful review of the literature on rural poverty (Subbarao 1985; Alhuwalia 1986; Bardhan 1986; Desai 1986; Mellor 1986; Mellor and Desai 1986; Vyas 1986; Hirway 1988; Hirway et.al. 1990; Minhas, Jain, and Tendulkar 1991; Rao 1992; Planning Commission 1993, 2002; Vyas and Sagar 1993; Kannan 1995; Parthasarathy 1995; Dev and Ranade 1997; Dreze and Sen 1999; Vyas and Bhargava 2000; Deaton and Dreze 2002; Srinivasan 2002; Basu 2003; Government of India 2004), it is hypothesized in this study that alleviation of rural poverty depends upon both public policy and socioeconomic factors.

The public policy factors include direct poverty alleviation programs, rural housing for the poor, public distribution systems, and loans by regional rural banks. The economic and social variables that influence rural poverty are rural nonfarm employment and rural literacy. With a view to capturing the overall contribution of all the policy variables and also that of other variables relating to the alleviation of rural poverty, multiple regression analysis has been used in this study.

For regression analysis, state-level data covering 14 major states have been used. Regression analysis has been carried out at 2 levels. At level 1, only policy variables are included in the model. The regression results of this level should help to identify the impact of public programs on rural poverty alleviation. At level 2, variables other than policy variables are also included. The results of this model should help to identify the collective role of both policy and nonpolicy variables in rural poverty alleviation. In addition to regression analysis, statistical techniques such as percentage, means, standard deviation, coefficient of variation (CV), and correlation have also been used to analyze the data.

PUBLIC PROGRAMS FOR RURAL POVERTY ALLEVIATION: AN OVERVIEW

The prominent direct rural poverty alleviation programs in India can be grouped into four categories:

Wage Employment Programs: The federal Government has launched various wage employment programs from time to time. The important wage employment programs include Jawahar Rozgar Yojana (JRY), Employment Assurance Scheme (EAS), Jawahar Gram Samridhi Yojana (JGSY) and Sampoorna Grameen Rozgar Yojana (SGRY). With a view to improving the effectiveness of these programs, from time to time the government has merged programs, restructured them, and also redesignated a couple of them. At present the SGRY is the only major wage employment generation program. It was launched in September 2001, by restructuring the erstwhile Jawahar Gram Samridhi Yojana (JGSY) and Employment Assurance Scheme (EAS). It has two streams, namely, EAS/ SGRY-I and JRY/JGSY/SGRY-II.

The objective of SGRY is to provide additional wage employment in rural areas as well as maintain food security and create durable community, social, and economic infrastructure. The rural poor who are in need of wage employment and desire to do manual and unskilled work in and around the village/habitat are eligible to get benefits from the SGRY. The scheme aims to generate 100 *crore* (1 billion) man-days of employment in a year. Central and state governments share the cost of each component in the ratio of 75:25 (Government of India 2003, 2004).

With a view to promoting participatory democracy and decentralization, the activities under SGRY are implemented by the Gram Panchayat (villagelevel democratically elected government). The District Rural Development Agencies (DRDAs)/Zila Parishad (ZPs) (democratically elected bodies at the district level) release funds directly to the Gram Panchayat. On the basis of the expressed needs of the area/people, the Gram Panchayat formulate the Annual Action Plan and implement activities with the approval of the Gram Sabha, the village assembly consisting of all eligible voters. Overall guidance, coordination, supervision, and periodical reporting are the responsibility of the DRDAs/ZPs.

Self-Employment Programs: The wage employment generation program mainly supplements the earnings of agricultural labour during lean seasons. However, the extent and nature of unemployment and underemployment in rural India necessitates having programs that aim to create assets for generating self-employment on a sustained basis. With this in view, the Government has introduced a number of programs like the Integrated Rural Development Programme, Training of Rural Youth for Self-Employment, Development of Women and Children in Rural Areas, the Ganga Kalyan Yojana, the Million Wells Scheme, and Supply of Improved Toolkits. Empirical evidence suggested that each program, instead of strengthening other programs through intended linkages, gradually started operating as a separate and independent program and as a consequence, the substantive issue of sustainable income generation was lost in the process (Government of India 2000). Recognizing this inadequacy of self-employment generation programs, the Government decided on 1 April 1999 to launch a new self-employment program, Swarn Jayanti Gram Swarozgar Yojana (SGSY), by merging earlier programs.

The major objective of SGSY was to bring every assisted family or group (self-help group) of rural poor above the poverty line within 3 years through the promotion of self-employment generation opportunities on a sustainable basis. Under this program, preference was given to those activities that generate self-employment in the vulnerable groups among the rural poor like the Scheduled Castes/Scheduled Tribes and women. The SGSY envisaged providing sustainable income through microenterprise development, both land-based and other. For this purpose, effective linkages were established between capacity building of the poor, credit, technology, marketing, and infrastructure.

The SGSY preferred activities to be undertaken through a group approach, with a stipulation that 40% of all self-help groups should be composed exclusively of women. The SGSY also preferred activity clusters. Under the activity cluster approach, the Block SGSY Committee identified four to five activities appropriate to the resource base for each block (cluster of villages).

This committee for the identification of cluster activities also made use of potential link plans prepared by National Bank for Agriculture and Rural Development, annual credit plans of commercial banks, and surveys carried out by technical organizations. The expertise of officials on local Khadi (a coarse homespun cotton cloth made in India) production and Village Industries and District Industry Centres was also available to the Block SGSY Committee.

The DRDA implemented the SGSY in association with the Panchayati Raj Institutions, particularly the Panchayat Samiti (the second tier of rural democratically elected bodies having headquarters at the block level), the banks, the line departments, and the nongovernment organizations. Under SGSY, the central and state governments shared the funds in the ratio of 75:25.

Rural Housing: The 1991 Census data revealed that around 3.1 million households were without shelter and another 10.31 million households resided in unserviceable *kutcha* (mud) houses (Government of India 2003). In view of the magnitude and severity of the problem, the central Government in 1998 announced a National Housing and Habitat Policy aiming to provide "Housing for All" and also facilitate construction of 2 million additional housing units annually, with an emphasis on extending benefits to the poor and the deprived (Government of India 2003).

The major rural housing programs under the Action Plan for Rural Housing are Indira Awaas Yojana (IAY), Credit-Cum-Subsidy Scheme for Rural Housing, Innovative Stream for Rural Housing and Habitat Development, Rural Building Centres, Samgara Awaas Yojana, enhancement of equity contributions by the Ministry of Rural Development to the Housing and Urban Development Corporation, and the National Mission for Rural Housing and Habitat.

IAY is the most important component of the Action Plan. It was launched in 1985–86 aiming to provide dwelling units free of cost to below-povertyline (BPL) families, subject to the condition that non-Scheduled Caste/ Scheduled Tribe families do not receive more than 40% of program allocations (Government of India 2003; Government of India 2004). Beneficiaries under IAY are selected by the Gram Sabha.

Public Distribution Schemes: The major objective of the Public Distribution System (PDS) is to provide food security to the poor by supplying food grains to them at subsidized prices. PDS, started during World War II, is one of the oldest and largest systems of its type in the world and has a network of around 500,000 fair price shops. These shops annually distribute food grains worth Rs. 300 billion. About 160 million BPL households are the beneficiaries of PDS both in urban and rural India. With a view to plugging the leakages in the PDS and specially targeting the poor, the PDS was revamped under the Target PDS (TPDS) in June 1997. In the new scheme, each poor household is entitled to 25 kgs of food grain per month at prices that are less than half the economic cost. For the poorest of the poor families (i.e., the most vulnerable sector of society), the price charged is less than one fourth the economic cost (Planning Commission 2001). In rural India, the beneficiaries of TPDS include landless agricultural labourers, marginal farmers, and rural artisans/craftsmen such as potters, weavers, blacksmiths, and carpenters.

RURAL POVERTY ACROSS STATES

The proportion of the BPL rural population at the national level has declined consistently over time. In 1973–74, more than half of the rural population (56.44%) was BPL. This percentage has declined to one fourth (27.10%) during 1999–2000. The absolute numbers of the BPL rural population have also declined, from 261.3 million in 1973–74 to 193.2 million in 2000–2001.

A close look at interstate variations in estimates of rural poverty shows that in 1973–74, four states, namely Bihar, Madhya Pradesh, Orissa, and West Bengal, had a high (above 60%) percentage of BPL rural people. States such as Kerala, Maharashtra, Tamil Nadu, Uttar Pradesh, Karnataka, Andhra Pradesh, Gujarat, and Haryana belonged to the medium level of rural poverty (i.e., 30–60% BPL). Punjab, with 28.21% was the only low rural poverty (below 30%) state. After a gap of about 25 years (i.e., in the years 1999–2000), the states of Orissa, Bihar, Madhya Pradesh, and West Bengal remained in the high rural BPL category, i.e., above 30%. Uttar Pradesh was the new entry in this category. Maharashtra, Karnataka, and Tamil Nadu were in the medium category (between 15–30%) of poverty states.

The low level of poverty (below 15%) was a feature of Rajasthan, Gujarat, Andhra Pradesh, Kerala, Haryana and Punjab. Interestingly Punjab again had the lowest (6.4%) rural population below poverty line. The foregoing analysis shows that rural poverty has declined in all the states, but at different rates. This trend has resulted in the perpetuation of interstate disparities in rural poverty. This is confirmed by the notable increase in the value of CV of rural poverty from 22.97% in 1973–1974 to 60.84% in 1999–2000.

CONCLUSIONS AND POLICY RECOMMENDATIONS

In India, the proportion of rural BPL people has declined over time. The same trend is noticeable in all the selected states. The pace of decline, however, has varied considerably across states. Kerala has experienced maximum decline (49.79%), whereas Bihar has witnessed minimum decline (18.69%) between the study periods. Though the declining trend is noticeable in most of the states over time, interstate disparities have widened. Factors such as per capita public expenditure on wage employment and self-employment programs for the rural poor; per capita monthly PDS supply of rice and wheat for rural BPL people, per capita advances by RRBs to the rural poor, and rural nonfarm employment have helped in reducing the percentage of rural poor in the country. In contrast, rural housing schemes and rural literacy programs have adversely affected rural poverty. From the policy perspective, the study recommends allocation of more public funds for wage employment and self-employment programs and for the PDS. Nonfarm activities should be promoted in the villages to provide employment to the rural poor.

The number of rural regional banks should also be increased; this would play an important role in reducing the numbers of the rural poor. The leakages and corruption in housing programs for the rural poor need to be reduced or stopped, with a view to improving their delivery. Introduction of a focused literacy program for the rural poor could also help in mitigating rural poverty in India.

11

Institutional Design and Citizen Participation in Local Governance

INTRODUCTION

Local government is the frontier of governance, and the quality of local government is related to the welfare and benefits of the citizens. Local governance plays a very important role in modern public administration. Public administration stresses the views of New Public Management (NPM) at the end of the 20th century, and it emphasizes the importance of customer orientation to enhance the effectiveness of and competition within local government. However, it is not apparent that a scenario where NPM principles dominate the administrative functions of a local government is compatible with an increasing demand for citizen participation.

Recently, research into local governance has become a popular subject. Scholars of public administration, however, do not define the core values and concepts of local governance clearly. Besides, there is no doubt that at this time local governance has some institutional problems of its own. It is most important to note that if we use the term without the concept of citizen participation, local governance will in fact become a source of troubles. In this paper, several points will be discussed. First, we will review the formation of local governance using the approach of NPM, and will review the related problems. Second, we will discuss institutional problems and solutions from the viewpoint of institutional design and reform when local government adopts the measures of local governance. Third, we will discuss measures related to how local governance connects with citizen participation; and finally, we will analyze the case of local governance in Taipei, China.

FORMATION OF LOCAL GOVERNANCE WITH A NEW PUBLIC MANAGEMENT APPROACH

Starting in the early 1980s, some countries were under financial pressure, and a wave of reorganizing the structures of government began to occur. New ideas emerged. Some scholars stressed the importance of effective management and of redefining government functions. What emerged was a new paradigm, known almost universally as NPM. Its main idea is to re-establish democratic principles in governments by reducing the ambiguities of delegation. Its main features:

- devolving authority and added flexibility;
- ensuring performance, control, and accountability;
- developing competition and choice;
- providing responsive service;
- improving the management of human resources;
- optimizing information technology;
- improving the quality of regulation; and
- strengthening steering functions at the centre (Jan 1999: 75).

From these features, we may infer that NPM is about achieving higher levels of performance by governments. Some countries have adopted NPM style government reforms to improve governmental and managerial performance.

The general mission of NPM thinking is achieving better governmental performance in democratic regimes. A key concept of NPM is managerialism. Managerialism stresses the following: hands-on professional management, explicit standards and measures of performance; managing by results; value for money; and, more recently, closeness to the customer (Rhodes 1997: 48). This transformation of the government involves less government but more governance (Osborne and Gaebler 1992: 34). Some organization experts had introduced the NPM-inspired government model and a set of government roles during the final decade of the 20th century. Around the same time, in Taipei, China, some consultants or scholars, such as C. Jan (1999) and T. Lee (1999), had also introduced the NPM-inspired governance models and roles. Above all, local government transforms the main governance issue into an interagency working group or partnerships among organizations. NPM advocates less input control and more emphasis on evaluation and performance, with the criteria used in the evaluation largely driven by the private sector rather than by bureaucratic theories. It accords a lesser role to the state and more to market forces. So the government's reform emphasis on the boundaries among organizations has become very blurred (Pierre and Peters 2000: 64– 65). The Organisation for Economic Cooperation and Development (OECD) notes that for the public sector to remain responsive to the needs of those it serves, governments must be willing and able to learn about client needs and adjust the provision of services accordingly (OECD 1995). Decentralized management would provide feedback from clients and ultimately enhance consumer choice (Yeatman 1990: 3). Incrementally, some scholars and proponents have taken off from NPM techniques and philosophies to improve upon the public sector's performance.

In recent years, some public administration scholars have questioned and even criticized the NPM approach. Although NPM ideas and reforms help provide multiple opportunities to local government, they blot out the role of local government and decrease the connection between local government and citizens. So, many scholars have also suggested strengthening local governance to offset the disadvantages of NPM (Pierre and Peters 1998: 231–233). Governance can be defined as "the tradition, institutions, and processes that determine how power is exercised, how citizens are given voice, and how decisions are made on the issues of public concern" (Denhardt 2002: 4). Bovaird and Löffler (2002: 16) define local governance as "the set of formal and informal rules, structures and processes defining the measures with which individuals and organizations can exercise power over the decisions by other stakeholders capable of affecting their welfare at the local levels." According to the definition, perfect local governance involves six groups of stakeholders: citizens, third sector (such as nonprofit organizations, nongovernment organizations, etc.), business, media, higher-level government, and local authorities. This means that governance includes cooperation, competition, and conflict management. The main issue for governance is whether it constitutes a new paradigm of how to solve common problems and create win-win situations for all stakeholders. However, just as NPM is not a panacea for all conditions, governance also does not provide a complete answer to all current challenges to the public sector.

THE INSTITUTIONAL PERSPECTIVE OF LOCAL GOVERNANCE

From an institutional perspective, governance involves creating capable political actors who understand how political institutions work and are able to deal effectively with them (Anderson 1990: 196–197). Institutional governance involves building and supporting cultures of rights and rules that make possible the agreements represented in coalition understandings. It involves building and supporting identities, preferences, and resources that can make a polity possible (March and Olsen 1995: 28). It is related to many institutions that are not suitable when the idea of governance is propagated. So we have to consider the institutional issue of local governance.

Local governance will influence the existing framework of local government. When the idea of governance is propagated, some mechanisms have to be adjusted. Such institutional reforms have to stress the relationship among local governments in a political system: on the one hand, it is a subordinated level expected to effectively implement the objectives of the higher levels of government; on the other hand, local government has to offer space for democratic choice for local actors in accordance with local preferences (Page and Goldsmith 1987). These reflections point to institutional reforms in local government as one approach to solve government failures in participation, transparency, and effectiveness.

One way to guarantee efficiency is to monitor performance through continuous policy evaluation. Parts of these budget-oriented reforms are changes in the organizational structure, especially changes that seek to strike a new balance between the public and private sectors: in other words, the introduction of market-type mechanisms to public tasks. This has become a key part of management reform strategies: government positioning in a competitive environment. Among the various reforms mentioned, there are several that stand out (OECD 1995: 36–44). In Taipei, China, for example, we can see some cases; these include the "build-operate-transfer" model (such as the Taiwan High Speed Railroad Company) and the public-private partnership (such as contracting out). In addition, models are still being developed. These models will help take the evaluation of local governance further. For example, the Commonwealth Association for Public Administration and Management (CAPAM) has, as of this year, initiated an award for innovations in governance. There are nine criteria in the CAPAM evaluation process:

- partnering,
- accountability,
- communication and information revolutions,
- demands for citizen engagement,
- integration of horizontal and vertical management,
- maintenance of policy coherence in a fragmented policy community,
- political or parliamentary structures,
- evolution in required human resource competencies, and
- values and ethics.

Promoting local governance, therefore, means local government accepting the influence from outside and amending the existing laws. Then, local government has to combine the ideas of governance with laws to create new mechanisms. Citizens would disapprove and resist if local government promoted new mechanisms that would negatively affect their benefits. So there is a focus of tasks at the local level as well as of the expectations of citizens toward local government.

Hood (1995: 15) observes that "unintended effects of policy and management measures are a recurring theme in social science." Local government reforms also tend to emphasize legitimacy. A traditional reform path has stressed the accountability of officeholders. Local governance focuses on the efficiency of local politics and administration, while "alternative modernizers" have stressed the element of direct citizen participation.

As Blair (1998: 13) notes: "Local government will still deliver some services but their distinctive leadership role will be to weave and knit together the contribution of the various local stakeholders." One of the important stakeholders is the citizens; we will therefore discuss the ties between local governance and citizen participation in the next section.

LOCAL GOVERNANCE AND CITIZEN PARTICIPATION

New governance institutions are being developed at the local level that require local authorities to consult with, and directly involve, the general public on an ongoing basis. It is important to recognize a number of practical issues that concern participatory mechanisms. Among those questions that have been raised in debates about participation and local participative structures in a number of countries are the following: (Beauchamp and Dionne 1997: 112–118):

- the need for continuity, and for processes to be institutionalized;
- the frequently very high financial costs of consultation and participation;
- whether the complexity of some issues for decision is compatible with participation;
- whether to involve in decisions a large group of people, which might result in relatively superficial opinions, or a small group, to obtain more developed opinions;
- the prospect of creating new elites, and processes being captured by minority groups or the well mobilized; and
- opposition from the professional bureaucracy to increased participation.

Local government is the frontier of governance, and the quality of local government is related to the welfare and benefits of the citizen. Local government is experimenting with "finding new forms of legitimacy for decisions made in loose networks of relationships. This strategy requires trials and errors and constantly searching for solutions that work in both the functional and democratic senses" (John 2001: 166). But because unlimited citizen participation will become populism, public administration scholars have aimed at "deliberative democracy." The philosophy of deliberative democracy is social justice. It means that everyone should have equal opportunity to participate in public affairs. In the context of deliberative democracy, local governance would play a very important role in affording citizens an opportunity to participate and in establishing some norms. Lindblom (1965) noted that effective governance is actually generated by participation. So "participation is the most valuable element of representative democracy. In that context, accountable representatives have the authority to evaluate needs, balance demands, arrange priorities, and monitor the outcomes of the political system" (Lowndes 1995: 169).

Clay researched the process of public institution building and pointed out the meanings of citizen participation in local governance (1996: 109–110):

- serving as an important means of meaningful negotiation, both within the public institution and with its policy subsystem;
- building relationships within the public institution and among institutions;
- resting on a degree of trust among the participants;
- requiring both explicit and implicit rules and norms to guide performance and behaviour;
- becoming institutionalized through the infusion of institutional values; and
- requiring continuous interaction to be maintained but with some degree of institutional memory.

Some scholars agree that citizen participations has two advantages. One is that participation is in the first place important in defining the expected outcomes of political interventions, together with the policy; the other is that participation is effective in the realization of policy objectives because it can help solve problems associated with making and implementing policy (Haus and Heinelt 2004).

Citizen participation can certainly contribute to good governance, if it is targeted at enhancing the deliberative quality of policy making and at activating the endogenous potential of local communities. If local communities could contribute to citizen participation by making the public sector closer to the citizens at the local government level, neighbourhood and grassroots organizations are important for more responsive governance.

Therefore, citizen participation could act as a real source of strength for a public sphere well informed of its responsibility to safeguard its interest in establishing a system of accountable and transparent governance (Salih 2003). Hence, the connection between decision making and deliberative democracy is very important. Local government has to prepare and build well-designed institutional and managerial mechanisms. One of OECD's projects picks up on this renewed recognition of citizen agency. The project is entitled "Strengthening Government-Citizen Connections." It recapitulates that the conditions of local governance have made the policy-making process highly complex and virtually unfathomable to the ordinary citizen. At the same time, some scholars are noting, "Many citizens are faced with such complexity and the perception of a loss of influence over national and local policy decisions, and they are complaining of a democratic deficit" (PUMA 1999).

However, even though citizen participation could assure effective governance and increase legitimacy, it has some disadvantages as well. First, governance and legitimacy depend on their forms, in that they are selective of the citizens involved, but citizen participation seldom covers all levels of citizens, and instead groups only those who would be affected. Thus, the principle of political equality, requiring equal opportunities to participate in the decisionmaking process, is not fulfilled (Dahl 1989). Second, while in most cases at least some of the outcomes must be transformed into binding decisions by representative bodies, the crucial difference between i) a traditional process of government, and ii) a process resting on interactive governance as well as some component of formalized government is that in the latter case the particular outcomes would not have been possible without the participation of societal actors (Haus 2003). Third, there is always the danger that those who are not well mobilized to represent their views may become even more marginalized by the process.

The most marginalized citizens in society are not heard through participatory mechanisms. On the other hand, those who shout the loudest and whose voice is heard may not always be the most representative. One potential solution to overcoming this distance might be to put in place arrangements by which representative democracy is complemented by increased mechanisms for public participation and increased contacts between government and civil society (Boyle and Humphreys 2001: 80).

Some scholars have suggested that local government should propose some mechanisms to encourage citizen participation. One of the mechanisms is a measure to build up the local citizen participation network through information and communication technology (ICT). Such a mechanism is called "digital democracy." The measure of digital democracy includes the following (Clift 2002):

- e-mail notice,
- in-person public hearing recordings and materials,
- online public hearings and consultations,
- wired politicians who reach out and serve,
- local civic deliberations and global networking, and
- e-voting.

One of the bases for the reform process is the introduction of ICT for all employees in government, especially in local government. The organizationwide use of ICT not only makes service delivery more efficient; it also breaks down communication barriers between professional groups within the local authority. Nevertheless, the local councils are only interested in the ICT project to the extent that it helps to reduce the budget deficit. In particular, they have not been able to use ICT as an instrument to improve the information basis for political decision making. Furthermore, ICT has not been used as a means to improve communication with citizens. Even though some basic information about local services is provided to the citizens on the Internet, the local authority has taken no steps to open up real dialogues with citizens through ICT (Bovaird, Löffler, and Parrado-Diez 2001: 8).

In particular, e-voting in public elections seems to be an extension of digital democracy. We view it as tinkering around the edges of digital democracy, having the technical capacity to make voting more convenient for citizens. With the proliferation of e-voting methods, we should put more emphasis on the participation of citizens. Furthermore, we should focus more on such groups as the youth, who tend to be less involved in political activities. The participation by voters that is essential to a healthy democracy could be increased with the use of Internet technology. The digital divide between those who do and do not have computers and access to the Internet decreases every day as Internet technology becomes more affordable. Internet voting could also create gains in efficiency and effectiveness for voting technology, democracy, and the voting process. Internet voter registration could efficiently and effectively accomplish this and could also increase overall voter registration, especially among young people, who have always had the lowest levels of voter registration.

Thus, e-channels could create a more efficient and effective voting process. The efficiency and effectiveness of e-channels could also result in increased voter participation. Clearly, e-voting could increase voter participation rates among those who have never voted or have voted infrequently. However, while the Internet could yield many potential benefits to the democratic process, some shortcomings may need to be overcome first.

Conclusion and Recommendations: The issues of local governance are structure, process, and analysis framework (Rhodes 1997). The study and planning of local governance should focus on institutional design, and local governance should play the most important role of integrating and aggregating citizens.

Local governance is related to the interaction of citizens and promotes the structure and process of citizen participation. So we have to connect different citizens, aggregate more social capital, and allow for sufficient government information.

There is little doubt that the integrating function of the local governance process is the ability to transfer resources. If we want to enhance that ability, the central Government should offer more incentive mechanisms and encourage citizens to participate in local government activities. When we discuss the issues of local governance, one topic focuses on enhancing citizen participation, and this is what we mean when we talk about "increasing the degree of direct democracy." In Taipei, China, we have been promoting citizen participation and e-democracy programs. But the most important thing is that we believe these are "oxymorons," mechanisms are not general ideas, and principles are generally not detailed.

□□□

Bibliography

Adam, R.: *Elements of Government,* New York, Random House, 1960.

Ali, A.: *Mandal Commission Controversy*, Delhi, Ajanta Publications, 1991.

Ashton, S.R.: *British Policy Towards the Indian States, 1905-1939*, London, Curzon, 1982.

Austin, Granville: *The Indian Constitution: Cornerstone of a Nation*, Oxford, Clarendon Press, 1966.

Bhuyan, B. C.: *Political Development of the North East,* New Delhi, Omsons Publications, 1989.

Blau, M.: *Bureaucracy in Modern Society,* New York, Random House, 1956.

Brierly, L.: *The Law of Nations,* New York, Oxford University Press, 1955.

Brown, M.: *Modern India: The Origins of an Asian Democracy*, New Delhi, Oxford University Press, 1985.

Chandra, R.: *Judicial System in India,* Lucknow, Print House (India), 1992.

Charles Howard McIlwain: *Constitutionalism: Ancient and Modern,* N.Y., Cornell University Press, 1958.

Chitta, R.: *Mixo Polity and Political Modernisation,* New Delhi, Vikas Publishing House PVT LTD, 1998.

Coleman, S.: *The Promise of Representative Bureaucracy: Diversity and Responsiveness in a Government Agency*, New York, M. E. Sharpe, 1997.

Cooper, T. L. : *Handbook of Administrative Ethics*, New York, Marcel Dekker, 2001.

David, H. : *Handbook of Regulation and Administrative Law*, New York, Marcel Dekker, 1994.

Dennis, L.: *Public Policy Management and Public Policy*, New York, Longman, 1999.

Derrett, J. : *Religion, Law, and the State in India*, London, Faber, 1968.

Dipak, K.: *Administration Report of the Political Agency*, Agartala, Tripura State Cultural Research Institute & Museum, 1995.

Dixit, Prabla: *Communalism: A Struggle for Power*, New Delhi, Orient Longman, 1981.

Donald E. : *Public Personnel Management: Contexts and Strategies*, Upper Saddle River, NJ: Prentice Hall, 1998.

Dwight Waldo: *Study of Public Administration*, New York, Random House, 1955.

Eldridge, P.J.: *The Politics of Foreign Aid in India*, New York, Schocken, 1970.

Fernandes, Walter: *Voluntary Action and Government Control*, New Delhi, Indian Social Institute, 1986.

Francis, E.: *Bureaucratic Power in National Politics*, Boston, Little Brown and Company, 1978.

Friedrich, J.: *Constitutional Government and Democracy*, Boston, Ginn, 1950.

Ganggopadhyay, D. K.: *Revenue Administration in Assam*, Assam, Revenue Department, Government of Assam, 1990.

Gawthrop, L.C. : *Public Sector Management Systems and Ethics*, Bloomington, Indiana University Press, 1984.

George, H.: *Toward a New Public Administration: The Minnowbrook Perspective*, San Francisco, Chandler, 1971.

Gerald, J. : *Handbook of Research Methods in Public Administration*, New York, Marcel Dekker, 1999.

Hans J. : *Politics Among Nations: The Struggle for Power and Peace*, New York, Knopf, 1960.

Jones, W.H.: *The Government and Politics of India*, London, Hutchinson, 1971.

Joseph, B.: *Scheduled Castes in Indian Politics and Society*, New Delhi, Ess Ess Publications, 1989.

Kenneth C. Wheare: *Modern Constitutions*, New York, Oxford University Press, 1951.

Kiel, L. D. : *Managing Chaos and Complexity in Government*, San Francisco, Jossey-Bass, 1994.

Kingsley, D. : *Representative Bureaucracy: An Interpretation of the British Civil Service*, Yellow Springs, Antioch University Press, 1944.

Kumar, D.: *Administration Report of the Political Agency*, Agartala, Tripura State Cultural Research Institute & Museum, 1995.

Lenneal, J. : *Urban Administrators: The Politics of Role Elasticity*, Westport, CT, Greenwood Press, 1988.

Luthra, P. N.: *Constitutional and Administrative Growth of the Arunachal Pradesh*, Itanagar, Directorate of Research, Government of Arunachal Pradesh, 1993.

Manpong, C. M.: *District Administration in Arunachal Pradesh*, New Delhi, Omsons Publications, 1993.

Marini, Frank: *Toward a New Public Administration: The Minnowbrook Perspective*, San Francisco, Chandler, 1971.

Morris, W.H.: *The Government and Politics of India*, London, Hutchinson, 1971.

Peddleton, E.: *Public Administration and the Public Interest*, New York, McGraw-Hill, 1936.

Piketo, S.: *British Policy and Administration in Nagaland 1881-1947*, New Delhi, Scholar Publishing House, 1992.

Prahlad, K.: *Governance and Public Administration for Poverty Reduction*, Salvador, Brazil, 1997.

Riggs, F.: *Administrative Reform and Political Responsiveness*, Beverly Hills, Sage Publications, 1970.

Robert, T.: *Practical Public Management*, New York, Marcel Dekker, 1995.

Robert, W.: *Public Bureaucracy and the Incentive Problem*, Washington, D.C., World Bank, 1994.

Rosenblum, G.: *Law as a Political Instrument*, New York, Random House, 1955.

Rourke, E.: *Bureaucratic Power in National Politics*, Boston, Little Brown and Company, 1978.

Selden, C.: *The Promise of Representative Bureaucracy: Diversity and Responsiveness in a Government Agency*, New York, M. E. Sharpe, 1997.

Simon, D. : *Public Administration,* New York, Knopf, 1950.

Srivastava, R.C.: *Judicial System in India*, Lucknow, Print House (India), 1992.

Sullivan, N.: *Bureaucrats and Policy Making,* New York, Holmes & Meier, 1984.

Uphoff, N.: *Local Organizations: Intermediaries in Rural Development*, Ithaca, Cornell University Press, 1984.

Victor G. : *Law as a Political Instrument,* New York, Random House, 1955.

Wade, R.: *Public Bureaucracy and the Incentive Problem*, Washington, D.C., World Bank, 1994.

Ziring, L.: *An Introduction to Asian Politics,* N.J., Prentice-Hall, 1977.

Index

E

F

G

H

I

J

□□□